WORDSWORTH
OF WORLD LITERATURE

General Editor: Tom Griffith

TWILIGHT OF THE IDOLS

FRIEDRICH NIETZSCHE

Twilight of the Idols

with The Antichrist and Ecce Homo

Translated by Antony M. Ludovici

With an Introduction by
Ray Furness

WORDSWORTH CLASSICS
OF WORLD LITERATURE

In loving memory of
MICHAEL TRAYLER
the founder of Wordsworth Editions

2

For customers interested in other titles from
Wordsworth Editions visit out website at
www.wordsworth-editions.com

For our latest list and a full mail order service contact
Bibliophile Books, 5 Thomas Road, London E14 7BN
Tel: +44 0207 515 9222
Fax: +44 0207 538 4115
e-mail: orders@bibliophilebooks.com

This edition published 2007 by Wordsworth Editions Limited
8B East Street, Ware, Hertfordshire SG12 9HJ

ISBN 978 1 84022 613 3

This edition © Wordsworth Editions Limited 2007
Introduction © Ray Furness 2007

Wordsworth® is a registered trademark of
Wordsworth Editions Limited

All rights reserved. This publication may not be reproduced,
stored in a retrieval system or transmitted, in any form or by any
means, electronic, mechanical, photocopying, recording or
otherwise, without the prior permission of the publishers.

Typeset in Great britain by Chrissie Madden
Printed and bound by Clays Ltd, St Ives plc

CONTENTS

INTRODUCTION

On 15 October 1888, Nietzsche reached his forty-fourth year and inserted the following into that extraordinary autobiography to which he had given the title *Ecce Homo*: 'On this perfect day, when everything is ripening, and not only the grapes are getting brown, a ray of sunshine has fallen on my life: I looked behind me, I looked before me, and never have I seen so many good things all at once.' The reason for this mellow gratitude? 'The first book of the *Transvaluation of all Values* [Nietzsche meant *The Antichrist* here], the *Songs of Zarathustra* [these are better known as the *Dionysus-Dithyrambs*] and *The Twilight of the Idols*, my attempt to philosophise with the hammer – all these things are the gift of this year, and even of its last quarter. *How could I help being thankful for the whole of my life?*'

These are indeed remarkable works, and one of the finest stylists in the German language rightly draws our attention to their quality. Some prefer to see these books, together with *The Wagner Case* (also 1888), as a stormy finale, tumbling precipitately in rapid succession before abruptly breaking off into silence; I would rather talk of dazzlingly euphoric, self-referential *tours de force* which refresh, baffle, astonish, infuriate and provoke the reader. And Nietzsche frequently plays with this putative reader, overwhelming him with a scintillating kaleidoscope of insights, maxims, epigrams, aphorisms and witty *bons mots*; he ironically advances and retracts propositions; he exhorts and harries. It is tempting, but inexcusable, to seek with hindsight symptoms of incipient madness in the amazing self-apotheosis of *Ecce Homo* and elsewhere, but there is no loss of self-control in these late writings. There is, rather, much self-creation: an experimentalist is at work here, a prestidigitator almost who dazzles and astonishes. The three works chosen for our collection demonstrate Nietzsche's remarkable dramatisation of ideas where there is much wit, daring, hyperbolic vivisection and ironic playfulness. A plurality of perspectives, of 'truths'? The reader is frequently confused but always refreshed by the daring and the panache; in the few lucid months left to him Nietzsche achieved an intensity and a brilliance hitherto unsurpassed, and it is with relish and gratitude that we read him.

Twilight of the Idols

In *Ecce Homo* Nietzsche describes the *Twilight of the Idols, or How to Philosophise with the Hammer* as a book cheerful and fateful in tone, like a laughing demon: 'there is no work more rich in substance, more independent, more upsetting – more wicked.' (The original title was to have been *A Psychologist at Leisure*, but his friend, the musician Peter Gast, urged him to use a more dramatic title which Nietzsche did, neatly punning on Wagner's *Götterdämmerung*). The preface insists upon cheerfulness, also *war*; in letters (to Gast and Overbeck) Nietzsche refers to his new book as a summary of his 'essential philosophical heterodoxies', a point of departure (*Auszug*), a starting point. An attack will be launched against those idols hitherto worshipped by man – but the hammer which Nietzsche uses is not a sledge-hammer, but a geologist's tool used to sound out that which is solid and that which is hollow: the idols will be touched with the hammer as with a tuning-fork.

Nietzsche's images are pithy and terse here, and a sparkling shower of 'maxims and missiles' are then unleashed at these idols as a rain of arrows, some forty-four of them which strike with deadly accuracy. Here as in *Beyond Good and Evil* (1886), Nietzsche shows himself to be the finest aphorist in the German language since Lichtenberg (he has also learnt much from La Rochefoucauld). The twenty-sixth is a very pertinent one, directed as it is against those thinkers such as Hegel who create vast systems of thought and live in a hovel outside them. 'I distrust all systematisers and avoid them. The will to a system shows a lack of honesty.' For philosophy must be *lived*, not merely *thought*: insights must come as lightning flashes to illuminate and sear, not as comfortable palliatives in reassuringly logical progression.

The book continues in a series of miniature essays attacking Socrates, philosophical errors, morality, the paucity of the German cultural scene, nationalism and culminates in Nietzsche's attitude to classical antiquity. Nietzsche brings his biggest guns (he had referred to himself as an old artillerist in a letter of 18 October 1888, hence the cliché may be allowed) to bear against Socrates, a figure who had fascinated and annoyed him ever since *The Birth of Tragedy* in 1872. The gravamen of Nietzsche's attack consists of the charge that Socrates had turned his back on the instincts and embraced rationalism, also dialectics: he brought about the end of the glories of Greek tragedy and, in 'owing a cock to Asclepius', implied that life was a disease and that he would be well out of it.

We may be surprised to hear that in fighting against the instincts of his age, Socrates was, in Nietzsche's eyes, a *décadent*. This opprobrious term will be used with increasing frequency in the texts we are dealing with here (and also in *The Wagner Case* and *Nietzsche contra Wagner*, 1889); Nietzsche had found it in Paul Bourget's essay dealing with Baudelaire and seized upon it with obvious delight. The terms *décadent* and *décadence* are of course protean and mutable, denoting literary labels and moralising evaluations, but in Nietzsche they come to describe that which is life-denying, which saps the will and cripples healthy instincts. Nietzsche claimed in a letter (18 October 1888) that in matters of *décadence* he was the highest authority at present on earth; in *The Wagner Case* he admitted that, like Wagner, he had been a child of his age, that is, a *décadent*, but he differed from Wagner essentially in that he had fought against it and overcome it.

In the *Twilight of the Idols* Socrates is also castigated as an ugly plebeian who had rejected the drama and glory of Dionysian life and extolled ratiocination; with him 'the mob comes to the top'. With Socrates Plato is also attacked for his belief in a world of absolute reality beyond the realm of phenomena, and with obvious delight Nietzsche attacks mummified philosophers who denied the validity of the senses: those who claim that God is the *ens realissimum* are nothing more than morbid cobweb-spinners, sickly *décadents*, and Dionysus is again extolled as a counter-weight and adversary, an artist-god delighting in power and terror, affirming life in all its manifestations. The great artist, then, provides a stimulus to life even at its most dreadful, and this section ends with undeniable echoes of *The Birth of Tragedy* but without the Wagnerian presence.

The short interlude 'How the "true world" ultimately became a fable' shows Nietzsche at his most witty, even hilarious, yet there is a sting in the tail, a dart which brilliantly startles us. The topic is the idea of the 'true world' (that is, the world of some transcendental realm, of Platonic forms) from its hegemony in Plato, Christianity and Kant (where, admittedly, it becomes rather pale in the mists of Königsberg) until its final rejection by pragmatists and materialists who enjoy a hearty breakfast as the sun rises at cockcrow. The idea of some 'true' or 'real' world beyond this transient one is abolished, reason has prevailed. But, Nietzsche insists, it is fallacious to assume that the 'apparent' world (the world of the senses, of materialism) can now go its merry way as if nothing had happened: if there is no 'beyond', no 'God', then *this* world can never be the same again, for the pillars which had hitherto supported all moral precepts have collapsed. Nietzsche, the 'free spirit' of the time of *Human, All-Too-Human*, now realises that the numinous and the phenomenal worlds are so enmeshed that the former cannot be rejected without far-reaching convulsions in the other. We are forcibly reminded here of the fable of the madman with his lantern seeking God in *The Joyful Science* (1882) where Nietzsche transcends platitudinous atheism and points to a far more urgent dispensation. If man is deprived of all the earlier certainties ('errors') he must now face the fact that there is nothing at all in existence to rely on but himself; this in mystical terms is the Great Midday, the moment of terrifying illumination which Zarathustra heralds and which will separate the *Übermensch* from the dross of mankind.

It is insights such as these, and the ebullience with which Nietzsche expresses them, that make him such an abrasive thinker. (In claiming, wittily, that he fears that we shall never be rid of God as long as we still believe in grammar, he continues to emphasise the hopeless entanglement of metaphysics and other human constructs and implies that to extirpate the former will never be an easy task.) Another pungent observation which anticipates many of the pre-occupations of twentieth-century existentialism is found in section eight of 'The four great errors'. An individual, Nietzsche explains, is simply thrown into the world: there is no purpose to his existence. He is not accountable to a god, to any providential being, to society, family or tribe. Teleology is a lie; one is simply there, in existence – *and this is the great liberation*. Nietzsche emphasises this fact: the 'innocence of Being' is here made manifest, and this innocence exults in godlessness and the concomitant wreckage of all ethical, metaphysical and logical worlds, creating new values, blessed and endorsed by none but the liberated self.

The 'improvers of mankind' – are they not responsible for man's emasculation? This is the question posed by Nietzsche in the following section where morality is unmasked as a misrepresent-ation of certain phenomena, for *there are no moral facts whatever* (Nietzsche's emphasis). Christianity, in attempting to tame man-kind, has weakened and made man sick: the 'blond beast' was curbed, domesticated and weakened. Those who were great, powerful and ruthless, became 'sinners' and crippled by conscience and ill will towards themselves. Nietzsche had written at length on this, with frequently reckless exuberance, in *The Genealogy of Morals* of the previous year, reassuring us, however, that there is no connection between the proposed blond beast of some shadowy past and 'us Germans' of today. This 'blond beast' which Nietzsche adumbrates was manifestly not a racial construct but an 'ideogram' (Kaufmann) used to symbolise those with strong animal impulses; when Christianity is condemned as an anti-Aryan religion the epithet has none of the racist associations bestowed by suspect *völkisch* thinkers (that is Nordic, proto-Germanic etc.) but simply denotes lack of nobility. The masterstroke of the priesthood of biblical times (and, again, Nietzsche's attack on historical Judaism is utterly remote from the strident anti-Semitism of, say, his brother-in-law Förster) was to direct man's cruelty, animosity and predatory instincts and direct them inwards against himself with, for Nietzsche, dire consequences. Christianity is consequently seen as the religion of the underprivileged, the Chandala. To a large extent the *Twilight of the Idols* may be seen as a preparation for the massive onslaught to follow in *The Antichrist*: the attack may not be so concentrated but the old artillerist in *Twilight* seeks a wider field of fire.

Nietzsche is above all a critic of culture, seeking to extol that which was life-enhancing and expunge all that was mendacious, pusillanimous or morbid, failing to exemplify what he would term 'the great health'. A broadside is now launched against con-temporary German life, as if to reinforce the contrast between earlier Germanic energies and the vulgarity of the present age:

some manly virtues may still be found, but '*Deutschland, Deutsch-land über alles* – I fear this was the death-blow to German philosophy'. How much beer, Nietzsche jokes, there is in the German intellect! German seriousness, German profundity and the German passion for things of the mind were sadly lacking in Bismarck's *Reich*, and philistinism prevailed. With great vivacity and obvious glee Nietzsche criticises German education (and teachers and academics in Britain today would thoroughly endorse his findings): higher education is no longer a privilege, and the democratisation of culture has resulted in banal superficiality. An *élite* is impossible, for high schools have been ruined by too many pupils. At university there is an indecent haste as if something had been neglected if a young man of twenty-three is not yet 'finished'. The scene is depressing indeed, yet '*Heiterkeit*' or cheer-fulness survives and indeed prevails for the one able to expose the specious, and apply hammer and tuning-fork with audacity.

Our cheerful psychologist becomes the 'untimely man' again and embarks on further skirmishes and sallies against various illustrious names hitherto lauded as the highest manifestations of European culture: many are already familiar to us. But it is in the attack on George Eliot where Nietzsche, who has seen far more deeply than others, shows that to remove God from a system of moral beliefs such as Christianity means necessarily to bring down the whole structure of morality which that system implies. Michael Tanner has called it one of the most magnificent passages in the *Twilight of the Idols*, indeed, in all of Nietzsche's writing. The English reader may find Eliot's inclusion in Nietzsche's shooting range puzzling, but Nietzsche knew her not as a novelist but as a moral philosopher who had translated Feuerbach and David Friedrich Strauss. Eliot and others solemnly believed that it was possible to do away with the concept 'God' and yet still preserve Christian morality. Here Nietzsche rounds on her with great vehemence and insists that this is impossible, and he writes with a conviction that all true Christians would surely applaud. Christianity, we read, is a system, a complete view of things, and if one removes the linch-pin then everything must disintegrate, whatever the English 'shallowpates' might say, these bluestock-ings *à la* Eliot. One seems to hear the voice of Nietzsche *père*, Lutheran pastor of the vicarage at Röcken.

The last pages of *Twilight* are devoted primarily to art and its value in life. Art at its most profound praises, glorifies and strengthens. It is indifferent to morality, it is a stimulus to life and therefore, Nietzsche argues, it is the opposite of Christianity which denies the here and now and shifts the emphasis to some spurious after-life. Art, and nothing but art! Nietzsche writes elsewhere: it is the great life-enhancer, the great seducer, and, intensifying life and the will to power, it is *Dionysian*. It is amoral; there is no hint of debility, of *décadence* about it. But 'Christian art'? This, for Nietzsche, is a contradiction in terms and he states provocatively that there is no such thing as a Christian who is also an artist. Let no-one be so puerile, we read, as to suggest Raphael 'or any other homeopathic Christian of the nineteenth century' as an objection to this statement, for Raphael blessed, affirmed and praised; Christian denial was unknown to him. And *Twilight*, this sparkling little book full of enthusiasms and fulminations, some brilliant, some wayward, ends, almost, with a paean of praise for Goethe, a writer of power and one emancipated from petty considerations. What he aspired to, Nietzsche tells us, was *totality*: he fought against the separation of reason, sensuality, freedom and will (most horribly preached by Kant, Goethe's antipodes), he disciplined himself to a whole, he *created* himself. And this attitude Nietzsche baptises with the name Dionysus.

Goethe – and the Greeks. The final comments are on Nietzsche's indebtedness to the classical world, to his vision of Dionysus above all, to life affirmation at its strongest and strangest. Christian morbidity is as nothing compared with the superabundance of joy and energy experienced in the Dionysian orgy and Nietzsche, 'the last disciple of the philosopher Dionysus', announces in a rhapsodic climax that he is the teacher of the Eternal Recurrence, that mystical, pseudoscientific substitute for infinity which, he will tell us in *Ecce Homo*, came to him as a vision 'six thousand feet above man and time'. Happy is he who affirms the endless cycle of existence, existence that will return with its joy and pain, that touchstone to determine who is strong enough to bless and to accept. And the last invigorating words, exuberant and self-indulgent, are uttered by Zarathustra's hammer castigating the crumbling worthlessness of charcoal and celebrating instead the infrangibility of the radiant diamond.

The Antichrist

Our next book, *The Antichrist*, was written in September 1888 and intended as the first part of a substantial work *The Transvaluation of All Values* which Nietzsche had planned but never completed (he had also contemplated a vast work with the overarching title *The Will to Power* which remained a mass of jottings). *The Antichrist* had originally received the subtitle 'Transvaluation of all Values'; this, however, became 'an attempted critique of Christianity' and, later 'a curse on Christianity'.

A brief word on the term 'transvaluation' (the German word is *Umwerthung*). With increasing urgency (indeed, excitement) Nietzsche sees that his task is nothing less than a radical reinterpretation of traditional morality, a revaluation which must serve to exterminate those attitudes which he regarded as *décadent* or life-denying, and to reinstate life-enhancing or Dionysian values. Christianity, as we have noted, is condemned as the ultimate blight and curse in its insistence on the ascetic ideal, on man's fallenness and depravity, also in its praise of pity and its rejection of pride, strength and aristocratic imperiousness. This transvaluation is in many ways a restitution of that earlier evaluation which Nietzsche posited in *The Genealogy of Morals* where, as we noted, some ill-defined assemblage of powerful rulers cultivated an iron self-control and imposed their own morality on those weaker: strength, health, beauty and pride were called 'good' and the attitudes of the servile were deemed to be base or 'bad'. Christianity will invert this and enable the poor and the dispossessed to compensate for their wretchedness by dreaming of the equality of all before the eyes of the Lord in heaven: the meek will now inherit the earth and the aristocratic values of pride and cruelty are now deemed 'evil' whilst pity, meekness and humility are 'good'.

Nietzsche's transvaluation would extirpate the baleful influence of Christianity and seek to undo the harm perpetrated by an ascetic priesthood which forced man's natural predatory instincts inwards, weakening the strong by creating self-hatred and 'bad conscience'. That 'pathos of distance' which gave the noble and the strong their justification for creating and imposing values has been discredited and must now be restored: if only the poor, the powerless, the lowly, the sick and the ugly may be 'saved', then, Nietzsche writes, there is very little hope for mankind.

The preface to *The Antichrist* insists that the book belongs to very few, to those spiritual aristocrats capable of living metaphorically in ice and loneliness. Nietzsche's interest is only in greatness, certainly not 'goodness', if 'goodness' is that which Christianity has inculcated into the herd. Maudlin altruism is rejected out of hand as Nietzsche has the courage to strike out on a lonely and dangerous path. The book begins with a formulaic definition of 'good' (that which increases the feeling of power), 'bad' (that which proceeds from weakness) and 'happiness' (the feeling that power increases). The weak and the botched, we read, should perish and, indeed, be helped on their way; more harmful than any vice is pity, sympathy for the weak or, in other words, Christianity. Nietzsche's words are provocative indeed and, with knowledge and hindsight of twentieth century barbarism, unsettling, but a daring and stimulating mind is at work here, storming the reader with an intellectual barrage which is deliberately shocking but also a valuable corrective to complacency and to tepid acquiescence in platitudes.

Nietzsche does not shrink from repudiating all forms of egalitarianism, all that levels out, whether it be socialism or Christianity. For Christianity has waged war against the higher type of man, and pity thwarts the law of selection, preserving as it does that which is ripe for destruction. (Schopenhauer, like Wagner an earlier mentor, is necessarily rejected with his praise of pity; indeed, German philosophy as a whole, Nietzsche cunningly suggests, has been contaminated by theologians' blood, with the Protestant pastor standing as its godfather.) In Christianity the instincts of the subjugated and the oppressed come to the foreground: it is the lowest classes who seek their salvation in it, the Chandala. Buddhism is preferred for its sophistication, its dignity and its serenity, and Hinduism is praised for its insistence on a hierarchical caste system; Islam is likewise extolled as a virile religion, a religion for *men*. The sickly Christian, racked with guilt, told that his body is a teeming mass of worms, that sexuality is a sin, that beauty is evil and that eternal damnation awaits, cuts a very sorry figure indeed.

The central section of *The Antichrist* consists of a recapitulation of certain preoccupations of *The Genealogy of Morals* but also contains an idiosyncratic and in many ways a sympathetic portrayal of Jesus who became, we are informed, a hapless victim of political machinations. Christianity was not a counter-movement against the Jews but a continuation of the Jewish drive for world domination; to turn the Jew on the cross into a redeemer, to see him as a sacrifice sent by God for the forgiveness of sins, to insist upon a resurrection, a Second Coming was, according to Nietzsche, a Jewish master-trick instigated by Paul in his rabbinical insolence to gain believers, to force the Gentiles to kneel before a lacerated, hanging Jew. In Christianity Judaism found its most sublime continuation, a religion of vindictiveness and resentment propagated by an ascetic priesthood. To object that it was the Jews who plotted Jesus' crucifixion due to his heretical views is unsubtle: this was a supremely political act, a means of apparently denying Jesus whilst at the same time using him as an indispensable means to assure that believers would fall before him and that the world would be conquered by three Jews and a Jewess – Jesus of Nazareth, Peter the fisherman, Paul the carpet-weaver and Mary. Thus Judea conquered Rome and ultimately the whole of Western civilisation; the *evangel* became the *dysangel* through Paul's crusade against life-enhancing aristocratic values, and the original symbolism of Jesus became debased into a 'diseased barbarism' utterly remote from the example and message of Jesus himself.

Nietzsche is fascinated by 'this most interesting *décadent*', regretting that there was no Dostoevsky living in the neighbourhood of Jesus of Nazareth who could have experienced and described that thrilling combination of the sublime, the sick and the childish which surrounded him. (The use of the term 'idiot' to describe Jesus may also be an oblique reference to Dostoevsky's novel and not simply a term of abuse.) It is to be regretted that Nietzsche only got to know Dostoevsky in French translations in later life; the section on criminality in *Twilight of the Idols* refers to the Russian novelist as the only psychologist from whom he, Nietzsche, had anything to learn. How is it possible, Nietzsche asks, that the man Jesus should extol blessedness in peace and gentleness and preach that the kingdom of heaven should belong to children? Jesus was neither hero nor genius, as the 'buffoon' Ernest Renan had claimed, but a man of wincing sensitivity who shrank from conflict and taught a religion of love.

Was Jesus a 'free spirit'? The 'glad tidings' spoke of a kingdom of heaven within us not interpreted through scripture but as a state of existential transfiguration where all differences are obliterated and all Jewish religious teaching is abolished. 'The very word "Christianity",' we read, 'is a misunderstanding – truth to tell, there never was more than one Christian and he died on the cross. The "gospel" died on the cross.' (It should be noted that '*Christ*' in German means 'Christian' and only archaically 'Christ', for which the normal word is '*Christus*'. Does Nietzsche's title for his book deliberately contain an ambiguity?) Paul, we remember, is the target of Nietzsche's most corrosive venom, Paul, who twisted Jesus' gently anarchic visions into a monstrous travesty, a religion of guilt and sin where the priest rules supreme. A 'new testament' was concocted, a document so subversive that 'one does well to put gloves on when reading it', and Nietzsche, inexhaustible it seems in his intellectual elation, his self-confidence, rejoices in the ferocity of his iconoclasm, while his readers, stunned, appalled perhaps but always invigorated by his sheer energy and in the undeniable brilliance of his ferocity, get caught up in the headlong rush of his effervescent hatred.

As in *The Twilight of the Idols* Nietzsche inserts a flippant yet very telling story to vary his pungent philippics. Section 48 asks the reader if he has really understood the story at the beginning of the bible – the story of God's panic, his terror even, when confronted by science, by the desire for knowledge? Out of boredom God creates man, but man, too, is bored and God creates the animals for his amusement. This is God's first blunder, for man is not amused, and God creates woman. This is his second blunder, for Eve is of the serpent and man is tempted to eat of the fruit of the tree of knowledge. The old God is seized by mortal terror: man now becomes his rival, for science makes him equal to God and hence sin, the original sin, is committed. Man must be punished, and the Lord heaps distress and every kind of misery upon him and his helpmeet – guilt, sickness, age and toil. But man triumphs despite these afflictions and builds the tower of Babel to equal God, so the 'Old Man' invents war and divides the peoples, creating an ascetic priesthood to assist him. But knowledge increases, emancipation from the vindictive priesthood increases, and the 'Old Man' comes to his final decision: man knows too much, so there is nothing for it: *he will have to be drowned*!

Amongst the afflictions which God has heaped upon Eve Nietzsche includes the suffering and danger to life which could accompany childbirth, thus ironically demonstrating his great mercy. Nietzsche will vigorously attack the Church's attitude to sex and procreation. A very telling aphorism from *Beyond Good and Evil* reads as follows: 'Christianity gave Eros poison to drink; he did not die of it, to be sure, but degenerated into lust'. A religion such as Christianity which 'throws mud' at sexuality and regards procreation as a base act is a sick religion, and the doctrine of the Immaculate Conception of Mary, the dogma which proclaimed that 'the Blessed Virgin Mary, from the first moment of Her conception was, by the singular grace and privilege of Almighty God and in view of the merits of Jesus Christ, Saviour of mankind, kept free from all stain of original sin' (1854) is further proof of Christianity's neurosis. Christianity, we hear, vents its abysmal vulgarity on procreation, woman and marriage, for the origins of man are sullied by such a dogma.

The *Law-book of Manu*, a book ascribed to the mythical patriarch (the *Manusmriti* had appeared in a translation and a critical edition by Julius Jolly in 1887), is held up as an antidote to such notions, an incomparably superior work, not an 'evil-smelling Jewish distillation of Rabbinism and superstition'. It is a book, Nietzsche writes, which expounds laws by which a noble and discerning aristocracy keeps the mob under control, where there is perfection and an affirmation of life, a feeling of well-being where woman and marriage are treated with respect and trust (how different from Paul's grudging admission that it is better to marry than to burn). In *Manu* Nietzsche finds dignity, purity and praise, a world utterly remote from that created by a God who increases the affliction of woman in childbirth and where a revengeful priesthood revels in original sin, exorcisms, commination and a neurotic cult of morbid relics.

Manu saw the need for an order of rank with the lawgiver at the top, the mediocre in the middle and the Chandala at the bottom, and Nietzsche's violent repudiation of egalitarianism is anticipated here. He now assails Christianity for undermining hierarchical orders in its doctrine of the equality of all before God. A high culture is a pyramid with the strongest at the top and the broad base below, and those who seek to loosen the stones comprising this pyramid, the socialist agitators and anarchists of his day, are vilified mercilessly. 'Whom do I most hate among the rabble of the present day? The socialistic rabble, the Chandala apostles who undermine the working man's instinct, who make him envious and who teach him revenge.' The anarchist and the Christian have a common origin and purpose for they are both desirous of overturning the pyramid in their hatred of the highest man. It was the same in Rome, Nietzsche explains: that magnificent edifice, the *imperium Romanum*, was undermined and destroyed by cunning, secretive and vindictive vampires who sucked its marrow from its bones – by Christians. 'Nihilist and Christian they rhyme and they do not only rhyme . . . ' In German they do (*Nihilist* and *Christ*) and Nietzsche links them with undeniable relish.

This remarkable critique of, and curse on, Christianity draws to an end with a eulogy, a condemnation and a curse. The Renaissance is seen by Nietzsche as an attempt to overthrow Christian values and to restore triumphant art upon the throne, the worship of earthly splendour in all its amoral glory, infinitely remote from Christian humility, morbidity and self-laceration. And then, Nietzsche impishly suggests, in Rome itself, at the very heart of Christianity, where popes glorified life and life's apotheosis in art, a vision arises which would make the gods in Olympus roar with laughter: Cesare Borgia as pope! Ruthlessness, power, energy and beauty upon the throne of St Peter – but it was not to be. A German monk, Luther, came to Rome and vindictive Christianity was reinstated, paving the way for the Reformation. 'If we shall never be able to get rid of Christianity the Germans will be to blame' – this is Nietzsche's bitter realisation. The final curse is pronounced on Christianity, that immortal blemish on mankind, the conspiracy against life itself. The last lines express the hope that the human race will ultimately come to its senses and no longer measure time from the *dies nefastus* on which this fatality arose, the *first* day of Christianity, but rather from its *last*, from today. Transvaluation of all values! But this transvaluation, as we have noted, would never be coherently formulated, and the writer who feared that he might blow the history of mankind into two with this work turned elsewhere.

Ecce Homo

We began this introduction by calling *Ecce Homo* an extraordinary autobiography; it is acknowledged to be the most amazing ever written but, unfortunately, its remarkable self-celebrations and dazzling literary exuberance are often taken, as we noted, as harbingers of Nietzsche's impending derangement. It is a relief that Max Nordau could not have known the book (published in a limited edition in 1908 and unlimited three years later) before writing his vulgar diatribe *Degeneration* (1892-3, English translation 1895) where Nietzsche is already portrayed as a 'raving madman with flashing eyes, wild gestures and foaming mouth', terrifying his listeners with threatening mien and flailing fists. *Ecce Homo* does indeed startle the reader with its high spirits but it is also a very mischievous book, mettlesome and mocking; this most readable of philosophers, writing with verve, high intelligence and unparalleled vivacity, tells us at breakneck speed of his achievements, his adversaries, his origins and his expectations. There is no febrile incandescence, no roaring rodomontade (*pace* Nordau) but a bracing and candid tone, tinged occasionally with elegiac nostalgia; the book is, indeed, refreshing and splendid in its imaginative brilliance (there is only one section, to be referred to later, of intolerable strain and lack of control).

It took Nietzsche three weeks to write, from his birthday on 15 October to 4 November: alterations and editions were added subsequently. The title has an obviously blasphemous resonance, possibly also a jocular one, in the use of Pilate's words: the subtitle is important. Nietzsche will insist that he must not be mistaken for what he is not, and that we must understand his provenance, his antecedents: the foreword will explain that he is neither bogeyman not monster but a disciple of Dionysus, a satyr, certainly not a saint. He has swept away idols and will force mankind to re-evaluate every belief hitherto held, and it is imperative that he be understood. He is the Antichrist, the iconoclast, the one standing beyond good and evil, for this is the slave's morality: this man now presents himself to us.

In the chapter 'Why I am so wise' Nietzsche speaks with great affection of his father who had died young, a delicate, lovable and tender man, a 'gracious reminder of life rather than life itself'. He died aged thirty-six, that age at which Nietzsche reached his lowest ebb. A discussion of Nietzsche's health ensues and those who recall Nietzsche's months of misery, his migraines and nausea, are surprised to read of the comments of a doctor who had once treated him as a nervous case declaring that there was nothing wrong with Nietzsche's nerves and it was only he, the doctor, who was nervous. Nietzsche denies ever having suffered from morbid disturbance of the intellect or any semi-stupor accompanying a fever; he *does*, however, admit of a delicate stomach and problems with his eyes but is adamant that these were merely the side-effects of a general exhaustion, nothing more. Far more important is the admission that he is prone to *décadence*: this we have already noticed together with Nietzsche's contention that he has over-come it. Serenity has been achieved, it seems, a joyful science, and the one who claimed that his ambition, his torment and his joy was to navigate the whole circumference of the modern soul and to sit in each of its corners – this man sought to conquer pessimism and thus achieve a Goethean vision full of love and affirmation.

And yet, and yet . . . In a correction to section 3 of this chapter, a correction sent by Nietzsche to Peter Gast shortly before the mental collapse of January 1889 (a correction which only came to light in Gast's papers in 1969 and survived because Gast had thoughtfully made a copy before sending it to Nietzsche's sister who subsequently destroyed it), a more strident note becomes evident which alarms the reader. Nietzsche praises his father's almost angelic nature and insists that he, his son, is a pure-blooded Polish nobleman in whose veins there was not one drop of German blood. A vicious attack follows on both mother and sister: it was a blasphemy against his dignity to be related to such *canaille* who are employing an infernal machine to destroy him. Even the most sympathetic reader must concede that there are undeniable traces of paranoia here, tinged, however, with the mournfully hilarious comment that his deepest objection to the doctrine of the Eternal Recurrence were his mother and sister: the prospect of encountering them for all eternity would be too much to bear. The section ends in incoherence, attacking the German Kaiser and extolling Cosima Wagner. The rest is silence, as a 'Dionysus-head' reaches him through the post.

The section 3 that we have here – which is not the altered one given to Gast – also speaks of a putative Polish ancestry: such is Nietzsche's hatred of Bismarck's *Reich*, of Europe's 'flatland' (Germany). The Goethean vision is remote indeed from late nineteenth-century Prussia with its sabre-rattling and *völkisch* gobbledygook. The chapter ends with the admonition to remain free of *ressentiment*, of sickness and morbidity and to accept *amor fati*: the pose now favoured by Nietzsche is that of an imperturbable and fastidious sage, a sage, however, who cannot refrain from despising mendacity, pusillanimity, cant and all forms of cultural malaise. And the autobiographer's good will is made manifest by the singular honour he bestows on Christianity by singling it out as the enemy most worthy of him: thus our spiritual aristocrat displays his magnaminity.

In 'Why I am so clever' Nietzsche disarmingly asserts that his greatness resides in transcending such bogus preoccupations as the existence of God or the immortality of the soul. What concerns him far more are questions concerning diet and climate: it was the heaviness of the cuisine of Leipzig (as well as reading Schopenhauer) which put into jeopardy his will to live. It is almost as a dandy that Nietzsche addresses us now: the need to prove the existence of a 'Beyond' is far less pressing than the avoidance of soup *before* the meal, greasy vegetables and puddings as heavy as paperweights. The thought of the gallons of beer consumed by the inhabitants of Munich (his 'antipodes') makes him shudder, as does the diet of the English which is little more than cannibalism and which causes a sluggish digestion and the clumsiness of gait best illustrated by the feet of English ladies. Nietzsche's coquettish individualism is reminiscent of Oscar Wilde, and his love of fine raiment in his Basel days (where Jakob Burckhardt considered him a fop), the preference for French culture above all, together with his insistence that art (and *l'art pour l'art* is included) was the highest manifestation of life, bring him tantalizingly close to the Irish writer and wit. The German *Geist* (or 'mind') was a contradiction in terms – nothing great could come of it. Yet the highest example of lyric poetry, Nietzsche admits, was given to him by Heinrich Heine, a poet who possessed that 'divine malice' without which perfection cannot be imagined. The surprising claim (and yet can the reader be surprised at anything now?) that he and Heine were by far the greatest artists of the German language that have ever existed may not, perhaps, be so fanciful.

A sage? A wit? An *homme de lettres*? A *flâneur* on the banks of the Po? Certainly, but also a bombardier obsessed with Richard Wagner, that garish monument on the German cultural scene. Was Wagner *reichsdeutsch*? Yet he shared much of the morbidity of the French *décadents*: he had even 'poisoned' Baudelaire. The philosopher-dandy of *Ecce Homo* who writes that the artist has no place in Europe but Paris suddenly expresses his eternal gratitude for the intimate association with Wagner, for the happiness of the early days in Tribschen which were never troubled, never clouded. And, amazingly, we read that Wagner had (metaphorically) provided the hashish for which Nietzsche yearned, that Wagner was the antidote to everything German and that *Tristan und Isolde* was the work above all to which Nietzsche succumbed, a work of sweet and shuddering infinity, of dangerous fascination, unique in all the arts. All the mysteries of Leonardo da Vinci, we read, fade at the first note of *Tristan* and the world is poorer for him who has never become sick enough for this 'voluptuousness of hell': it is permissible, Nietzsche writes, even necessary to employ the terminology of the mystic here. But Nietzsche then checks himself and rejects the rest of music for Chopin (for he, like Nietzsche, was Polish . . .).

Recalling Wagner's death in Venice five years previously, Nietzsche now addresses us as a poet, writing that Venice was simply another word for music, for the south – in fact the *only* word, and he quotes his poem 'Venice' (in German '*Venedig*') verbatim. Nietzsche wrote a considerable number of poems (short lyrics, odes, witty epigrams) but it is 'Venice' which is most frequently anthologised and acknowledged to be his best. Indeed, Nietzsche has been called by some the father of impressionism in German poetry, and 'Venice' is certainly a concatenation of highly concentrated statements enmeshed with traditional Romantic tropes (the drops of song on the water and the harp of the poet's soul). A *pointilliste* technique is employed and the effect of golden brilliance achieved. But the visual effect, we feel, is unimportant – it is the shimmering of a soul which is portrayed: the subject is a lonely individual consciousness. No ecstasy is achieved here, and the last line poses an unanswerable question. No *Übermensch* writes thus (and where *is* he in these last pamphlets?), no prophet, no *Untier* or monster, but a man of acute sensitivity, a hermit or recluse, alone on the Rialto bridge at dusk, the one who wrote of a mystical engulfment by *Tristan und Isolde* and who seeks in *Ecce Homo* to define himself before an uncomprehending and largely indifferent world.

Chapter three, 'Why I write such excellent books', is a self-congratulatory account of his published work, extolling its merits; it is extremely important, however, to recall the startling and pivotal statement with which it opens: 'I am one thing, my creations are another.' (The preface urged us not to confuse him with anyone else, and quoted Zarathustra's exhortation that we should lose him and find ourselves.) A letter to the musicologist Carl Fuchs, written from Sils Maria in the summer of 1888, is an important one. After mentioning the impact of his thinking in Scandinavia (on Brandes, on Strindberg) and the difficulties faced by the few who read him in categorising him (psychologist? immoralist? epigrammatist?), Nietzsche writes as follows: 'It is not at all necessary, not even desirable, to be on my side: on the contrary, a dose of curiosity as though one were confronted by some strange plant, a dose of ironic antipathy – this would seem an incomparably more *intelligent* attitude towards me'.

There is an increasing tension in the writings of 1888 between earnestness and play, a sense of ironical detachment and provocation. Are the descriptions of his books, especially *Thus Spake Zarathustra*, which is deemed to be a work beyond anything written by Goethe, Shakespeare and Dante, the eruptions of a self-absorbed psychotic or simply *jeux d'esprit*? The portrayal of the *Genealogy of Morals* is an excellent one and relevant to much else besides: there is an intention to mystify, Nietzsche writes, an ironic sally, followed by isolated flashes of lightning, then a dull rumbling until a fierce tempo is attained in which everything surges forward with tremendous tension. What does all this tell us? That Nietzsche is an enthralling and deeply problematic figure and that his intellectual and emotional magnetism is very hard to resist: the sympathetic reader will frequently feel unsettled by the strangeness of his thought, yet also liberated, refreshed and forced to come to terms with 'fifty worlds of strange and terrible delights'.

Behold, then, the man. We seek to but the man is, apparently, Dionysus, or dynamite, or a buffoon – this the last chapter suggests.

The final broadside is directed at the Church, at institutionalised, infamous Christianity, excoriated by Voltaire in his notorious '*écrasez l'infâme!*' and Dionysus now steps before his ultimate adversary. Is *Ecce Homo* the 'Jupiter symphony of German letters' (Hollingdale)? Perhaps, but there is also a sombre warning that the transvaluation of all values will bring unheard-of cataclysms in the coming century: there will be wars the like of which have never been seen on earth. (Are there echoes here of the rhapsodic utterances of the madman where the consequences of godlessness are seen?) Then the fizzing Catherine wheel stops, the endless self-propulsive images and word associations cease: this most fascinating of thinkers, wayward, infectious, endlessly invigorating, endlessly elusive and exemplary in his courage, finishes his apologia.

RAY FURNESS

FURTHER READING

Aschheim, Steven, *The Nietzsche Legacy in Germany 1890–1990*, Berkeley 1992

Blackham, Harold, *Six Existentialist Thinkers*, London 1956, 1961

Bridgwater, Patrick, *Nietzsche in Anglosaxony*, Leicester 1972

Deleuze, Gilles, *Nietzsche and Philosophy* (tr. Tomlinson), London 1983

Heller, Erich, *The Disinherited Mind*, London 1952

Heller, Erich, *The Importance of Nietzsche*, Chicago 1988

Hollingdale, R.J., *Nietzsche: The Man and his Philosophy*, London 1965

Kaufmann, Walter, *Nietzsche: Philosopher, Psychologist, Antichrist* (4th edition), Princeton 1974

Nietzsche, F., *Daybreak: Thoughts on the Prejudices of Morality* (tr. Hollingdale), Cambridge 1972

Nietzsche, F., *Beyond Good and Evil: Prelude to a Philosophy of the Future* (tr. Hollingdale), London 1973, 1990

Pasley, Malcolm (ed.), *Nietzsche: Imagery and Thought*, London 1978

Martin, Nicholas (ed.), *Nietzsche and the German Tradition*, Oxford and Berne 2003

Tanner, Michael, *Nietzsche*, Oxford 1994

TWILIGHT
OF THE IDOLS

or

How to Philosophise
with the Hammer

PREFACE

To maintain a cheerful attitude of mind in the midst of a gloomy and exceedingly responsible task, is no slight artistic feat. And yet, what could be more necessary than cheerfulness? Nothing ever succeeds which exuberant spirits have not helped to produce. Surplus power, alone, is the proof of power. A *transvaluation of all values* – this note of interrogation which is so black, so huge, that it casts a shadow even upon him who affixes it – is a task of such fatal import, that he who undertakes it is compelled every now and then to rush out into the sunlight in order to shake himself free from an earnestness that becomes crushing, far too crushing. This end justifies every means, every event on the road to it is a windfall. Above all *war*. War has always been the great policy of all spirits who have penetrated too far into themselves or who have grown too deep; a wound stimulates the recuperative powers. For many years, a maxim, the origin of which I withhold from learned curiosity, has been my motto:

increscunt animi, virescit volnere virtus.

At other times another means of recovery which is even more to my taste, is to cross-examine idols. There are more idols than realities in the world: this constitutes my 'evil eye' for this world: it is also my 'evil ear'. To put questions in this quarter with a hammer, and to hear perchance that well-known hollow sound which tells of blown-out frogs – what a joy this is for one who has ears even behind his ears, for an old psychologist and Pied Piper like myself in whose presence precisely that which would fain be silent *must betray itself*.

Even this treatise – as its title shows – is above all a recreation, a ray of sunshine, a leap sideways of a psychologist in his leisure moments. Maybe, too, a new war? And are we again cross-examining new idols? This little work is a great declaration of war;

and with regard to the cross-examining of idols, this time it is not the idols of the age but eternal idols which are here struck with a hammer as with a tuning fork – there are certainly no idols which are older, more convinced, and more inflated. Neither are there any more hollow. This does not alter the fact that they are believed in more than any others, besides they are never called idols – at least, not the most exalted among their number.

FRIEDRICH NIETZSCHE

Turin, 30 September 1888
on the day when the first
book of the Transvaluation
of all Values was finished.

MAXIMS AND MISSILES

1

Idleness is the parent of all psychology. What? Is psychology then a – vice?

2

Even the pluckiest among us has but seldom the courage of what he really knows.

3

Aristotle says that in order to live alone, a man must be either an animal or a god. The third alternative is lacking: a man must be both – a *philosopher*.

4

'All truth is simple.' – Is not this a double lie?

5

Once for all I wish to be blind to many things – Wisdom sets bounds even to knowledge.

6

A man recovers best from his exceptional nature – his intellectuality – by giving his animal instincts a chance.

7

Which is it? Is man only a blunder of God? Or is God only a blunder of man?

8

From the military school of life. – That which does not kill me, makes me stronger.

9

Help thyself, then everyone will help thee. A principle of neighbour-love.

10

A man should not play the coward to his deeds. He should not repudiate them once he has performed them. Pangs of conscience are indecent.

11

Can a donkey be tragic? – To perish beneath a load that one can neither bear nor throw off? This is the case of the Philosopher.

12

If a man knows the wherefore of his existence, then the manner of it can take care of itself. Man does not aspire to happiness; only the Englishman does that.

13

Man created woman – out of what? Out of a rib of his god – of his 'ideal'.

14

What? Art thou looking for something? Thou wouldst fain multiply thyself tenfold, a hundredfold? Thou seekest followers? Seek ciphers!

15

Posthumous men, like myself, are not so well understood as men who reflect their age, but they are heard with more respect. In plain English : we are never understood – hence our authority.

16

Among women. – 'Truth? Oh, you do not know truth! Is it not an outrage on all our *pudeurs*?' –

17

There is an artist after my own heart, modest in his needs: he really wants only two things, his bread and his art – *panem et Circen*.

18

He who knows not how to plant his will in things at least endows them with some meaning: that is to say, he believes that a will is already present in them. (A principle of faith.)

19

What? Ye chose virtue and the heaving breast, and at the same time ye squint covetously at the advantages of the unscrupulous. – But with virtue ye renounce all 'advantages' . . . (to be nailed to an Antisemite's door).

20

The perfect woman perpetrates literature as if it were a petty vice: as an experiment, *en passant*, and looking about her all the while to see whether anybody is noticing her, hoping that somebody *is* noticing her.

21

One should adopt only those situations in which one is in no need of sham virtues, but rather, like the tight-rope dancer on his tight rope, in which one must either fall or stand – or escape.

22

'Evil men have no songs.' * – How is it that the Russians have songs?

23

'German intellect'; for eighteen years this has been a *contradictio in adjecto*.

---

* This is a reference to Seume's poem 'Die Gesänge', the first verse of which is:
    Wo man singet, lass dich ruhig nieder,
    Ohne Furcht, was man im Lande glaubt;
    Wo man singet, wird kein Mensch beraubt:
    Bösewichter haben keine Lieder.
('Wherever people sing thou canst safely settle down without a qualm as to what the general faith of the land may be. Wherever people sing, no man is ever robbed; *rascals* have no songs.') Popular tradition, however, renders the lines thus:
    Wo man singt, da lass dich ruhig nieder;
    Böse Menschen [evil men] haben keine Lieder.
                                                                    – Tr.

24

By seeking the beginnings of things, a man becomes a crab. The historian looks backwards: in the end he also *believes* backwards.

25

Contentment preserves one even from catching cold. Has a woman who knew that she was well-dressed ever caught cold? – No, not even when she had scarcely a rag to her back.

26

I distrust all systematisers, and avoid them. The will to a system shows a lack of honesty.

27

Man thinks woman profound – why? Because he can never fathom her depths. Woman is not even shallow.

28

When woman possesses masculine virtues, she is enough to make you run away. When she possesses no masculine virtues, she herself runs away.

29

'How often conscience had to bite in times gone by! What good teeth it must have had! And today, what is amiss?' – A dentist's question.

30

Errors of haste are seldom committed singly. The first time a man always does too much. And precisely on that account he commits a second error, and then he does too little.

31

The trodden worm curls up. This testifies to its caution. It thus reduces its chances of being trodden upon again. In the language of morality: Humility.

32

There is such a thing as a hatred of lies and dissimulation, which is the outcome of a delicate sense of humour; there is also the selfsame hatred but as the result of cowardice, in so far as falsehood is forbidden by divine law. Too cowardly to lie . . .

33

What trifles constitute happiness! The sound of a bagpipe. Without music life would be a mistake. The German imagines even God as a songster.

34

On ne peut penser et écrire qu'assis (G. Flaubert). Here I have got you, you nihilist! A sedentary life is the real sin against the Holy Spirit. Only those thoughts that come by walking have any value.

35

There are times when we psychologists are like horses, and grow fretful. We see our own shadow rise and fall before us. The psychologist must look away from himself if he wishes to see anything at all.

36

Do we immoralists injure virtue in any way? Just as little as the anarchists injure royalty. Only since they have been shot at do princes sit firmly on their thrones once more. Moral: *morality must be shot at.*

37

Thou runnest *ahead*? – Dost thou do so as a shepherd or as an exception? A third alternative would be the fugitive. . . . First question of conscience.

38

Art thou genuine or art thou only an actor? Art thou a representative or the thing represented, itself? Finally, art thou perhaps simply a copy of an actor? . . . Second question of conscience.

39

The disappointed man speaks: I sought for great men, but all I found were the apes of their ideal.

40

Art thou one who looks on, or one who puts his own shoulder to the wheel? – Or art thou one who looks away, or who turns aside? . . . Third question of conscience.

41

Wilt thou go in company, or lead, or go by thyself? . . . A man should know what he desires, and that he desires something. – Fourth question of conscience.

42

They were but rungs in my ladder, on them I made my ascent: to that end I had to go beyond them. But they imagined that I wanted to lay myself to rest upon them.

43

What matters it whether I am acknowledged to be right! I am much too right. And he who laughs best today, will also laugh last.

44

The formula of my happiness: a yea, a nay, a straight line, a *goal* . . .

THE PROBLEM OF SOCRATES

I

In all ages the wisest have always agreed in their judgment of life: *it is no good.* At all times and places the same words have been on their lips – words full of doubt, full of melancholy, full of weariness of life, full of hostility to life. Even Socrates' dying words were: 'To live – means to be ill a long while: I owe a cock to the god Aesculapius.' Even Socrates had had enough of it. What does that prove? What does it point to? Formerly people would have said (oh, it has been said, and loudly enough too; by our Pessimists loudest of all!): 'In any case there must be some truth in this! The *consensus sapientium* is a proof of truth.' – Shall we say the same today? *May* we do so? 'In any case there must be some sickness here,' we make reply. These great sages of all periods should first be examined more closely! Is it possible that they were, every one of them, a little shaky on their legs, effete, rocky, decadent? Does wisdom perhaps appear on earth after the manner of a crow attracted by a slight smell of carrion?

2

This irreverent belief that the great sages were decadent types first occurred to me precisely in regard to that case concerning which both learned and vulgar prejudice was most opposed to my view. I recognised Socrates and Plato as symptoms of decline, as instruments in the disintegration of Hellas, as pseudo-Greek, as anti-Greek (*The Birth of Tragedy*, 1872). That *consensus sapientium*, as I perceived ever more and more clearly, did not in the least prove that they were right in the matter on which they agreed. It proved rather that these sages themselves must have been alike in some physiological particular, in order to assume the same negative attitude towards life – in order to be bound to assume that attitude. After all, judgments and valuations of life, whether for or against, cannot be true: their only value lies in the fact that they are symptoms; they can be considered only as symptoms – *per se* such judgments are nonsense. You must therefore endeavour by all means to reach out and try to grasp this astonishingly subtle axiom, *that the value of life cannot be estimated.* A living man cannot do so, because he is a contending party, or rather the very object in the dispute, and not a judge; nor can a dead man estimate it – for other reasons. For a philosopher to see a problem in the value of life, is almost an objection against him, a note of interrogation set against his wisdom – a lack of wisdom. What? Is it possible that all these great sages were not only decadents, but that they were not even wise? Let me however return to the problem of Socrates.

3

To judge from his origin, Socrates belonged to the lowest of the low: Socrates was mob. You know, and you can still see it for yourself, how ugly he was. But ugliness, which in itself is an objection, was almost a refutation among the Greeks. Was Socrates really a Greek? Ugliness is not infrequently the expression of thwarted development, or of development arrested by crossing. In other cases it appears as a decadent development. The anthropologists among the criminal specialists declare that the typical criminal is ugly: *monstrum in fronte, monstrum in animo.* But the criminal is a decadent.* Was Socrates a typical criminal? – At all events this would not clash with that famous physiognomist's judgment which was so repugnant to Socrates' friends. While on his way through Athens a certain foreigner who was no fool at judging by looks, told Socrates to his face that he was a monster, that his body harboured all the worst vices and passions. And Socrates replied simply: 'You know me, sir!'

4

Not only are the acknowledged wildness and anarchy of Socrates' instincts indicative of decadence, but also that preponderance of the logical faculties and that malignity of the misshapen which was

---

* It should be borne in mind that Nietzsche recognised two types of criminals – the criminal from strength, and the criminal from weakness. This passage alludes to the latter, Aphorism 45 of 'Skirmishes in a war with the age' alludes to the former. – Tr.

his special characteristic. Neither should we forget those aural delusions which were religiously interpreted as 'the demon of Socrates'. Everything in him is exaggerated, *buffo*, caricature, his nature is also full of concealment, of ulterior motives, and of underground currents. I try to understand the idiosyncrasy from which the Socratic equation: – Reason = Virtue = Happiness, could have arisen: the weirdest equation ever seen, and one which was essentially opposed to all the instincts of the older Hellenes.

5

With Socrates Greek taste veers round in favour of dialectics: what actually occurs? In the first place a noble taste is vanquished: with dialectics the mob comes to the top. Before Socrates' time, dialectical manners were avoided in good society: they were regarded as bad manners, they were compromising. Young men were cautioned against them. All such proffering of one's reasons was looked upon with suspicion. Honest things like honest men do not carry their reasons on their sleeve in such fashion. It is not good form to make a show of everything. That which needs to be proved cannot be worth much. Wherever authority still belongs to good usage, wherever men do not prove but command, the dialectician is regarded as a sort of clown. People laugh at him, they do not take him seriously. Socrates was a clown who succeeded in making men take him seriously: what then was the matter?

6

A man resorts to dialectics only when he has no other means to hand. People know that they excite suspicion with it and that it is not very convincing. Nothing is more easily dispelled than a dialectical effect: this is proved by the experience of every gathering in which discussions are held. It can be only the last defence of those who have no other weapons. One must require to extort one's right, otherwise one makes no use of it. That is why the Jews were dialecticians. Reynard the Fox was a dialectician: what? – and was Socrates one as well?

7

Is the Socratic irony an expression of revolt, of mob resentment? Does Socrates, as a creature suffering under oppression, enjoy his innate ferocity in the knife-thrusts of the syllogism? Does he wreak his revenge on the noblemen he fascinates? – As a dialectician a man has a merciless instrument to wield; he can play the tyrant with it: he compromises when he conquers with it. The dialectician leaves it to his opponent to prove that he is no idiot: he infuriates, he likewise paralyses. The dialectician cripples the intellect of his opponent. Can it be that dialectics was only a form of revenge in Socrates?

8

I have given you to understand in what way Socrates was able to repel: now it is all the more necessary to explain how he fascinated. – One reason is that he discovered a new kind of *agon*, and that he was the first fencing-master in the best circles in Athens. He fascinated by appealing to the combative instinct of the Greeks – he introduced a variation into the contests between men and youths. Socrates was also a great erotic.

9

But Socrates divined still more. He saw right through his noble Athenians; he perceived that his case, his peculiar case, was no exception even in his time. The same kind of degeneracy was silently preparing itself everywhere: ancient Athens was dying out. And Socrates understood that the whole world needed him – his means, his remedy, his special artifice for self-preservation. Everywhere the instincts were in a state of anarchy; everywhere people were within an ace of excess: the *monstrum in animo* was the general danger. 'The instincts would play the tyrant; we must discover a counter-tyrant who is stronger than they.' On the occasion when that physiognomist had unmasked Socrates, and had told him what he was – a crater full of evil desires – the great Master of Irony let fall one or two words more, which provide the key to his nature. 'This is true,' he said, 'but I overcame them all.' How did Socrates succeed in mastering himself? His case was at bottom only the extreme and most apparent example of a state of distress which was beginning to be general: that state in which no-one was able to master himself and in which the instincts turned one against the other. As the extreme example of this state, he fascinated – his terrifying ugliness made him conspicuous to every eye: it is quite obvious that he fascinated still more as a reply, as a solution, as an apparent cure of this case.

10

When a man finds it necessary, as Socrates did, to create a tyrant out of reason, there is no small danger that something else wishes to play the tyrant. Reason was then discovered as a saviour; neither Socrates nor his 'patients' were at liberty to be rational or not, as they pleased; at that time it was *de rigueur*, it had become a last shift. The fanaticism with which the whole of Greek thought plunges into reason betrays a critical condition of things: men were in danger; there were only two alternatives: either perish or else be absurdly rational. The moral bias of Greek philosophy from Plato onward is the outcome of a pathological condition, as is also its appreciation of dialectics. Reason = Virtue = Happiness, simply means: we must imitate Socrates, and confront the dark passions permanently with the light of day – the light of reason. We must at all costs be clever, precise, clear: all yielding to the instincts, to the unconscious, leads downwards.

11

I have now explained how Socrates fascinated: he seemed to be a doctor, a Saviour. Is it necessary to expose the errors which lay in his faith in 'reason at any price'? – It is a piece of self-deception on the part of philosophers and moralists to suppose that they can extricate themselves from degeneration by merely waging war upon it. They cannot thus extricate themselves: that which they choose as a means, as the road to salvation, is in itself again only an expression of degeneration – they only modify its mode of manifesting itself: they do not abolish it. Socrates was a misunderstanding. *The whole of the morality of amelioration – that of Christianity as well – was a misunderstanding.* The most blinding light of day: reason at any price; life made clear, cold, cautious, conscious, without instincts, opposed to the instincts, was in itself only a disease, another kind of disease – and by no means a return to 'virtue', to 'health', and to happiness. To be obliged to fight the instincts – this is the formula of degeneration: as long as life is in the ascending line, happiness is the same as instinct.

12

Did he understand this himself, this most intelligent of self-deceivers? Did he confess this to himself in the end, in the wisdom of his courage before death? Socrates wished to die. Not Athens, but his own hand gave him the draught of hemlock; he drove Athens to the poisoned cup. 'Socrates is not a doctor,' he whispered to himself, 'death alone can be a doctor here. . . . Socrates himself has only been ill a long while.'

'REASON' IN PHILOSOPHY

I

You ask me what all idiosyncrasy is in philosophers? . . . For instance their lack of the historical sense, their hatred even of the idea of Becoming, their Egyptianism. They imagine that they do honour to a thing by divorcing it from history *sub specie æterni* – when they make a mummy of it. All the ideas that philosophers have treated for thousands of years have been mummied concepts; nothing real has ever come out of their hands alive. These idolaters of concepts merely kill and stuff things when they worship – they threaten the life of everything they adore. Death, change, age, as well as procreation and growth, are in their opinion objections – even refutations. That which is cannot evolve; that which evolves *is* not. Now all of them believe, and even with desperation, in Being. But, as they cannot lay hold of it, they try to discover reasons why this privilege is withheld from them. 'Some merely apparent quality, some deception must be the cause of our not being able to ascertain the nature of Being: where is the deceiver?' 'We have him,' they cry rejoicing, 'it is sensuality!' These senses, *which in other things are so immoral*, cheat us concerning the true world. Moral: we must get rid of the deception of the senses, of Becoming, of history, of falsehood. – History is nothing more than the belief in the senses, the belief in falsehood. Moral: we must say 'no' to everything in which the senses believe: to all the rest of mankind: all that belongs to the 'people'. Let us be philosophers, mummies, monotono-theists, grave-diggers! – And above all, away with the *body*, this wretched *idée fixe* of the senses, infected with all the faults of logic that exist, refuted, even impossible, although it be impudent enough to pose as if it were real!

2

With a feeling of great reverence I except the name of *Heraclitus*. If the rest of the philosophic gang rejected the evidences of the senses, because the latter revealed a state of multifariousness and change, he rejected the same evidence because it revealed things as if they possessed permanence and unity. Even Heraclitus did an injustice to the senses. The latter lie neither as the Eleatics believed them to lie, nor as he believed them to lie – they do not lie at all. The interpretations we give to their evidence is what first introduces falsehood into it; for instance the lie of unity, the lie of matter, of substance and of permanence. Reason is the cause of our falsifying the evidence of the senses. In so far as the senses show us a state of Becoming, of transiency, and of change, they do not lie. But in declaring that Being was an empty illusion, Heraclitus will remain eternally right. The 'apparent' world is the only world: the 'true world' is no more than a false adjunct thereto.

3

And what delicate instruments of observation we have in our senses! This human nose, for instance, of which no philosopher has yet spoken with reverence and gratitude, is, for the present, the most finely adjusted instrument at our disposal: it is able to register even such slight changes of movement as the spectroscope would be unable to record. Our scientific triumphs at the present day extend precisely so far as we have accepted the evidence of our senses – as we have sharpened and armed them, and learned to follow them up to the end. What remains is abortive and not yet science – that is to say, metaphysics, theology, psychology, epistemology, or formal science, or a doctrine of symbols, like logic and its applied form mathematics. In all these things reality does not come into consideration at all, even as a problem; just as little as does the question concerning the general value of such a convention of symbols as logic.

4

The other idiosyncrasy of philosophers is no less dangerous; it consists in confusing the last and the first things. They place that which makes its appearance last – unfortunately! for it ought not to appear at all! – the 'highest concept', that is to say, the most general, the emptiest, the last cloudy streak of evaporating reality, at the beginning as the beginning. This again is only their manner of expressing their veneration: the highest thing must not have grown out of the lowest, it must not have grown at all. . . . Moral: everything of the first rank must be *causa sui*. To have been derived from something else, is as good as an objection, it sets the value of a thing in question. All superior values are of the first rank, all the highest concepts – that of Being, of the Absolute, of Goodness, of Truth, and of Perfection; all these things cannot have been evolved, they must therefore be *causa sui*. All these things cannot however be unlike one another, they cannot be opposed to one another. Thus they attain to their stupendous concept 'God'. The last, most attenuated and emptiest thing is postulated as the first thing, as the absolute cause, as *ens realissimum*. Fancy humanity having to take the brain diseases of morbid cobweb-spinners seriously! – And it has paid dearly for having done so.

5

Against this let us set the different manner in which we (you observe that I am courteous enough to say 'we') conceive the problem of the error and deceptiveness of things. Formerly people regarded change and evolution in general as the proof of appearance, as a sign of the fact that something must be there that leads us astray. Today, on the other hand, we realise that precisely as far as the rational bias forces us to postulate unity, identity, permanence, substance, cause, materiality and being, we are in a measure involved in error, driven necessarily to error; however certain we may feel, as the result of a strict examination of the matter, that the error lies here. It is just the same here as with the motion of the sun: In its case it was our eyes that were wrong; in the matter of the concepts above mentioned it is our language itself that pleads most constantly in their favour. In its origin language belongs to an age of the most rudimentary forms of psychology: if we try to conceive of the first conditions of the metaphysics of language, i.e., in plain English, of reason, we immediately find ourselves in the midst of a system of fetishism. For here, the doer and his deed are seen in all circumstances, will is believed in as a cause in general; the ego is taken for granted, the ego as Being, and as substance, and the faith in the ego as substance is projected into all things – in this way, alone, the concept 'thing' is created. Being is thought into and insinuated into everything as cause; from the concept 'ego', alone, can the concept 'Being' proceed. At the beginning stands the tremendously fatal error of supposing the will to be something that actuates – a faculty. Now we know that it is only a word.* Very much later, in a world a thousand times more enlightened, the assurance, the subjective certitude, in the handling of the categories of reason came into the minds of philosophers as a surprise. They concluded that these categories could not be derived from experience – on the contrary, the whole of experience rather contradicts them. *Whence do they come therefore?* In India, as in Greece, the same mistake was made: 'we must already once have lived in a higher world (instead of in a much lower one, which would have been the truth!), we must have been divine, for we possess reason!' . . . Nothing indeed has exercised a more simple power of persuasion hitherto than the error of Being, as it was formulated by the Eleatics for instance: in its favour are every word and every sentence that we utter! – Even the opponents of the Eleatics succumbed to the seductive powers of their concept of Being. Among others there was Democritus in his discovery of the atom. 'Reason' in language! – oh what a deceptive old witch it has been! I fear we shall never be rid of God, so long as we still believe in grammar.

6

People will feel grateful to me if I condense a point of view, which is at once so important and so new, into four theses: by this means I shall facilitate comprehension, and shall likewise challenge contradiction.

Proposition One. The reasons upon which the apparent nature of 'this' world have been based, rather tend to prove its reality – any other kind of reality defies demonstration.

Proposition Two. The characteristics with which man has endowed the 'true Being' of things, are the characteristics of non-Being, of *nonentity.* The 'true world' has been erected upon a contradiction of

* Nietzsche here refers to the concept 'free will' of the Christians; this does not mean that there is no such thing as will – that is to say a powerful determining force from within. – Tr.

the real world; and it is indeed an apparent world, seeing that it is merely a *moralo-optical* delusion.

Proposition Three. There is no sense in spinning yarns about another world, provided, of course, that we do not possess a mighty instinct which urges us to slander, belittle, and cast suspicion upon this life: in this case we should be avenging ourselves on this life with the phantasmagoria of 'another', of a 'better' life.

Proposition Four. To divide the world into a 'true' and an 'apparent' world, whether after the manner of Christianity or of Kant (after all a Christian in disguise), is only a sign of decadence — a symptom of *degenerating* life. The fact that the artist esteems the appearance of a thing higher than reality, is no objection to this statement. For 'appearance' signifies once more reality here, but in a selected, strengthened and corrected form. The tragic artist is no pessimist — he says *Yea* to everything questionable and terrible, he is Dionysian.

HOW THE 'TRUE WORLD' ULTIMATELY BECAME A FABLE

The History of an Error

1. The true world, attainable to the sage, the pious man and the man of virtue – he lives in it, *he is it*.

(The most ancient form of the idea was relatively clever, simple, convincing. It was a paraphrase of the proposition 'I, Plato, am the truth.')

2. The true world which is unattainable for the moment, is promised to the sage, to the pious man and to the man of virtue ('to the sinner who repents').

(Progress of the idea: it becomes more subtle, more insidious, more evasive – *it becomes a woman*, it becomes Christian.)

3. The true world is unattainable, it cannot be proved, it cannot promise anything; but even as a thought, alone, it is a comfort, an obligation, a command.

(At bottom this is still the old sun; but seen through mist and scepticism: the idea has become sublime, pale, northern, Königsbergian.)*

4. The true world – is it unattainable? At all events it is unattained. And as unattained it is also *unknown*. Consequently it no longer comforts, nor saves, nor constrains: what could something unknown constrain us to?

(The grey of dawn. Reason stretches itself and yawns for the first time. The cock-crow of positivism.)

* Kant was a native of Königsberg and lived there all his life. Did Nietzsche know that Kant was simply a Scotch Puritan, whose family had settled in Germany?

5. The 'true world' – an idea that no longer serves any purpose, that no longer constrains one to anything – a useless idea that has become quite superfluous, consequently an exploded idea: let us abolish it!

(Bright daylight; breakfast; the return of common sense and of cheerfulness; Plato blushes for shame and all free-spirits kick up a shindy.)

6. We have suppressed the true world: what world survives? The apparent world perhaps? . . . Certainly not! *In abolishing the true world we have also abolished the world of appearance!*

(Noon; the moment of the shortest shadows; the end of the longest error; mankind's zenith; *Incipit Zarathustra*.)

MORALITY AS THE ENEMY OF NATURE

I

There is a time when all passions are simply fatal in their action, when they wreck their victims with the weight of their folly – and there is a later period, a very much later period, when they marry with the spirit, when they 'spiritualise' themselves. Formerly, owing to the stupidity inherent in passion, men waged war against passion itself: men pledged themselves to annihilate it – all ancient moral-mongers were unanimous on this point, '*il faut tuer les passions*.' The most famous formula for this stands in the New Testament, in that Sermon on the Mount, where, let it be said incidentally, things are by no means regarded *from a height*. It is said there, for instance, with an application to sexuality: 'if thy eye offend thee, pluck it out': fortunately no Christian acts in obedience to this precept. To annihilate the passions and desires, simply on account of their stupidity, and to obviate the unpleasant consequences of their stupidity, seems to us today merely an aggravated form of stupidity. We no longer admire those dentists who extract teeth simply in order that they may not ache again. On the other hand, it will be admitted with some reason, that on the soil from which Christianity grew, the idea of the 'spiritualisation of passion' could not possibly have been conceived. The early Church, as everyone knows, certainly did wage war against the 'intelligent', in favour of the 'poor in spirit'. In these circumstances how could the passions be combated intelligently? The Church combats passion by means of excision of all kinds: its practice, its 'remedy', is *castration*. It never inquires 'how can a desire be spiritualised, beautified, deified?' – In all ages it has laid the weight of discipline in the process of extirpation (the extirpation of sensuality, pride, lust of dominion, lust of property, and revenge). – But to attack the passions at their roots means attacking life itself at its source: the method of the Church is hostile to life.

2

The same means, castration and extirpation, are instinctively chosen for waging war against a passion, by those who are too weak of will, too degenerate, to impose some sort of moderation upon it; by those natures who, to speak in metaphor (and without metaphor), need *la Trappe*, or some kind of ultimatum of war, a *gulf* set between themselves and a passion. Only degenerates find radical methods indispensable: weakness of will, or more strictly speaking, the inability not to react to a stimulus, is in itself simply another form of degeneracy. Radical and mortal hostility to sensuality, remains a suspicious symptom: it justifies one in being suspicious of the general state of one who goes to such extremes. Moreover, that hostility and hatred reach their height only when such natures no longer possess enough strength of character to adopt the radical remedy, to renounce their inner 'Satan'. Look at the whole history of the priests, the philosophers, and the artists as well: the most poisonous diatribes against the senses have not been said by the impotent, nor by the ascetics; but by those impossible ascetics, by those who found it necessary to be ascetics.

3

The spiritualisation of sensuality is called *love*: it is a great triumph over Christianity. Another triumph is our spiritualisation of hostility. It consists in the fact that we are beginning to realise very profoundly the value of having enemies: in short that with them we are forced to do and to conclude precisely the reverse of what we previously did and concluded. In all ages the Church wished to annihilate its enemies: we, the immoralists and Antichrists, see our advantage in the survival of the Church. Even in political life, hostility has now become more spiritual — much more cautious, much more thoughtful, and much more moderate. Almost every party sees its self-preservative interests in preventing the opposition from going to pieces; and the same applies to politics on a grand scale. A new creation, more particularly, like the new Empire, has more need of enemies than friends: only as a contrast does it begin to feel necessary, only as a contrast does it *become* necessary. And we behave in precisely the same way to the 'inner enemy': in this quarter too we have spiritualised enmity, in this quarter too we have understood its value. A man is productive only in so far as he is rich in contrasted instincts; he can remain young only on condition that his soul does not begin to take things easy and to yearn for peace. Nothing has grown more alien to us than that old desire – the 'peace of the soul', which is the aim of Christianity. Nothing could make us less envious than the moral cow and the plump happiness of a clean conscience. The man who has renounced war has renounced a grand life. In many cases, of course, 'peace of the soul' is merely a misunderstanding – it is something *very different* which has failed to find a more honest name for itself. Without either circumlocution or prejudice I will suggest a few cases. 'Peace of the soul' may for instance be the sweet effulgence of rich animality in the realm of morality (or religion). Or the first presage of weariness, the first shadow that evening, every kind of evening, is wont to cast. Or a sign that the air is moist, and that winds are blowing up from the south. Or unconscious gratitude for a good digestion (sometimes called 'brotherly love'). Or the serenity of the convalescent, on whose lips all things have a new taste, and who bides his time. Or the condition which follows upon a thorough gratification of our strongest passion, the well-being of unaccustomed satiety. Or the senility of our will, of our desires, and of our vices. Or laziness, coaxed by vanity into togging itself out in a moral garb. Or the ending of a state of long suspense and of agonising uncertainty, by a state of certainty, of even terrible certainty. Or the expression of ripeness and mastery in the midst of a task, of a creative work, of a production, of a thing willed, the calm breathing that denotes that 'freedom of will' has been attained. Who knows? – maybe the *Twilight of the Idols* is only a sort of 'peace of the soul'.

4

I will formulate a principle. All naturalism in morality – that is to say, every sound morality is ruled by a life instinct – any one of the laws of life is fulfilled by the definite canon 'thou shalt'; 'thou shalt not' and any sort of obstacle or hostile element in the road of life is thus cleared away. Conversely, the morality which is antagonistic to nature – that is to say, almost every morality that has been taught, honoured and preached hitherto, is directed precisely against the life-instincts – it is a condemnation, now secret, now blatant and impudent, of these very instincts. Inasmuch as it says

'God sees into the heart of man,' it says nay to the profoundest and most superior desires of life and takes God as the enemy of life. The saint in whom God is well pleased is the ideal eunuch. Life terminates where the 'Kingdom of God' begins.

5

Admitting that you have understood the villainy of such a mutiny against life as that which has become almost sacrosanct in Christian morality, you have fortunately understood something besides; and that is the futility, the fictitiousness, the absurdity and the falseness of such a mutiny. For the condemnation of life by a living creature is after all but the symptom of a definite kind of life: the question as to whether the condemnation is justified or the reverse is not even raised. In order even to approach the problem of the value of life, a man would need to be placed outside life, and moreover know it as well as one, as many, as all in fact, who have lived it. These are reasons enough to prove to us that this problem is an inaccessible one to us. When we speak of values, we speak under the inspiration and through the optics of life: life itself urges us to determine values: life itself values through us when we determine values. From which it follows that even that morality which is antagonistic to life, and which conceives God as the opposite and the condemnation of life, is only a valuation of life – of what life? of what kind of life? But I have already answered this question: it is the valuation of declining, of enfeebled, of exhausted and of condemned life. Morality, as it has been understood hitherto – as it was finally formulated by Schopenhauer in the words 'the denial of the will to life', is the instinct of degeneration itself, which converts itself into an imperative: it says: 'Perish!' It is the death sentence of men who are already doomed.

6

Let us at last consider how exceedingly simple it is on our part to say: 'Man should be thus and thus!' Reality shows us a marvellous wealth of types, and a luxuriant variety of forms and changes: and yet the first wretch of a moral loafer that comes along cries 'No! Man should be different!' He even knows what man should be like, does this sanctimonious prig: he draws his own face on the wall and declares: '*ecce homo!*' But even when the moralist addresses himself only to the individual and says 'thus and thus shouldst thou be!' he still makes an ass of himself. The individual in his past and future is a piece of fate, one law the more, one necessity the more for all that is to come and is to be. To say to him 'change thyself', is tantamount to saying that everything should change, even backwards as well. Truly these have been consistent moralists, they wished man to be different, i.e., virtuous; they wished him to be after their own image – that is to say sanctimonious humbugs. And to this end they denied the world! No slight form of insanity! No modest form of immodesty! Morality, in so far it condemns *per se*, and *not* out of any aim, consideration or motive of life, is a specific error, for which no-one should feel any mercy, a degenerate idiosyncrasy that has done an unutterable amount of harm. We others, we immoralists, on the contrary, have opened our hearts wide to all kinds of comprehension, understanding and approbation.* We do not deny readily, we glory in saying yea to things. Our eyes have opened ever wider and wider to that economy which still employs and knows how to use to its own advantage all that which the sacred craziness of priests and the morbid reason in priests rejects; to that economy in the law of life which draws its own advantage even out of the repulsive race of bigots, the priests and the virtuous – what advantage? But we ourselves, we immoralists, are the reply to this question.

---

* cf. Spinoza, who says in the *Tractatus politicus* (1677), Chap. 1, § 4: '*Sedulo curavi, humanas actiones non ridere, non lugere, neque detestari, sed intelligere.*' ('I have carefully endeavoured not to deride, or deplore, or detest human actions, but to understand them.') – TR.

I

The error of the confusion of cause and effect. – There is no more dangerous error than to confound the effect with the cause: I call this error the intrinsic perversion of reason. Nevertheless this error is one of the most ancient and most recent habits of mankind. In one part of the world it has even been canonised; and it bears the name of 'religion' and 'morality.' Every postulate formulated by religion and morality contains it. Priests and the promulgators of moral laws are the promoters of this perversion of reason. – Let me give you an example. Everybody knows the book of the famous Cornaro, in which he recommends his slender diet as the recipe for a long, happy and also virtuous life. Few books have been so widely read, and to this day many thousand copies of it are still printed annually in England. I do not doubt that there is scarcely a single book (the Bible of course excepted) that has worked more mischief, shortened more lives, than this well-meant curiosity. The reason of this is the confusion of effect and cause. This worthy Italian saw the cause of his long life in his diet: whereas the prerequisites of long life, which are exceptional slowness of molecular change, and a low rate of expenditure in energy, were the cause of his meagre diet. He was not at liberty to eat a small or a great amount. His frugality was not the result of free choice, he would have been ill had he eaten more. He who does not happen to be a carp, however, is not only wise to eat well, but is also compelled to do so. A scholar of the present day, with his rapid consumption of nervous energy, would soon go to the dogs on Cornaro's diet. *Crede experto.*

2

The most general principle lying at the root of every religion and morality, is this: 'Do this and that and avoid this and that – and thou wilt be happy. Otherwise — .' Every morality and every religion is this imperative – I call it the great original sin of reason – *immortal unreason*. In my mouth this principle is converted into its opposite – first example of my 'transvaluation of all values': a well-constituted man, a man who is one of 'nature's lucky strokes', *must* perform certain actions and instinctively fear other actions; he introduces the element of order, of which he is the physiological manifestation, into his relations with men and things. In a formula: his virtue is the consequence of his good constitution. Longevity and plentiful offspring are not the reward of virtue, virtue itself is on the contrary that retardation of the metabolic process which, among other things, results in a long life and in plentiful offspring, in short in *Cornarism*. The Church and morality say: 'A race, a people perish through vice and luxury.' My reinstated reason says: when a people are going to the dogs, when they are degenerating physiologically, vice and luxury (that is to say, the need of ever stronger and more frequent stimuli such as all exhausted natures are acquainted with) are bound to result. Such and such a young man grows pale and withered prematurely. His friends say this or that illness is the cause of it. I say: the fact that he became ill, the fact that he did not resist illness, was in itself already the outcome of impoverished life, of hereditary exhaustion. The newspaper reader says: such and such a party by committing such an error will meet its death. My superior politics say: a party that can make such mistakes, is in its last agony – it no longer possesses any certainty of instinct. Every mistake is in every sense the sequel to degeneration of the instincts, to disintegration of the will. This is almost the definition of evil, Everything valuable is instinct – and consequently easy, necessary, free. Exertion is an objection, the god is characteristically different from the hero (in my language: light feet are the first attribute of divinity).

3

The error of false causality. In all ages men have believed that they knew what a cause was: but whence did we derive this knowledge, or more accurately, this faith in the fact that we know? Out of the realm of the famous 'inner facts of consciousness', not one of which has yet proved itself to be a fact. We believed ourselves to be causes even in the action of the will; we thought that in this matter at least we caught causality red-handed. No-one doubted that all the *antecedentia* of an action were to be sought in consciousness, and could be discovered there – as 'motive' – if only they were sought. Otherwise we should not be free to perform them, we should not have been responsible for them. Finally who would have questioned that a thought is caused? that the ego causes the thought? Of these three 'facts of inner consciousness' by means of which causality seemed to be guaranteed, the first and most convincing is that of the will as cause; the conception of consciousness ('spirit') as a cause, and subsequently that of the ego (the 'subject') as a cause, were merely born afterwards, once the causality of the will stood established as 'given', as a fact of experience. Meanwhile we have come to our senses. Today we no longer believe a word of all this. The 'inner world' is full of phantoms and will-o'-the-wisps: the will is one of these. The will no longer actuates, consequently it no longer explains anything – all it does is to accompany processes; it may even be absent. The so-called 'motive' is another error. It is merely a ripple on the surface of consciousness, a side issue of the action, which is much more likely to conceal than to reveal the *antecedentia* of the latter. And as for the ego! It has become legendary, fictional, a play upon words: it has ceased utterly and completely from thinking, feeling, and willing! What is the result of it all? There are no such things as spiritual causes. The whole of popular experience on this subject went to the devil! That is the result of it all. For we had blissfully abused that experience, we had built the world upon it as a world of causes, as a world of will, as a world of spirit. The most antiquated and most traditional psychology has been at work here, it has done nothing else: all phenomena were deeds in the light of this psychology, and all deeds were the result of will; according to it the world was a complex mechanism of agents, an agent (a 'subject') lay at the root of all things. Man projected his three 'inner facts of consciousness', the will, the spirit, and the ego in which he believed most firmly, outside himself. He first deduced the concept Being out of the concept Ego, he supposed 'things' to exist as he did himself, according to his notion of the ego as cause. Was it to be wondered at that later on he always found in things only that which he had laid in them? – The thing itself, I repeat, the concept 'thing' was merely a reflex of the belief in the ego as cause. And even your atom, my dear good mechanists and physicists, what an amount of error, of rudimentary psychology still adheres to it! – Not to speak of the 'thing-in-itself', of the *horrendum pudendum* of the metaphysicians! The error of spirit regarded as a cause, confounded with reality! And made the measure of reality! And called *God!*

4

The error of imaginary causes. Starting out from dreamland, we find that to any definite sensation, like that produced by a distant cannon shot for instance, we are wont to ascribe a cause after the fact (very often quite a little romance in which the dreamer himself is, of course, the hero). Meanwhile the sensation becomes protracted like a sort of continuous echo, until, as it were, the instinct of causality allows it to come to the front rank, no longer however as a chance occurrence, but as a thing which has some meaning. The cannon shot presents itself in a *causal* manner, by means of an apparent reversal in the order of time. That which occurs last, the motivation, is experienced first, often with a hundred details which flash past like lightning, and the shot is the *result*. What has happened? The ideas suggested by a particular state of our senses, are misinterpreted as the cause of that state. As a matter of fact we proceed in precisely the same manner when we are awake. The greater number of our general sensations – every kind of obstacle, pressure, tension, explosion in the interplay of the organs, and more particularly the condition of the *nervus sympathicus* – stimulate our instinct of causality: we will have a reason which will account for our feeling thus or thus – for feeling ill or well. We are never satisfied by merely ascertaining the fact that we feel thus or thus: we admit this fact – we become conscious of it – only when we have attributed it to some kind of motivation. Memory, which, in such circumstances unconsciously becomes active, adduces former conditions of a like kind, together with the causal interpretations with which they are associated – but not their real cause. The belief that the ideas, the accompanying processes of consciousness, have been the causes, is certainly produced by the agency of memory. And in this way we become *accustomed* to a particular interpretation of causes which, truth to tell, actually hinders and even utterly prevents the investigation of the proper cause.

5

The psychological explanation of the above fact. To trace something unfamiliar back to something familiar is at once a relief, a comfort and a satisfaction, while it also produces a feeling of power. The unfamiliar involves danger, anxiety and care – the fundamental instinct is to get rid of these painful circumstances. First principle: any explanation is better than none at all. Since, at bottom, it is only a question of shaking one's self free from certain oppressive ideas, the means employed to this end are not selected with overmuch punctiliousness: the first idea by means of which the unfamiliar is revealed as familiar produces a feeling of such comfort that it is 'held to be true'. The proof of happiness ('of power') as the criterion of truth. The instinct of causality is therefore conditioned and stimulated by the feeling of fear. Whenever possible, the question 'why?' should not only educe the cause as cause, but rather a certain kind of cause – a comforting, liberating and reassuring cause. The first result of this need is that something known or already experienced, and recorded in the memory, is posited as the cause. The new factor, that which has not been experienced and which is unfamiliar, is excluded from the sphere of causes. Not only do we try to find a certain kind of explanation as the cause, but those kinds of explanations are selected and preferred which dissipate most rapidly the sensation of strangeness, novelty and unfamiliarity – in fact the most ordinary explanations. And the result is that a certain manner of postulating causes tends to predominate ever more and more, becomes concentrated into a system, and finally reigns supreme, to the complete exclusion of all other causes and explanations. The banker thinks immediately of business, the Christian of 'sin', and the girl of her love affair.

6

The whole domain of morality and religion may be classified under the rubric 'imaginary causes'. The 'explanation' of general unpleasant sensations. These sensations are dependent upon certain creatures who are hostile to us (evil spirits: the most famous example of this – the mistaking of hysterical women for witches). These sensations are dependent upon actions which are reprehensible (the feeling of 'sin', 'sinfulness' is a manner of accounting for a certain physiological disorder – people always find reasons for being dissatisfied with themselves). These sensations depend upon punishment, upon compensation for something which we ought not to have done, which we ought not to have been (this idea was generalised in a more impudent form by Schopenhauer, into that principle in which morality appears in its real colours – that is to say, as a veritable poisoner and slanderer of life: 'all great suffering, whether mental or physical, reveals what we deserve: for it could not visit us if we did not deserve it,' – *The World as Will and Idea*, vol. 2, p. 666). These sensations are the outcome of ill-considered actions, having evil consequences (the passions, the senses, postulated as causes, as guilty. By means of other calamities distressing physiological conditions are interpreted as 'merited'). – The 'explanation' of pleasant sensations. These sensations are dependent upon a trust in God. They may depend upon our consciousness of having done one or two good actions (a so-called 'good conscience' is a physiological condition, which may be the outcome of good digestion). They may depend upon the happy issue of certain undertakings (an ingenuous mistake: the happy issue of an undertaking certainly does not give a hypochondriac or a Pascal any general sensation of pleasure). They may depend upon faith, love and hope – the Christian virtues. As a matter of fact all these pretended explanations are but the results of certain states, and as it were translations of feelings of pleasure and pain into a false dialect: a man is in a condition of hopefulness because the dominant physiological sensation of his being is again one of strength and wealth; he trusts in God because the feeling of abundance and power gives him a peaceful state of mind. Morality and religion are completely and utterly parts of the psychology of error: in every particular case cause and effect are confounded; as truth is confounded with the effect of that which is believed to be true; or a certain state of consciousness is confounded with the chain of causes which brought it about.

7

The error of free will. At present we no longer have any mercy upon the concept 'free will': we know only too well what it is – the most egregious theological trick that has ever existed for the purpose of making mankind 'responsible' in a theological manner – that is to say, to make mankind dependent upon theologians. I will now explain to you only the psychology of the whole process of inculcating the sense of responsibility. Wherever men try to trace responsibility home to anyone, it is the instinct of punishment and of the desire to judge which is active. Becoming is robbed of its innocence when any particular condition of things is traced to a will, to intentions and to responsible actions. The doctrine of the will was invented principally for the purpose of punishment – that is to say, with the intention of tracing guilt. The whole of ancient psychology, or the psychology of the will, is the outcome of the fact that its originators, who were the priests at the head of ancient communities, wanted to create for themselves a right to administer punishments – or the right for God to do so. Men were thought of as 'free' in order that they might be judged and punished – in order that they might be held guilty: consequently every action had to be regarded as voluntary, and the origin of every action had to be imagined as lying in consciousness (in this way the most fundamentally fraudulent character of psychology was established as the very principle of psychology itself). Now that we have entered upon the opposite movement, now that we immoralists are trying with all our power to eliminate the concepts of guilt and punishment from the world once more, and to cleanse psychology, history, nature and all social institutions and customs of all signs of those two concepts, we recognise no more radical opponents than the theologians, who with their notion of 'a moral order of things' still continue to pollute the innocence of Becoming with punishment and guilt. Christianity is the metaphysics of the hangman.

8

What then, alone, can our teaching be? – That no-one gives man his qualities, neither God, society, his parents, his ancestors, nor himself (this nonsensical idea which is at last refuted here was taught as 'intelligible freedom' by Kant, and perhaps even as early as Plato himself). No-one is responsible for the fact that he exists at all, that he is constituted as he is, and that he happens to be in certain circumstances and in a particular environment. The fatality of his being cannot be divorced from the fatality of all that which has been and will be. This is not the result of an individual intention, of a will, of an aim, there is no attempt at attaining to any 'ideal man', or 'ideal happiness' or 'ideal morality' with him – it is absurd to wish him to be careering towards some sort of purpose. *We* invented the concept 'purpose'; in reality purpose is altogether lacking. One is necessary, one is a piece of fate, one belongs to the whole, one is in the whole – there is nothing that could judge, measure, compare, and condemn our existence, for that would mean judging, measuring, comparing and condemning the whole. *But there is nothing outside the whole!* The fact that no-one shall any longer be made responsible, that the nature of existence may not be traced to a *causa prima*, that the world is an entity neither as a sensorium nor as a spirit – *this alone is the great deliverance* – thus alone is the innocence of Becoming restored. . . . The concept 'God' has been the greatest objection to existence hitherto. . . . We deny God, we deny responsibility in God: thus alone do we save the world.

THE 'IMPROVERS' OF MANKIND

I

You are aware of my demand upon philosophers, that they should take up a stand beyond Good and Evil – that they should have the illusion of the moral judgment beneath them. This demand is the result of a point of view which I was the first to formulate: *that there are no such things as moral facts*. Moral judgment has this in common with the religious one, that it believes in realities which are not real. Morality is only an interpretation of certain phenomena: or, more strictly speaking, a misinterpretation of them. Moral judgment, like the religious one, belongs to a stage of ignorance in which even the concept of reality, the distinction between real and imagined things, is still lacking: so that truth, at such a stage, is applied to a host of things which today we call 'imaginary'. That is why the moral judgment must never be taken quite literally: as such it is sheer nonsense. As a sign code, however, it is invaluable: to him at least who knows, it reveals the most valuable facts concerning cultures and inner conditions, which did not know enough to 'understand' themselves. Morality is merely a sign-language, simply symptomatology: one must already know what it is all about in order to turn it to any use.

2

Let me give you one example, quite provisionally. In all ages there have been people who wished to 'improve' mankind: this above all is what was called morality. But the most different tendencies are concealed beneath the same word. Both the taming of the beast man, and the rearing of a particular type of man, have been called 'improvement': these zoological *termini* alone represent real things – real things of which the typical 'improver', the priest, naturally knows nothing, and will know nothing. To call the taming of an animal 'improving' it, sounds to our ears almost like a joke. He who knows what goes on in menageries, doubts very much whether an animal is improved in such places. It is certainly weakened, it is made less dangerous, and by means of the depressing influence of fear, pain, wounds, and hunger, it is converted into a sick animal. And the same holds good of the tamed man whom the priest has 'improved'. In the early years of the Middle Ages, during which the Church was most distinctly and above all a menagerie, the most beautiful examples of the 'blond beast' were hunted down in all directions – the noble Germans, for instance, were 'improved'. But what did this 'improved' German, who had been lured to the monastery, look like after the process? He looked like a caricature of man, like an abortion: he had become a 'sinner', he was caged up, he had been imprisoned behind a host of appalling notions. He now lay there, sick, wretched, malevolent even toward himself: full of hate for the instincts of life, full of suspicion in regard to all that is still strong and happy. In short a 'Christian'. In physiological terms: in a fight with an animal, the only way of making it weak may be to make it sick. The Church understood this: it ruined man, it made him weak – but it laid claim to having 'improved' him.

3

Now let us consider the other case which is called morality, the case of the rearing of a particular race and species. The most magnificent example of this is offered by Indian morality, and is sanctioned religiously as the 'Law of Manu'. In this book the task is set of rearing no less than four races at once: a priestly race, a warrior race, a merchant and agricultural race, and finally a race of servants – the Sudras. It is quite obvious that we are no longer in a circus watching tamers of wild animals in this book. To have conceived even the plan of such a breeding scheme presupposes the existence of a man who is a hundred times milder and more reasonable than the mere lion-tamer. One breathes more freely, after stepping out of the Christian atmosphere of hospitals and prisons, into this more salubrious, loftier and more spacious world. What a wretched thing the New Testament is beside Manu, what an evil odour hangs around it! – But even this organisation found it necessary to be terrible – not this time in a struggle with the animal-man, but with his opposite, the non-caste man, the hotch-potch man, the Chandala. And once again it had no other means of making him weak and harmless, than by making him sick – it was the struggle with the greatest 'number'. Nothing perhaps is more offensive to our feelings than these measures of security on the part of Indian morality. The third edict, for instance (Avadana-Sastra I), which treats 'of impure vegetables', ordains that the only nourishment that the Chandala should be allowed must consist of garlic and onions, as the holy scriptures forbid their being given corn or grain-bearing fruit, water and fire. The same edict declares that the water which they need must be drawn neither out of rivers, wells or ponds, but only out of the ditches leading to swamps and out of the holes left by the footprints of animals. They are likewise forbidden to wash either their linen or themselves, since the water which is graciously granted to them must only be used for quenching their thirst. Finally Sudra women are forbidden to assist Chandala women at their confinements, while Chandala women are also forbidden to assist each other at such times. The results of sanitary regulations of this kind could not fail to make themselves felt; deadly epidemics and the most ghastly venereal diseases soon appeared, and in consequence of these again 'the law of the knife', that is to say circumcision, was prescribed for male children and the removal of the small labia from the females. Manu himself says: 'the Chandala are the fruit of adultery, incest, and crime (this is the necessary consequence of the idea of breeding). Their clothes shall consist only of the rags torn from corpses, their vessels shall be the fragments of broken pottery, their ornaments shall be made of old iron, and their religion shall be the worship of evil spirits; without rest they shall wander from place to place. They are forbidden to write from left to right or to use their right hand in writing: the use of the right hand and writing from left to right are reserved to people of virtue, to people of race.'

4

These regulations are instructive enough: we can see in them the absolutely pure and primeval humanity of the Aryans – we learn that the notion 'pure blood' is the reverse of harmless. On the other hand it becomes clear among which people the hatred, the Chandala hatred of this humanity has been immortalised, among which people it has become religion and genius. From this point of view the gospels are documents of the highest value; and the Book of Enoch is still more so. Christianity as sprung from Jewish roots and comprehensible only as grown upon this soil, represents the counter-movement against that morality of breeding, of race and of privilege: it is essentially an anti-Aryan religion: Christianity is the transvaluation of all Aryan values, the triumph of Chandala values, the proclaimed gospel of the poor and of the low, the general insurrection of all the down-trodden, the wretched, the bungled and the botched, against the 'race' – the immortal revenge of the Chandala as the *religion of love*.

5

The morality of breeding and the morality of taming, in the means which they adopt in order to prevail, are quite worthy of each other: we may lay down as a leading principle that in order to create morality a man must have the absolute will to immorality. This is the great and strange problem with which I have so long been occupied: the psychology of the 'improvers' of mankind. A small, and at bottom perfectly insignificant fact, known as the *pia fraus*, first gave me access to this problem: the *pia fraus*, the heirloom of all philosophers and priests who 'improve' mankind. Neither Manu, nor Plato, nor Confucius, nor the teachers of Judaism and Christianity, have ever doubted their right to falsehood. They have never doubted their right to quite a number of other things. To express oneself in a formula, one might say: all means which have been used heretofore with the object of making man moral, were through and through immoral.

THINGS THE GERMANS LACK

I

Among Germans at the present day it does not suffice to have intellect; one is actually forced to appropriate it, to lay claim to it.

Maybe I know the Germans, perhaps I may tell them a few home truths. Modern Germany represents such an enormous store of inherited and acquired capacity, that for some time it might spend this accumulated treasure even with some prodigality. It is no superior culture that has ultimately become prevalent with this modern tendency, nor is it by any means delicate taste, or noble beauty of the instincts; but rather a number of virtues more manly than any that other European countries can show. An amount of good spirits and self-respect, plenty of firmness in human relations and in the reciprocity of duties; much industry and much perseverance – and a certain inherited soberness which is much more in need of a spur than of a brake. Let me add that in this country people still obey without feeling that obedience humiliates. And no-one despises his opponent.

You observe that it is my desire to be fair to the Germans: and in this respect I should not like to be untrue to myself – I must therefore also state my objections to them. It costs a good deal to attain to a position of power; for power *stultifies*. The Germans – they were once called a people of thinkers: do they really think at all at present? Nowadays the Germans are bored by intellect, they mistrust intellect; politics have swallowed up all earnestness for really intellectual things – 'Germany, Germany above all'.[*] I fear this was the death-blow to German philosophy. 'Are there any German philosophers? Are there any German poets? Are there any good German books?' people ask me abroad. I

* The German national hymn: '*Deutschland, Deutschland über alles*'. – Tr.

blush; but with that pluck which is peculiar to me, even in moments of desperation, I reply: 'Yes, Bismarck!' – Could I have dared to confess what books *are* read today? Cursed instinct of mediocrity!

2

What might not German intellect have been! – who has not thought sadly upon this question! But this nation has deliberately stultified itself for almost a thousand years: nowhere else have the two great European narcotics, alcohol and Christianity, been so viciously abused as in Germany. Recently a third opiate was added to the list, one which in itself alone would have sufficed to complete the ruin of all subtle and daring intellectual animation, I speak of music, our costive and constipating German music. How much peevish ponderousness, paralysis, dampness, dressing-gown languor, and beer is there not in German intelligence!

How is it really possible that young men who consecrate their whole lives to the pursuit of intellectual ends, should not feel within them the first instinct of intellectuality, the *self-preservative instinct of the intellect* – and should drink beer? The alcoholism of learned youths does not incapacitate them for becoming scholars – a man quite devoid of intellect may be a great scholar – but it is a problem in every other respect. Where can that soft degeneracy not be found, which is produced in the intellect by beer! I once laid my finger upon a case of this sort, which became almost famous – the degeneration of our leading German free-spirit, the *clever* David Strauss, into the author of a suburban gospel and New Faith. Not in vain had he sung the praises of 'the dear old brown liquor' in verse – true unto death.

3

I have spoken of German intellect. I have said that it is becoming coarser and shallower. Is that enough? – In reality something very different frightens me, and that is the ever steady decline of German earnestness, German profundity, and German passion in things intellectual. Not only intellectuality, but also pathos has altered. From time to time I come in touch with German uni-versities; what an extraordinary atmosphere prevails among their scholars! what barrenness! and what self-satisfied and lukewarm intellectuality! For anyone to point to German science as an argument against me would show that he grossly misunderstood my meaning, while it would also prove that he had not read a word of my writings. For seventeen years I have done little else than expose the de-intellectualising influence of our modern scientific studies. The severe slavery to which every individual nowadays is condemned by the enormous range covered by the sciences, is the chief reason why fuller, richer and profounder natures can find no education or educators that are fit for them. Nothing is more deleterious to this age than the superfluity of pretentious loafers and fragmentary human beings; our universities are really the involuntary forcing houses for this kind of withering-up of the instincts of intellectuality. And the whole of Europe is beginning to know this – politics on a large scale deceive no-one. Germany is becoming ever more and more the Flat-land of Europe. I am still in search of a German with whom I could be serious after my own fashion. And how much more am I in search of one with whom I could be cheerful – *Twilight of the Idols:* ah! what man today would be capable of understanding the kind of seriousness from which a philosopher is recovering in this work! It is our cheerfulness that people understand least.

4

Let us examine another aspect on the question: it is not only obvious that German culture is declining, but adequate reasons for this decline are not lacking. After all, nobody can spend more than he has: this is true of individuals, it is also true of nations. If you spend your strength in acquiring power, or in politics on a large scale, or in economy, or in universal commerce, or in parliament-arism, or in military interests – if you dissipate the modicum of reason, of earnestness, of will, and of self-control that constitutes your nature in one particular fashion, you cannot dissipate it in another. Culture and the state – let no-one be deceived on this point – are antagonists: A 'culture-state'* is merely a modern idea. The one lives upon the other, the one flourishes at the expense of the other. All great periods of culture have been periods of political decline; that which is great from the standpoint of culture

* The word *Kultur-Staat* 'culture-state' had become a standard expression in the German language, and was applied to the leading European states. – TR.

was always unpolitical – even anti-political. Goethe's heart opened at the coming of Napoleon – it closed at the thought of the 'Wars of Liberation'. At the very moment when Germany arose as a great power in the world of politics, France won new importance as a force in the world of culture. Even at this moment a large amount of fresh intellectual earnestness and passion has emigrated to Paris; the question of pessimism, for instance, and the question of Wagner; in France almost all psychological and artistic questions are considered with incomparably more subtlety and thoroughness than they are in Germany – the Germans are even incapable of this kind of earnestness. In the history of European culture the rise of the Empire signifies, above all, a displacement of the centre of gravity. Everywhere people are already aware of this: in things that really matter – and these after all constitute culture – the Germans are no longer worth considering. I ask you, can you show me one single man of brains who could be mentioned in the same breath with other European thinkers, like your Goethe, your Hegel, your Heinrich Heine, and your Schopenhauer? – The fact that there is no longer a single German philosopher worth mentioning is an increasing wonder.

5

Everything that matters has been lost sight of by the whole of the higher educational system of Germany: the end quite as much as the means to that end. People forget that education, the process of cultivation itself, is the end – and not 'the Empire' – they forget that the *educator* is required for this end – and not the public-school teacher and university scholar. Educators are needed who are themselves educated, superior and noble intellects, who can prove that they are thus qualified, that they are ripe and mellow products of culture at every moment of their lives, in word and in gesture – not the learned louts who, like 'superior wetnurses,' are now thrust upon the youth of the land by public schools and universities. With but rare exceptions, that which is lacking in Germany is the first prerequisite of education – that is to say, the educators; hence the decline of German culture. One of those rarest exceptions is my highly respected friend Jacob Burckhardt of Basle: to him above all is Basle indebted for its foremost position in human culture. What the higher schools of Germany really do accomplish is this, they brutally train a vast crowd of young men, in the smallest amount of time possible, to become useful and exploitable servants of the state. 'Higher education' and a vast crowd – these terms contradict each other from the start. All superior education can only concern the exception: a man must be privileged in order to have a right to such a great privilege. All great and beautiful things cannot be a common possession: *pulchrum est paucorum hominum.* – What is it that brings about the decline of German culture? The fact that 'higher education' is no longer a special privilege – the democracy of a process of cultivation that has become 'general', *common.* Nor must it be forgotten that the privileges of the military profession by urging many too many to attend the higher schools, involve the downfall of the latter. In modern Germany nobody is at liberty to give his children a noble education: in regard to their teachers, their curricula, and their educational aims, our higher schools are one and all established upon a fundamentally doubtful mediocre basis. Everywhere, too, a hastiness which is unbecoming rules supreme; just as if something would be forfeited if the young man were not 'finished' at the age of twenty-three, or did not know how to reply to the most essential question, 'which calling to choose?' – The superior kind of man, if you please, does not like 'callings', precisely because he knows himself to be called. He has time, he takes time, he cannot possibly think of becoming 'finished' – in the matter of higher culture, a man of thirty years is a beginner, a child. Our overcrowded public schools, our accumulation of foolishly manufactured public-school masters, are a scandal: maybe there are very serious *motives* for defending this state of affairs, as was shown quite recently by the professors of Heidelberg; but there can be no reasons for doing so.

6

In order to be true to my nature, which is affirmative and which concerns itself with contradictions and criticism only indirectly and with reluctance, let me state at once what the three objects are for which we need educators. People must learn to see; they must learn to think, and they must learn to speak and to write: the object of all three of these pursuits is a noble culture. To learn to see – to accustom the eye to calmness, to patience, and to allow things to come up to it; to defer judgment, and to acquire the habit of approaching and grasping an individual case from all sides. This is the first preparatory schooling of intellectuality. One must not respond immediately to a stimulus; one must acquire a command of the obstructing and isolating instincts. To learn to see, as I understand this matter, amounts almost to that which in popular language is called 'strength of will': its essential feature is precisely *not* to *wish* to see, to be able to postpone one's decision. All lack of intellectuality, all vulgarity, arises out of the inability to resist a stimulus: one must respond or react, every impulse is indulged. In many cases such necessary action is already a sign of morbidity, of decline, and a symptom of exhaustion. Almost everything that coarse popular language characterises as vicious, is merely that physiological inability to refrain from reacting. – As an instance of what it means to have learnt to see, let me state that a man thus trained will as a learner have become generally slow, suspicious, and refractory. With hostile calm he will first allow every kind of strange and *new* thing to come right up to him – he will draw back his hand at its approach. To stand with all the doors of one's soul wide open, to lie slavishly in the dust before every trivial fact, at all times of the day to be strained ready for the leap, in order to deposit one's self, to plunge one's self, into other souls and other things, in short, the famous 'objectivity' of modern times, is bad taste, it is essentially vulgar and cheap.

7

As to learning how to think – our schools no longer have any notion of such a thing. Even at the universities, among the actual scholars in philosophy, logic as a theory, as a practical pursuit, and as a business, is beginning to die out. Turn to any German book: you will not find the remotest trace of a realisation that there is such a thing as a technique, a plan of study, a will to mastery, in the matter of thinking – that thinking insists upon being learnt, just as dancing insists upon being learnt, and that thinking insists upon being learnt as a form of dancing. What single German can still say he knows from experience that delicate shudder which *light footfalls* in matters intellectual cause to pervade his whole body and limbs! Stiff awkwardness in intellectual attitudes, and the clumsy fist in grasping – these things are so essentially German, that outside Germany they are absolutely confounded with the German spirit. The German has no fingers for delicate *nuances*. The fact that the people of Germany have actually tolerated their philosophers, more particularly that most deformed cripple of ideas that has ever existed – the great Kant – gives one no inadequate notion of their native elegance. For, truth to tell, dancing in all its forms cannot be excluded from the curriculum of all noble education: dancing with the feet, with ideas, with words, and need I add that one must also be able to dance with the pen – that one must learn how to write? – But at this stage I should become utterly enigmatical to German readers.

I

My Impossible People. – Seneca, or the toreador of virtue. – Rousseau, or the return to nature, *in impuris naturalibus.* – Schiller, or the Moral-Trumpeter of Säckingen. – Dante, or the hyena that writes poetry in tombs. – Kant, or *cant* as an intelligible character. – Victor Hugo, or the lighthouse on the sea of nonsense. – Liszt, or the school of racing – after women. – George Sand, or *lactea ubertas*, in plain English: the cow with plenty of beautiful milk. – Michelet, or enthusiasm in its shirt sleeves. – Carlyle, or Pessimism after undigested meals. – John Stuart Mill, or offensive lucidity. – The brothers Goncourt, or the two Ajaxes fighting with Homer. Music by Offenbach. – Zola, or the love of stinking.

2

Renan. – Theology, or the corruption of reason by original sin (Christianity). Proof of this – Renan who, even in those rare cases where he ventures to say either yes or no on a general question, invariably misses the point with painful regularity. For instance, he would fain associate science and nobility: but surely it must be obvious that science is democratic. He seems to be actuated by a strong desire to represent an aristocracy of intellect: but at the same time he grovels on his knees, and not only on his knees, before the opposite doctrine, the gospel of the humble. What is the good of all free-spiritedness, modernity, mockery and acrobatic suppleness, if in one's belly one is still a Christian, a Catholic, and even a priest! Renan's forte, precisely like that of a Jesuit and father confessor, lies in his seductiveness. His intellectuality is not devoid of that unctuous complacency of a parson – like all priests, he becomes dangerous only when he loves. He is second to none in the art of skilfully worshipping a dangerous thing. This intellect of Renan's, which in its action is enervating, is one calamity the more for poor, sick France with her will-power all going to pieces.

3

Sainte-Beuve. – There is naught of man in him; he is full of petty spite towards all virile spirits. He wanders erratically; he is subtle, inquisitive, a little bored, for ever with his ear to keyholes – at bottom a woman, with all woman's revengefulness and sensuality. As a psychologist he is a genius of slander; inexhaustively rich in means to this end; no-one understands better than he how to introduce a little poison into praise. In his fundamental instincts he is plebeian and next of kin to Rousseau's resentful spirit: consequently he is a Romanticist – for beneath all romanticism Rousseau's instinct for revenge grunts and frets. He is a revolutionary, but kept within bounds by 'funk'. He is embarrassed in the face of everything that is strong (public opinion, the Academy, the court, even Port Royal). He is embittered against everything great in men and things, against everything that believes in itself. Enough of a poet and of a female to be able to feel greatness as power, he is always turning and twisting, because, like the proverbial worm, he constantly feels that he is being trodden upon. As a critic he has no standard of judgment, no guiding principle, no backbone. Although he possesses the tongue of the cosmopolitan libertine which can chatter about a thousand things, he has not the courage even to acknowledge his *libertinage*. As a historian he has no philosophy, and lacks the power of philosophical vision – hence his refusal to act the part of a judge, and his adoption of the mask of 'objectivity' in all important matters. His attitude is better in regard to all those things in which subtle and effete taste is the highest tribunal: in these things he really does have the courage of his own personality – he really does enjoy his own nature – he actually is a *master*. – In some respects he is a prototype of Baudelaire.

4

The Imitation of Christ is one of those books which I cannot even take hold of without physical loathing: it exhales a perfume of the eternally feminine, which to appreciate fully one must be a Frenchman or a Wagnerite. This saint has a way of speaking about love which makes even Parisiennes feel a little curious. – I am told that that *most intelligent* of Jesuits, Auguste Comte, who wished to lead his compatriots back to Rome by the circuitous route of science, drew his inspiration from this book. And I believe it: 'the religion of the heart'.

5

G. Eliot. – They are rid of the Christian God and therefore think it all the more incumbent upon them to hold tight to Christian morality: this is an English way of reasoning; but let us not take it ill in moral females *à la* Eliot. In England, every man who indulges in any trifling emancipation from theology, must retrieve his honour in the most terrifying manner by becoming a moral fanatic. That is how they do penance in that country. – As for us, we act differently. When we renounce the Christian faith, we abandon all right to Christian morality. This is not by any means self-evident, and in defiance of English shallow-pates the point must be made ever more and more plain. Christianity is a system, a complete outlook upon the world, conceived as a whole. If its leading concept, the belief in God, is wrenched from it, the whole is destroyed; nothing vital remains in our grasp. Christianity presupposes that man does not and cannot know what is good or bad for him: the Christian believes in God who alone can know these things. Christian morality is a command, its origin is transcendental. It is beyond all criticism, all right to criticism; it is true only on condition that God is truth – it stands or falls with the belief in God. If the English really believe that they know intuitively, and of their own accord, what is good and evil; if, therefore, they assert that they no longer need Christianity as a guarantee of morality, this in itself is simply the outcome of the dominion of Christian valuations, and a proof of the strength and profundity of this dominion. It only shows that the origin of English morality has been forgotten, and that its exceedingly relative right to exist is no longer felt. For Englishmen morality is not yet a problem.

6

George Sand. – I have been reading the first *Lettres d'un Voyageur*: like everything that springs from Rousseau's influence it is false, made-up, blown out, and exaggerated! I cannot endure this bright wallpaper style, any more than I can bear the vulgar striving after generous feelings. The worst feature about it is certainly the coquettish adoption of male attributes by this female, after the manner of ill-bred schoolboys. And how cold she must have been inwardly all the while, this insufferable artist! She wound herself up like a clock – and wrote. As cold as Hugo and Balzac, as cold as all Romanticists are as soon as they begin to write! And how self-complacently she must have lain there, this prolific ink-yielding cow. For she had something German in her (German in the bad sense), just as Rousseau, her master, had; – something which could only have been possible when French taste was declining! – and Renan adores her! . . .

7

A Moral for Psychologists. Do not go in for any note-book psychology! Never observe for the sake of observing! Such things lead to a false point of view, to a squint, to something forced and exaggerated. To experience things on purpose – this is not a bit of good. In the midst of an experience a man should not turn his eyes upon himself; in such cases any eye becomes the 'evil eye'. A born psychologist instinctively avoids seeing for the sake of seeing. And the same holds good of the born painter. Such a man never works 'from nature' – he leaves it to his instinct, to his *camera obscura* to sift and to define the 'fact', 'nature', the 'experience'. The general idea, the conclusion, the result, is the only thing that reaches his consciousness. He knows nothing of that wilful process of deducing from particular cases. What is the result when a man sets about this matter differently? – when, for instance, after the manner of Parisian novelists, he goes in for notebook psychology on a large and small scale? Such a man is constantly spying on reality, and every evening he bears home a handful of fresh curios. . . . But look at the result! – a mass of daubs, at best a piece of mosaic, in any case something heaped together, restless and garish. The Goncourts are the greatest sinners in this respect: they cannot put three sentences together which are not absolutely painful to the eye – the eye of the psychologist. From an artistic standpoint, nature is no model. It exaggerates, distorts, and leaves gaps. Nature is the *accident*. To study 'from nature' seems to me a bad sign: it betrays submission, weakness, fatalism – this lying in the dust before trivial facts is

unworthy of a thorough artist. To see *what is* – is the function of
another order of intellects, the *anti-artistic*, the matter-of-fact. One
must know *who* one is.

8

Concerning the psychology of the artist. For art to be possible at all –
that is to say, in order that an aesthetic mode of action and of
observation may exist, a certain preliminary physiological state is
indispensable: *ecstasy.** This state of ecstasy must first have intensified the susceptibility of the whole machine: otherwise, no art is
possible. All kinds of ecstasy, however differently produced, have
this power to create art, and above all the state dependent upon
sexual excitement – this most venerable and primitive form of
ecstasy. The same applies to that ecstasy which is the outcome of
all great desires, all strong passions; the ecstasy of the feast, of the
arena, of the act of bravery, of victory, of all extreme action; the
ecstasy of cruelty; the ecstasy of destruction; the ecstasy following
upon certain meteorological influences, as for instance that of
spring-time, or upon the use of narcotics; and finally the ecstasy of
will, that ecstasy which results from accumulated and surging will-
power. – The essential feature of ecstasy is the feeling of increased
strength and abundance. Actuated by this feeling a man gives of
himself to things, he *forces* them to partake of his riches, he does
violence to them – this proceeding is called *idealising*. Let us
rid ourselves of a prejudice here: idealising does not consist, as is
generally believed, in a suppression or an elimination of detail or of
unessential features. A stupendous *accentuation* of the principal
characteristics is by far the most decisive factor at work, and in
consequence the minor characteristics vanish.

9

In this state a man enriches everything from out his own abundance: what he sees, what he wills, he sees distended, compressed,
strong, overladen with power. He transfigures things until they
reflect his power – until they are stamped with his perfection. This
compulsion to transfigure into the beautiful is – Art. Everything –
even that which he is not – is nevertheless to such a man a means

* The German word *Rausch* as used by Nietzsche here suggests a blend of our
two English words 'intoxication' and 'elation'. – TR.

of rejoicing over himself; in Art man rejoices over himself as perfection. – It is possible to imagine a contrary state, a specifically anti-artistic state of the instincts – a state in which a man impoverishes, attenuates, and draws the blood from everything. And, truth to tell, history is full of such anti-artists, of such creatures of low vitality who have no choice but to appropriate everything they see and to suck its blood and make it thinner. This is the case with the genuine Christian, Pascal for instance. There is no such thing as a Christian who is also an artist. . . . Let no-one be so childish as to suggest Raphael or any homeopathic Christian of the nineteenth century as an objection to this statement: Raphael said yea, Raphael *did* yea – consequently Raphael was no Christian.

10

What is the meaning of the antithetical concepts *Apollonian* and *Dionysian* which I have introduced into the vocabulary of Aesthetic, as representing two distinct modes of ecstasy? – Apollonian ecstasy acts above all as a force stimulating the eye, so that it acquires the power of vision. The painter, the sculptor, the epic poet are essentially visionaries. In the Dionysian state, on the other hand, the whole system of passions is stimulated and intensified, so that it discharges itself by all the means of expression at once, and vents all its power of representation, of imitation, of transfiguration, of transformation, together with every kind of mimicry and histrionic display at the same time. The essential feature remains the facility in transforming, the inability to refrain from reaction (a similar state to that of certain hysterical patients, who at the slightest hint assume any role). It is impossible for the Dionysian artist not to understand any suggestion; no outward sign of emotion escapes him, he possesses the instinct of comprehension and of divination in the highest degree, just as he is capable of the most perfect art of communication. He enters into every skin, into every passion: he is continually changing himself. Music as we understand it today is likewise a general excitation and discharge of the emotions; but notwithstanding this, it is only the remnant of a much richer world of emotional expression, a mere residuum of Dionysian histrionism. For music to be made possible as a special art, quite a number of senses, and particularly the muscular sense, had to be paralysed (at least relatively: for all rhythm still appeals to

our muscles to a certain extent): and thus man no longer imitates
and represents physically everything he feels, as soon as he feels it.
Nevertheless that is the normal Dionysian state, and in any case its
primitive state. Music is the slowly attained specialisation of this
state at the cost of kindred capacities.

11

The actor, the mime, the dancer, the musician, and the lyricist, are
in their instincts fundamentally related; but they have gradually
specialised in their particular branch, and become separated – even
to the point of contradiction. The lyricist remained united with the
musician for the longest period of time; and the actor with the
dancer. The architect manifests neither a Dionysian nor an Apollonian state: In his case it is the great act of will, the will that moveth
mountains, the ecstasy of the great will which aspires to art. The
most powerful men have always inspired architects; the architect has
always been under the suggestion of power. In the architectural
structure, man's pride, man's triumph over gravitation, man's will
to power, assume a visible form. Architecture is a sort of oratory of
power by means of forms. Now it is persuasive, even flattering, and
at other times merely commanding. The highest sensation of power
and security finds expression in grandeur of style. That power
which no longer requires to be proved, which scorns to please;
which responds only with difficulty; which feels no witnesses
around it; which is oblivious of the fact that it is being opposed;
which relies on itself fatalistically, and is a law among laws: – such
power expresses itself quite naturally in grandeur of style.

12

I have been reading the life of Thomas Carlyle, that unconscious
and involuntary farce, that heroico-moral interpretation of dyspeptic moods. – Carlyle, a man of strong words and attitudes, a
rhetorician by necessity, who seems ever to be tormented by the
desire of finding some kind of strong faith, and by his inability to
do so (in this respect a typical Romanticist!). To yearn for a strong
faith is not the proof of a strong faith, but rather the reverse. If a
man have a strong faith he can indulge in the luxury of scepticism;
he is strong enough, firm enough, well-knit enough for such a
luxury. Carlyle stupefies something in himself by means of the

fortissimo of his reverence for men of a strong faith, and his rage over those who are less foolish: he is in sore need of noise. An attitude of constant and passionate dishonesty towards himself – this is his *proprium*; by virtue of this he is and remains interesting. – Of course, in England he is admired precisely on account of his honesty. Well, that is English; and in view of the fact that the English are the nation of consummate cant, it is not only comprehensible but also very natural. At bottom, Carlyle is an English atheist who makes it a point of honour not to be one.

· 13 ·

Emerson. – He is much more enlightened, much broader, more versatile, and more subtle than Carlyle; but above all, he is happier. He is one who instinctively lives on ambrosia and who leaves the indigestible parts of things on his plate. Compared with Carlyle he is a man of taste. – Carlyle, who was very fond of him, nevertheless declared that 'he does not give us enough to chew.' This is perfectly true but it is not unfavourable to Emerson. – Emerson possesses that kindly intellectual cheerfulness which deprecates overmuch seriousness; he has absolutely no idea of how old he is already, and how young he will yet be – he could have said of himself, in Lope de Vega's words: '*yo me sucedo a mi mismo.*' His mind is always finding reasons for being contented and even thankful; and at times he gets preciously near to that serene superiority of the worthy bourgeois who returning from an amorous rendezvous *tamquam re bene gesta*, said gratefully '*Ut desint vires, tamen est laudanda voluptas.*'

14

Anti-Darwin. – As to the famous 'struggle for existence', it seems to me, for the present, to be more of an assumption than a fact. It does occur, but as an exception. The general condition of life is not one of want or famine, but rather of riches, of lavish luxuriance, and even of absurd prodigality – where there is a struggle, it is a struggle for power. We should not confound Malthus with nature. – Supposing, however, that this struggle exists – and it does indeed occur – its result is unfortunately the very reverse of that which the Darwinian school seems to desire, and of that which in agreement with them we also might desire:

that is to say, it is always to the disadvantage of the strong, the privileged, and the happy exceptions. Species do not evolve towards perfection: the weak always prevail over the strong – simply because they are the majority, and because they are also the more crafty. Darwin forgot the intellect (that is English!), the weak have more intellect. In order to acquire intellect, one must be in need of it. One loses it when one no longer needs it. He who possesses strength flings intellect to the deuce ('let it go hence!' * say the Germans of the present day, 'the *Empire* will remain'). As you perceive, intellect to me means caution, patience, craft, dissimulation, great self-control, and everything related to mimicry (what is praised nowadays as virtue is very closely related to the latter).

15

Casuistry of a Psychologist. – This man knows mankind: to what purpose does he study his fellows? He wants to derive some small or even great advantages from them – he is a politician! . . . That man yonder is also well versed in human nature: and ye tell me that he wishes to draw no personal profit from his knowledge, that he is a thoroughly disinterested person? Examine him a little more closely! Maybe he wishes to derive a more wicked advantage from his possession; namely, to feel superior to men, to be able to look down upon them, no longer to feel one of them. This 'disinterested person' is a despiser of mankind; and the former is of a more humane type, whatever appearances may seem to say to the contrary. At least he considers himself the equal of those about him, at least he classifies himself with them.

16

The psychological tact of Germans seems to me to have been set in doubt by a whole series of cases which my modesty forbids me to enumerate. In one case at least I shall not let the occasion slip for substantiating my contention: I bear the Germans a grudge for having made a mistake about Kant and his 'backstairs philosophy', as I call it. Such a man was not the type of intellectual uprightness. Another thing I hate to hear is a certain infamous 'and': the

* An allusion to a verse in Luther's hymn, *Lass fahren dahin . . . das Reich muss uns doch bleiben*, which Nietzsche applies to the German Empire. – Tr.

Germans say, 'Goethe *and* Schiller', – I even fear that they say, 'Schiller and Goethe'. . . . Has nobody found Schiller out yet? – But there are other 'ands' which are even more egregious. With my own ears I have heard – only among university professors, it is true! – men speak of 'Schopenhauer *and* Hartmann'.*

17

The most intellectual men, provided they are also the most courageous, experience the most excruciating tragedies: but on that very account they honour life, because it confronts them with its most formidable antagonism.

18

Concerning '*the Conscience of the Intellect*'. – Nothing seems to me more uncommon today than genuine hypocrisy. I strongly suspect that this growth is unable to flourish in the mild climate of our culture. Hypocrisy belongs to an age of strong faith – one in which one does not lose one's own faith in spite of the fact that one has to make an outward show of holding another faith. Nowadays a man gives it up; or, what is still more common, he acquires a second faith – in any case, however, he remains honest. Without a doubt it is possible to have a much larger number of convictions at present than it was formerly: *possible* – that is to say, allowable – that is to say, *harmless*. From this there arises an attitude of toleration towards one's self. Toleration towards one's self allows of a greater number of convictions: the latter live comfortably side by side, and they take jolly good care, as all the world does today, not to compromise themselves. How does a man compromise himself today? When he is consistent; when he pursues a straight course; when he has anything less than five faces; when he is genuine. . . . I very greatly fear that modern man is much too fond of comfort for certain vices; and the consequence is that the latter are dying out. Everything evil which is the outcome of strength of will – and maybe there is nothing evil without the strength of will – degenerates, in our muggy atmosphere, into virtue. The few hypocrites I have known only imitated hypocrisy: like almost every tenth man today, they were actors. –

* A disciple of Schopenhauer who blunted the sharpness of his master's Pessimism and watered it down for modern requirements. – Tr.

19

Beautiful and Ugly. – Nothing is more relative, let us say, more restricted, than our sense of the beautiful. He who would try to divorce it from the delight man finds in his fellows, would immediately lose his footing. 'Beauty in itself', is simply a word, it is not even a concept. In the beautiful, man postulates himself as the standard of perfection; in exceptional cases he worships himself as that standard. A species has no other alternative than to say 'yea' to itself alone, in this way. Its lowest instinct, the instinct of self-preservation and self-expansion, still radiates in such sublimities. Man imagines the world itself to be overflowing with beauty – he forgets that he is the cause of it all. He alone has endowed it with beauty. Alas! and only with human all-too-human beauty! Truth to tell, man reflects himself in things, he thinks everything beautiful that throws his own image back at him. The judgment 'beautiful' is the 'vanity of his species'. . . . A little demon of suspicion may well whisper into the sceptic's ear: is the world really beautified simply because man thinks it beautiful? He has only humanised it – that is all. But nothing, absolutely nothing proves to us that it is precisely man who is the proper model of beauty. Who knows what sort of figure he would cut in the eyes of a higher judge of taste? He might seem a little *outré*? Perhaps even somewhat amusing? perhaps a trifle arbitrary? 'O Dionysus, thou divine one, why dost thou pull mine ears?' Ariadne asks on one occasion of her philosophic lover, during one of those famous conversations on the island of Naxos. 'I find a sort of humour in thine ears, Ariadne: why are they not a little longer?'

20

Nothing is beautiful; man alone is beautiful: all aesthetic rests on this piece of ingenuousness, it is the first axiom of this science. And now let us straightway add the second to it: nothing is ugly save the degenerate man – within these two first principles the realm of aesthetic judgments is confined. From the physiological standpoint, everything ugly weakens and depresses man. It reminds him of decay, danger, impotence; he literally loses strength in its presence. The effect of ugliness may be gauged by the dynamometer. Whenever man's spirits are downcast, it is a sign that he scents the proximity of something 'ugly'. His feeling of power, his will to power, his courage and his pride – these things collapse at the sight of what is ugly, and rise at the sight of what is beautiful. In both cases an inference is drawn; the premises to which are stored with extraordinary abundance in the instincts. Ugliness is understood to signify a hint and a symptom of degeneration: that which reminds us however remotely of degeneracy impels us to the judgment 'ugly'. Every sign of exhaustion, of gravity, of age, of fatigue; every kind of constraint, such as cramp, or paralysis; and above all the smells, colours and forms associated with decomposition and putrefaction, however much they may have been attenuated into symbols – all these things provoke the same reaction, which is the judgment 'ugly'. A certain hatred expresses itself here: what is it that man hates? Without a doubt it is the *decline of his type*. In this regard his hatred springs from the deepest instincts of the race: there is horror, caution, profundity and far-reaching vision in this hatred – it is the most profound hatred that exists. On its account alone Art is profound.

21

Schopenhauer. – Schopenhauer, the last German who is to be reckoned with (who is a European event like Goethe, Hegel, or Heinrich Heine, and who is not merely local, national), is for a psychologist a case of the first rank: I mean as a malicious though masterly attempt to enlist on the side of a general nihilistic depreciation of life the very forces which are opposed to such a movement – that is to say, the great self-affirming powers of the 'will to live', the exuberant forms of life itself. He interpreted Art, heroism, genius, beauty, great sympathy, knowledge, the will to truth, and tragedy, one after the other, as the results of the denial, or of the need of the denial, of the 'will' – the greatest forgery, Christianity always excepted, which history has to show. Examined more carefully, he is in this respect simply the heir of the Christian interpretation; except that he knew how to approve in a Christian fashion (i.e., nihilistically) even of the great facts of human culture, which Christianity completely repudiates. (He approved of them as paths to 'salvation', as preliminary stages to 'salvation', as *appetisers* calculated to arouse the desire for 'salvation'.)

22

Let me point to one single instance. Schopenhauer speaks of beauty with melancholy ardour – why in sooth does he do this? Because in beauty he sees a bridge on which one can travel further, or which stimulates one's desire to travel further. According to him it constitutes a momentary emancipation from the 'will' – it lures to eternal salvation. He values it more particularly as a deliverance from the 'burning core of the will' which is sexuality – in beauty he recognises the negation of the procreative instinct. Singular saint! Someone contradicts thee; I fear it is Nature. Why is there beauty of tone, colour, aroma, and of rhythmic movement in Nature at all? What is it forces beauty to the fore? Fortunately, too, a certain philosopher contradicts him. No less an authority than the divine Plato himself (thus does Schopenhauer call him) upholds another proposition: that all beauty lures to procreation – that this precisely is the chief characteristic of its effect, from the lowest sensuality to the highest spirituality.

23

Plato goes further. With an innocence for which a man must be Greek and not 'Christian', he says that there would be no such thing as Platonic philosophy if there were not such beautiful boys in Athens: it was the sight of them alone that set the soul of the philosopher reeling with erotic passion, and allowed it no rest until it had planted the seeds of all lofty things in a soil so beautiful. He was also a singular saint! – One scarcely believes one's ears, even supposing one believes Plato. At least one realises that philosophy was pursued differently in Athens; above all, publicly. Nothing is less Greek than the cobweb-spinning with concepts by an anchorite, *amor intellectualis dei* after the fashion of Spinoza. Philosophy according to Plato's style might be defined rather as an erotic competition, as a continuation and a spiritual-isation of the old agonal gymnastics and the conditions on which they depend. . . . What was the ultimate outcome of this philo-sophic eroticism of Plato's? A new art-form of the Greek *agon*, dialectics. – In opposition to Schopenhauer and to the honour of Plato, I would remind you that all the higher culture and literature of classical France, as well, grew up on the soil of sexual interests. In all its manifestations you may look for gallantry, the senses, sexual competition, and 'woman', and you will not look in vain.

24

L'art pour l'art. – The struggle against a purpose in art is always a struggle against the moral tendency in art, against its subordination to morality. *L'art pour l'art* means, 'let morality go to the devil!' – But even this hostility betrays the preponderating power of the moral prejudice. If art is deprived of the purpose of preaching morality and of improving mankind, it does not by any means follow that art is absolutely pointless, purposeless, senseless, in short *l'art pour l'art* – a snake which bites its own tail. 'No purpose at all is better than a moral purpose!' – thus does pure passion speak. A psychologist, on the other hand, puts the question: what does all art do? does it not praise? does it not glorify? does it not select? does it not bring things into prominence? In all this it strengthens or weakens certain valuations. Is this only a secondary matter? an accident? something in which the artist's instinct has no share? Or is it not rather the very prerequisite which enables the artist to accomplish something? . . . Is his most fundamental instinct concerned with art? Is it not rather concerned with the purpose of art, with life? with a certain desirable kind of life? Art is the great stimulus to life: how can it be regarded as purposeless, as pointless, as *l'art pour l'art?* – There still remains one question to be answered: Art also reveals much that is ugly, hard and questionable in life – does it not thus seem to make life intolerable? – And, as a matter of fact, there have been philosophers who have ascribed this function to art. According to Schopenhauer's doctrine, the general object of art was to 'free one from the Will'; and what he honoured as the great utility of tragedy was that it 'made people more resigned'. – But this, as I have already shown, is a pessimistic standpoint; it is the 'evil eye': the artist himself must be appealed to. What is it that the soul of the tragic artist communicates to others? Is it not precisely his fearless attitude towards that which is terrible and questionable? This attitude is in itself a highly desirable one; he who has once experienced it honours it above everything else. He communicates it. He must communicate, provided he is an artist and a genius in the art of communication. A courageous and free spirit, in the presence of a mighty foe, in the presence of a sublime misfortune, and face to face with a problem that inspires horror – this is the triumphant attitude which the tragic artist selects and which he glorifies. The martial elements in our soul celebrate their Saturnalia in tragedy; he who is used to suffering, he who looks out for suffering, the heroic man, extols his existence by means of tragedy – to him alone does the tragic artist offer this cup of sweetest cruelty.

25

To associate in an amiable fashion with anybody; to keep the house of one's heart open to all, is certainly liberal: but it is nothing else. One can recognise the hearts that are capable of noble hospitality, by their wealth of screened windows and closed shutters: they keep their best rooms empty. Whatever for? – Because they are expecting guests who are somebodies.

26

We no longer value ourselves sufficiently highly when we communicate our soul's content. Our real experiences are not at all garrulous. They could not communicate themselves even if they wished to. They are at a loss to find words for such confidences. Those things for which we find words are things we have already overcome. In all speech there lies an element of contempt. Speech, it would seem, was only invented for average, mediocre and communicable things. – Every spoken word proclaims the speaker vulgarised. – (Extract from a moral code for deaf-and-dumb people and other philosophers.)

27

'This picture is perfectly beautiful!'* The dissatisfied and exasperated literary woman with a desert in her heart and in her belly, listening with agonised curiosity every instant to the imperative which whispers to her from the very depths of her being: *aut liberi, aut libri:* the literary woman, sufficiently educated to understand the voice of nature, even when nature speaks Latin, and moreover enough of a peacock and a goose to speak even French with herself in secret. *'Je me verrai, je me lirai, je m'extasierai et je dirai: Possible, que j'aie eu tant d'esprit?'* . . .

* Quotation from the libretto of Mozart's *Magic Flute*, Act 1, Sc. 3. – Tr.

28

The objective ones speak. – 'Nothing comes more easily to us, than to be wise, patient, superior. We are soaked in the oil of indulgence and of sympathy, we are absurdly just, we forgive everything. Precisely on that account we should be severe with ourselves; for that very reason we ought from time to time to go in for a little emotion, a little emotional vice. It may seem bitter to us; and between ourselves we may even laugh at the figure which it makes us cut. But what does it matter? We have no other kind of self-control left. This is our asceticism, our manner of performing penance.' *To become personal* – the virtues of the 'impersonal and objective one'.

29

Extract from a doctor's examination paper. – 'What is the task of all higher schooling?' – To make man into a machine. 'What are the means employed?' – He must learn how to be bored. 'How is this achieved?' – By means of the concept of duty. 'What example of duty has he before his eyes?' – The philologist: it is he who teaches people how to swat. 'Who is the perfect man?' – The government official. 'Which philosophy furnishes the highest formula for the government official?' – Kant's philosophy: the government official as thing-in-itself made judge over the government official as appearance.

30

The right to stupidity. – The worn-out worker, whose breath is slow, whose look is good-natured, and who lets things slide just as they please: this typical figure which in this age of labour (and of 'Empire!') is to be met with in all classes of society, has now begun to appropriate even Art, including the book, above all the newspaper – and how much more so beautiful, nature, Italy! This man of the evening, with his 'savage instincts lulled', as Faust has it, needs his summer holiday, his sea-baths, his glacier, his Bayreuth. In such ages Art has the right to be *purely foolish* – as a sort of vacation for spirit, wit and sentiment. Wagner understood this. Pure foolishness* is a pick-me-up.

---

* An allusion to Parsifal. – Tʀ.

31

Yet another problem of diet. – The means, with which Julius Cæsar preserved himself against sickness and headaches: heavy marches, the simplest mode of living, uninterrupted sojourns in the open air, continual hardships – generally speaking these are the self-preservative and self-defensive measures against the extreme vulnerability of those subtle machines working at the highest pressure, which are called geniuses.

32

The immoralist speaks. – Nothing is more distasteful to true philosophers than man when he begins to wish . . . If they see man only at his deeds; if they see this bravest, craftiest and most enduring of animals even inextricably entangled in disaster, how admirable he then appears to them! They even encourage him . . . But true philosophers despise the man who wishes, as also the 'desirable' man – and all the desiderata and *ideals* of man in general. If a philosopher could be a nihilist, he would be one; for he finds only nonentity behind all human ideals. Or, not even nonentity, but vileness, absurdity, sickness, cowardice, fatigue and all sorts of dregs from out the quaffed goblets of his life . . . How is it that man, who as a reality is so estimable, ceases from deserving respect the moment he begins to desire? Must he pay for being so perfect as a reality? Must he make up for his deeds, for the tension of spirit and will which underlies all his deeds, by an eclipse of his powers in matters of the imagination and in absurdity? Hitherto the history of his desires has been the *partie honteuse* of mankind: one should take care not to read too deeply in this history. That which justifies man is his reality – it will justify him to all eternity. How much more valuable is a real man than any other man who is merely the phantom of desires, of dreams of stinks and of lies? – than any kind of ideal man? . . . And the ideal man, alone, is what the philosopher cannot abide.

33

The natural value of egoism. – Selfishness has as much value as the physiological value of him who practises it: its worth may be great, or it may be worthless and contemptible. Every individual may be classified according to whether he represents the ascending or the descending line of life. When this is decided, a canon is obtained by means of which the value of his selfishness may be determined. If he represent the ascending line of life, his value is of course extraordinary – and for the sake of the collective life which in him makes one step *forward*, the concern about his maintenance, about procuring his *optimum* of conditions may even be extreme. The human unit, the 'individual', as the people and the philosopher have always understood him, is certainly an error: he is nothing in himself, no atom, no 'link in the chain', no mere heritage from the past – he represents the whole direct line of mankind up to his own life . . . If he represent declining development, decay, chronic degeneration, sickness (illnesses are on the whole already the outcome of decline, and not the cause thereof), he is of little worth, and the purest equity would have him *take away* as little as possible from those who are lucky strokes of nature. He is then only a parasite upon them.

34

The Christian and the anarchist. – When the anarchist, as the mouthpiece of the decaying strata of society, raises his voice in splendid indignation for 'right', 'justice', 'equal rights', he is only groaning under the burden of his ignorance, which cannot understand *why* he actually suffers – what his poverty consists of – the poverty of life. An instinct of causality is active in him: someone must be responsible for his being so ill at ease. His 'splendid indignation' alone relieves him somewhat, it is a pleasure for all poor devils to grumble – it gives them a little intoxicating sensation of power. The very act of complaining, the mere fact that one bewails one's lot, may lend such a charm to life that on that account alone one is ready to endure it. There is a small dose of revenge in every lamentation. One casts one's afflictions, and, under certain circumstances, even one's baseness, in the teeth of those who are different, as if their condition were an injustice, an *iniquitous* privilege. 'Since I am *a blackguard* you ought to be one too.' It is upon such reasoning that revolutions are based. – To bewail one's lot is always despicable: it is always the outcome of weakness. Whether one ascribes one's afflictions to others or to *one's self*, it is all the same. The socialist does the former, the Christian, for instance, does the latter. That which is common to both attitudes, or rather that which is equally ignoble in them both, is the fact that somebody must be to *blame* if one suffers – in short that the sufferer drugs himself with the honey of revenge to allay his anguish. The objects towards which this lust of vengeance, like a lust of pleasure, is directed, are purely accidental causes. In all directions the sufferer finds reasons for cooling his petty passion for revenge. If he is a Christian, I repeat, he finds these reasons in himself. The Christian and the anarchist – both are decadents. But even when the Christian condemns, slanders, and sullies the world, he is actuated by precisely the same instinct as that which leads the socialistic workman to curse, calumniate and cast dirt at society. The last 'Judgment' itself is still the sweetest solace to revenge – revolution, as the socialistic workman expects it, only thought of as a little more remote . . . The notion of a 'Beyond,' as well – why a Beyond, if it be not a means of splashing mud over a 'Here', over this world?

35

A criticism of the morality of decadence. – An 'altruistic' morality, a morality under which selfishness withers, is in all circumstances a bad sign. This is true of individuals and above all of nations. The best are lacking when selfishness begins to be lacking. Instinctively to select that which is harmful to one, to be *lured* by 'disinterested' motives – these things almost provide the formula for decadence. 'Not to have one's own interests at heart' – this is simply a moral fig-leaf concealing a very different fact, a physiological one, to wit: 'I no longer know how to find what is to my interest.'. . . Disintegration of the instincts! – All is up with man when he becomes altruistic. – Instead of saying ingenuously 'I am no longer any good,' the lie of morality in the decadent's mouth says: 'Nothing is any good – life is no good.' – A judgment of this kind ultimately becomes a great danger; for it is infectious, and it soon flourishes on the polluted soil of society with tropical luxuriance, now as a religion (Christianity), anon as a philosophy (Schopenhauerism). In certain circumstances the mere effluvia of such a venomous vegetation, springing as it does out of the very heart of putrefaction, can poison life for thousands and thousands of years.

36

A moral for doctors. – The sick man is a parasite of society. In certain cases it is indecent to go on living. To continue to vegetate in a state of cowardly dependence upon doctors and special treatments, once the meaning of life, the right to life, has been lost, ought to be regarded with the greatest contempt by society. The doctors, for their part, should be the agents for imparting this contempt – they should no longer prepare prescriptions, but should every day administer a fresh dose of *disgust* to their patients. A new responsibility should be created, that of the doctor – the responsibility of ruthlessly suppressing and eliminating *degenerate* life, in all cases in which the highest interests of life itself, of ascending life, demand such a course – for instance in favour of the right of procreation, in favour of the right of being born, in favour of the right to live. One should die proudly when it is no longer possible to live proudly. Death should be chosen freely – death at the right time, faced clearly and joyfully and embraced while one is surrounded by one's children and other witnesses. It should be affected in such a way that a proper farewell is still possible, that he who is about to take leave of us is still *himself*, and really capable not only of valuing what he has achieved and willed in life, but also of *summing-up* the value of life itself. Everything precisely the opposite of the ghastly comedy which Christianity has made of the hour of death. We should never forgive Christianity for having so abused the weakness of the dying man as to do violence to his conscience, or for having used his manner of dying as a means of valuing both man and his past! – In spite of all cowardly prejudices, it is our duty, in this respect, above all to reinstate the proper – that is to say, the physiological – aspect of so-called *natural* death, which after all is perfectly 'unnatural' and nothing else than suicide. One never perishes through anybody's fault but one's own. The only thing is that the death which takes place in the most contemptible circumstances, the death that is not free, the death which occurs at the wrong time, is the death of a coward. Out of the very love one bears to life, one should wish death to be different from this – that is to say, free, deliberate, and neither a matter of chance nor of surprise. Finally let me whisper a word of advice to our friends the pessimists and all other decadents. We have not the power to prevent ourselves from being born: but this error – for sometimes it is an error – can be rectified if we choose. The man who does away with himself, performs the most estimable of deeds: he almost deserves to live for having done so. Society – nay, life itself – derives more profit from such a deed than from any sort of life spent in renunciation, anaemia and other virtues – at least the suicide frees others from the sight of him, at least he removes one objection against life. Pessimism *pur et vert*, can *be proved only* by the self-refutation of the pessimists themselves: one should go a step further in one's consistency; one should not merely deny life with 'the World as Will and Idea', as Schopenhauer did; one should in the first place *deny Schopenhauer* . . . Incidentally, Pessimism, however infectious it may be, does not increase the morbidness of an age or of a whole species; it is rather the expression of that morbidness. One falls a victim to it in the same way as one falls a victim to cholera; one must already be predisposed to the disease. Pessimism in itself does not increase the number of the world's *decadents* by a single unit. Let me remind you of the statistical fact that in those years in which cholera rages, the total number of deaths does not exceed that of other years.

37

Have we become more moral? – As might have been expected, the whole *ferocity* of moral stultification, which, as is well known, passes for morality itself in Germany, hurled itself against my concept 'Beyond Good and Evil'. I could tell you some nice tales about this. Above all, people tried to make me see the 'incontestable superiority' of our age in regard to moral sentiment, and the *progress* we had made in these matters. Compared with us, a Caesar Borgia was by no means to be represented as 'higher man', the sort of *Superman*, which I declared him to be. The editor of the Swiss paper the *Bund* went so far as not only to express his admiration for the courage displayed by my enterprise, but also to pretend to 'understand' that the intended purpose of my work was to abolish all decent feeling. Much obliged ! – In reply, I venture to raise the following question: *have we really become more moral?* The fact that everybody believes that we have is already an objection to the belief. We modern men, so extremely delicate and susceptible, full of consideration one for the other, actually dare to suppose that the pampering fellow-feeling which we all display, this unanimity which we have at last acquired in sparing and helping and trusting one another, marks a definite step forward, and shows us to be far ahead of the man of the Renaissance. But every age thinks the same, it is *bound* to think the same. This at least is certain, that we should not dare to stand amid the conditions which prevailed at the Renaissance, we should not even dare to imagine ourselves in those conditions: our nerves could not endure that reality, not to speak of our muscles. The inability to do this however does not denote any progress; but simply the different and more senile quality of our particular nature, its greater weakness, delicateness, and suscept- ibility, out of which a morality *more rich in consideration* was bound to arise. If we imagine our delicateness and senility, our physio- logical decrepitude as non-existent, our morality of 'humanisation' would immediately lose all value – no morality has any value *per se* – it would even fill us with scorn. On the other hand, do not let us doubt that we moderns, wrapped as we are in the thick cotton wool of our humanitarianism which would shrink even from grazing a stone, would present a comedy to Caesar Borgia's con- temporaries which would literally make them die of laughter. We are indeed, without knowing it, exceedingly ridiculous with our modern 'virtues'. . . . The decline of the instincts of hostility and of those instincts that arouse suspicion – for this if anything is what constitutes our progress – is only one of the results manifested by the general decline in *vitality:* it requires a hundred times more trouble and caution to live such a dependent and senile existence. In such circumstances everybody gives everybody else a helping hand, and, to a certain extent, everybody is either an invalid or an invalid's attendant. This is then called 'virtue': among those men who knew a different life – that is to say, a fuller, more prodigal, more superabundant sort of life – it might have been called by another name – possibly 'cowardice', or 'vileness', or 'old woman's morality' . . . . Our mollification of morals – this is my cry; this if you will is my *innovation* – is the outcome of our decline; conversely hardness and terribleness in morals may be the result of a surplus of life. When the latter state prevails, much is dared, much is challenged, and much is also *squandered*. That which formerly was simply the salt of life, would now be our *poison*. To be indifferent – even this is a form of strength – for that, likewise, we are too senile, too decrepit: our morality of fellow-feeling, against which I was the first to raise a finger of warning, that which might be called *moral impressionism*, is one symptom the more of the excessive physiological irritability which is peculiar to everything decadent. That movement which attempted to introduce itself in a scientific manner on the shoulders of Schopenhauer's morality of pity – a very sad attempt! – is in its essence the movement of decadence in morality, and as such it is intimately related to Christian morality. Strong ages and noble cultures see something contemptible in pity, in the 'love of one's neighbour', and in a lack of egoism and of self-esteem. – Ages should be measured according to their *positive forces;* valued by this standard that prodigal and fateful age of the Renaissance appears as the last *great* age, while we moderns with our anxious care of ourselves and love of our neighbours, with all our unassuming virtues of industry, equity, and scientific method – with our lust of collection, of economy and of mechanism – represent a *weak* age . . . Our virtues are necessarily determined, and are even stimulated, by our weakness. 'Equality', a certain definite process of making everybody uniform, which only finds its expression in the theory of equal rights, is essentially bound up with a declining culture: the chasm between man and man, class and class, the multiplicity of types, the will to be one's self, and to distinguish one's self – that, in fact, which I call the *pathos of distance* is proper to all *strong* ages. The force of tension – nay, the tension itself, between extremes grows slighter every day – the extremes themselves are tending to become obliterated to the point of becoming identical. All our political theories and state constitutions, not by any means excepting 'the German Empire', are the logical consequences, the necessary consequences of decline; the unconscious effect of *decadence* has begun to dominate even the ideals of the various sciences. My objection to the whole of English and French sociology still continues to be this, that it knows only the *decadent form* of society from experience, and with perfectly childlike innocence takes the instincts of decline as the *norm*, the standard, of sociological valuations. *Descending* life, the decay of all organising power – that is to say, of all that power which separates, cleaves gulfs, and establishes rank above and below, formulated itself in modern sociology as *the* ideal. Our socialists are decadents: but Herbert Spencer was also a *decadent* – he saw something to be desired in the triumph of altruism! . . .

38

My concept of freedom. – Sometimes the value of a thing does not lie in that which it helps us to achieve, but in the amount we have to pay for it – what it *costs* us. For instance, liberal institutions straightway cease from being liberal the moment they are soundly established: once this is attained no more grievous and more thorough enemies of freedom exist than liberal institutions! One knows, of course, what they bring about: they undermine the Will to Power, they are the levelling of mountain and valley exalted to a morality, they make people small, cowardly and pleasure-loving – by means of them the gregarious animal invariably triumphs. Liberalism, or in plain English the *transformation of mankind into cattle.* The same institutions, so long as they are fought for, produce quite other results; then indeed they promote the cause of freedom quite powerfully. Regarded more closely, it is war which produces these results, war in favour of liberal institutions, which, as war, allows the illiberal instincts to subsist. For war trains men to be free. What in sooth is freedom? Freedom is the will to be responsible for ourselves. It is to preserve the distance which separates us from other men. To grow more indifferent to hardship, to severity, to privation, and even to life itself. To be ready to sacrifice men for one's cause, one's self included. Freedom denotes that the virile instincts which rejoice in war and in victory prevail over other instincts; for instance, over the instincts of 'happiness'. The man who has won his freedom, and how much more so, therefore, the spirit that has won its freedom, tramples ruthlessly upon that contemptible kind of comfort which tea-grocers, Christians, cows, women, Englishmen and other democrats worship in their dreams. The free man is a *warrior.* – How is freedom measured in individuals as well as in nations? According to the resistance which has to be overcome, according to the pains which it costs to remain *uppermost.* The highest type of free man would have to be sought where the greatest resistance has continually to be overcome: five paces away from tyranny, on the very threshold of the danger of thraldom. This is psychologically true if, by the word 'tyrants' we mean inexorable and terrible instincts which challenge the *maximum* amount of authority and discipline to oppose them – the finest example of this is Julius Cæsar; it is also true politically: just examine the course of history. The nations which were worth anything, which *got to be* worth anything, never attained to that condition under liberal institutions: *great danger* made out of them something which deserves reverence, that danger which alone can make us aware of our resources, our virtues, our means of defence, our weapons, our *genius* – which *compels* us to be strong. *First* principle: a man must need to be strong, otherwise he will never attain it. – Those great forcing-houses of the strong, of the strongest kind of men that have ever existed on earth, the aristocratic communities like those of Rome and Venice, understood freedom precisely as I understand the word: as something that one has and that one has *not*, as something that one *will* have and that one *seizes by force*.

39

A criticism of modernity. – Our institutions are no longer any good; on this point we are all agreed. But the fault does not lie with them; but with *us*. Now that we have lost all the instincts out of which institutions grow, the latter on their part are beginning to disappear from our midst because we are no longer fit for them. Democracy has always been the death agony of the power of organisation: already in *Human All-too-Human*, Part I, Aph. 472, I pointed out that modern democracy, together with its half-measures, of which the 'German Empire' is an example, was a decaying form of the state. For institutions to be possible there must exist a sort of will, instinct, imperative, which cannot be otherwise than antiliberal to the point of wickedness: the will to tradition, to authority, to responsibility for centuries to come, to *solidarity* in long family lines forwards and backwards *in infinitum*. If this will is present, something is founded which resembles the *imperium Romanum*: or Russia, the *only* great nation today that has some lasting power and grit in her, that can bide her time, that can still promise something. – Russia the opposite of all wretched European petty-statism and neurasthenia, which the foundation of the German Empire has brought to a crisis. The whole of the Occident no longer possesses those instincts from which institutions spring, out of which a *future* grows: maybe nothing is more opposed to its 'modern spirit' than these things. People live for the present, they live at top speed – they certainly live without any sense of responsibility; and this is precisely what they call 'freedom'. Everything in institutions which makes them institutions, is scorned, loathed and repudiated: everybody is in mortal fear of a new slavery, wherever the word 'authority' is so much as whispered. The decadence of the valuing instinct, both in our politicians and in our political parties, goes so far, that they instinctively prefer that which acts as a solvent, that which precipitates the final catastrophe . . . As an example of this behold *modern* marriage. All reason has obviously been divorced from modern marriage: but this is no objection to matrimony itself but to modernity. The rational basis of marriage – it lay in the exclusive legal responsibility of the man: by this means some ballast was laid in the ship of matrimony, whereas nowadays it has a list, now on this side, now on that. The rational basis of marriage – it lay in its absolute indissolubleness: in this way it was given a gravity which knew how to make its influence felt, in the face of the accident of sentiment, passion and momentary impulse: it lay also in the fact that the responsibility of choosing the parties to the contract lay with the families. By showing ever more and more favour to *love*-marriages, the very foundation of matrimony, that which alone makes it an institution, has been undermined. No institution ever has been nor ever will be built upon an idiosyncrasy; as I say, marriage cannot be based upon 'love'. It can be based upon sexual desire; upon the instinct of property (wife and child as possessions); upon the instinct of dominion, which constantly organises for itself the smallest form of dominion – the family which *requires* children and heirs in order to hold fast, also in the physiological sense, to a certain quantum of acquired power, influence and wealth, so as to prepare for lasting tasks, and for solidarity in the instincts from one century to another. Marriage as an institution presupposes the affirmation of the greatest and most permanent form of organisation; if society cannot as a whole *stand security* for itself into the remotest generations, marriage has no meaning whatsoever. – Modern marriage *has lost* its meaning; consequently it is being abolished.

40

The question of the working-man. – The mere fact that there is such a thing as the question of the working-man is due to stupidity, or at bottom to degenerate instincts which are the cause of all the stupidity of modern times. Concerning certain things *no questions ought to be put:* the first imperative principle of instinct. For the life of me I cannot see what people want to do with the working-man of Europe, now that they have made a question of him. He is far too comfortable to cease from questioning ever more and more, and with ever less modesty. After all, he has the majority on his side. There is now not the slightest hope that an unassuming and contented sort of man, after the style of the Chinese, will come into being in this quarter: and this would have been the reasonable course, it was even a dire necessity. What has been done? Everything has been done with the view of nipping the very prerequisite of this accomplishment in the bud – with the most frivolous thoughtlessness those self-same instincts by means of which a working class becomes possible, and *tolerable* even to its members themselves, have been destroyed root and branch. The working-man has been declared fit for military service; he has been granted the right of combination, and of voting: can it be wondered at that he already regards his condition as one of distress (expressed morally, as an injustice)? But, again I ask, what do people want? If they desire a certain end, then they should desire the means thereto. If they will have slaves, then it is madness to educate them to be masters.

41

'The kind of freedom I do *not* mean . . .' * – In an age like the present, it simply adds to one's perils to be left to one's instincts. The instincts contradict, disturb, and destroy each other; I have already defined modernism as physiological self-contradiction. A reasonable system of education would insist upon at least one of these instinct-systems being *paralysed* beneath an iron pressure, in order to allow others to assert their power, to grow strong, and to dominate. At present, the only conceivable way of making the individual possible would be to *prune* him: of making him possible – that is to say, *whole*. The very reverse occurs. Independence, free development, and *laisser aller* are clamoured for most violently precisely by those for whom no restraint *could be too severe* – this is true *in politics*, it is true in Art. But this is a symptom of decadence: our modern notion of 'freedom' is one proof the more of the degeneration of instinct.

* This is a playful adaptation of Max von Schenkendorf's poem 'Freiheit'. The proper line reads: 'Freiheit die ich meine' (The freedom that I do mean). – TR.

42

Where faith is necessary. – Nothing is more rare among moralists and saints than uprightness; maybe they say the reverse is true, maybe they even believe it. For, when faith is more useful, more effective, more convincing than *conscious* hypocrisy, by instinct that hypocrisy forthwith becomes *innocent*: first principle towards the understanding of great saints. The same holds good of philosophers, that other order of saints; their whole business compels them to concede only certain truths – that is to say, those by means of which their particular trade receives the *public* sanction – to speak 'Kantingly': the truths of *practical* reason. They know what they *must* prove; in this respect they are practical – they recognise each other by the fact that they agree upon 'certain truths'. – 'Thou shalt not lie' – in plain English: *Beware*, Mr Philosopher, of speaking the truth . . .

43

A quiet hint to conservatives. – That which we did not know formerly, and know now, or might know if we chose – is the fact that a *retrograde formation*, a reversion in any sense or degree, is absolutely impossible. We physiologists, at least, are aware of this. But all priests and moralists have believed in it – they wished to drag and screw man back to a *former* standard of virtue. Morality has always been a Procrustean bed. Even the politicians have imitated the preachers of virtue in this matter. There are parties at the present day whose one aim and dream is to make all things adopt the *crab-march*. But not everyone can be a crab. It cannot be helped: we must go forward – that is to say step by step further and further into decadence (this is my definition of modern 'progress'). We can hinder this development, and by so doing dam up and accumulate degeneration itself and render it more convulsive, more *volcanic*: we cannot do more.

44

My concept of genius. – Great men, like great ages, are explosive material, in which a stupendous amount of power is accumulated; the first conditions of their existence are always historical and physiological; they are the outcome of the fact that for long ages energy has been collected, hoarded up, saved up and preserved for their use, and that no explosion has taken place. When the tension in the bulk has become sufficiently excessive, the most fortuitous stimulus suffices in order to call 'genius', 'great deeds', and momentous fate into the world. What then is the good of all environment, historical periods, '*Zeitgeist*' (Spirit of the age) and 'public opinion'? – Take the case of Napoleon. France of the Revolution, and still more of the period preceding the Revolution, would have brought forward a type which was the very reverse of Napoleon: it actually *did* produce such a type. And because Napoleon was something different, the heir of a stronger, more lasting and older civilisation than that which in France was being smashed to atoms, he became master there, he was the only master there. Great men are necessary, the age in which they appear is a matter of chance; the fact that they almost invariably master their age is accounted for simply by the fact that they are stronger, that they are older, and that power has been stored longer for them. The relation of a genius to his age is that which exists between strength and weakness and between maturity and youth: the age is relatively always very much younger, thinner, less mature, less resolute and more childish. The fact that the general opinion in France at the present day is utterly different on this very point (in Germany too, but that is of no consequence); the fact that in that country the theory of environment – a regular neuropathic notion – has become sacrosanct and almost scientific, and finds acceptance even among the physiologists, is a very bad and exceedingly depressing sign. In England too the same belief prevails: but nobody will be surprised at that. The Englishman knows only two ways of understanding the genius and the 'great man': either *democratically* in the style of Buckle, or *religiously* after the manner of Carlyle. – The danger which great men and great ages represent is simply extraordinary; every kind of exhaustion and of sterility follows in their wake. The great man is an end; the great age – the Renaissance for instance – is an end. The genius – in work and in deed – is necessarily a squanderer: the fact that he spends himself constitutes his greatness. The instinct of self-preservation is as it were suspended in him; the overpowering pressure of out-flowing energy in him forbids any such protection and prudence. People call this 'self-sacrifice', they praise his 'heroism', his indifference to his own well-being, his utter devotion to an idea, a great cause, a fatherland: All misunderstandings . . . He flows out, he flows over, he consumes himself, he does not spare himself – and does all this with fateful necessity, irrevocably, involuntarily, just as a river involuntarily bursts its dams. But, owing to the fact that humanity has been much indebted to such explosives, it has endowed them with many things, for instance, with a kind of *higher morality* . . . This is indeed the sort of gratitude that humanity is capable of: it *misunderstands* its benefactors.

45

The criminal and his like. – The criminal type is the type of the strong man amid unfavourable conditions, a strong man made sick. He lacks the wild and savage state, a form of nature and existence which is freer and more dangerous, in which everything that constitutes the shield and the sword in the instinct of the strong man takes a place by right. Society puts a ban upon his virtues; the most spirited instincts inherent in him immediately become involved with the depressing passions, with suspicion, fear and dishonour. But this is almost the recipe for physiological degeneration. When a man has to do that which he is best suited to do, which he is most fond of doing, not only clandestinely, but also with long suspense, caution and ruse, he becomes anaemic; and inasmuch as he is always having to pay for his instincts in the form of danger, persecution and fatalities, even his feelings begin to turn against these instincts – he begins to regard them as fatal. It is society, our tame, mediocre, castrated society, in which an un-tutored son of nature who comes to us from his mountains or from his adventures at sea, must necessarily degenerate into a criminal. Or almost necessarily: for there are cases in which such a man shows himself to be stronger than society: the Corsican Napoleon is the most celebrated case of this. Concerning the problem before us, Dostoevsky's testimony is of importance – Dostoevsky who, incidentally, was the only psychologist from whom I had anything to learn: he belongs to the happiest windfalls of my life, happier even than the discovery of Stendhal. This profound man, who was right ten times over in esteeming the superficial Germans low, found the Siberian convicts among whom he lived for many years – those thoroughly hopeless criminals for whom no road back to society stood open – very different from what even he had expected – that is to say carved from about the best, hardest and most valuable material that grows on Russian soil.* Let us generalise the case of the criminal; let us imagine creatures who for some reason or other fail to meet with public approval, who know that they are regarded neither as beneficent nor useful – the feeling of the Chandala, who are aware that they are not looked upon as equal, but as proscribed, unworthy, polluted. The thoughts and actions of all such natures are tainted with a subterranean mouldiness; everything in them is of a paler hue than in those on whose existence the sun shines. But almost all those creatures whom, nowadays, we honour and respect formerly lived in this semi-sepulchral atmosphere: the man of science, the artist, the genius, the free spirit, the actor, the businessman, and the great explorer. As long as the *priest* represented the highest type of man, every valuable kind of man was depreciated . . . The time is coming – this I guarantee – when he will pass as the *lowest* type, as our Chandala, as the falsest and most disreputable kind of man . . . I call your attention to the fact that even now, under the sway of the mildest customs and usages which have ever ruled on earth or at least in Europe, every form of standing aside, every kind of prolonged, excessively prolonged concealment, every unaccustomed and obscure form of existence tends to approximate to that type which the criminal exemplifies to perfection. All pioneers of the spirit have, for a while, the grey and fatalistic mark of the Chandala on their brows: *not* because they are regarded as Chandala, but because they themselves feel the terrible chasm which separates them from all that is traditional and honourable. Almost every genius knows the 'Catilinarian life' as one of the stages in his development, a feeling of hate, revenge and revolt against everything that exists, that has ceased to evolve . . . Catiline – the early stage of every Caesar.

46

Here the outlook is free. – When a philosopher holds his tongue it may be the sign of the loftiness of his soul: when he contradicts himself it may be love; and the very courtesy of a knight of knowledge may force him to lie. It has been said, and not without subtlety: *il est indigne des grands coeurs de répandre le trouble qu'ils*

* See *Memoirs of the House of the Dead*, by Dostoevsky – TR.

ressentent:* but it is necessary to add that there may also be *grandeur de coeur* in not shrinking *from the most undignified* proceeding. A woman who loves sacrifices her honour; a knight of knowledge who 'loves', sacrifices perhaps his humanity; a God who loved became a Jew . . .

47

Beauty no accident. – Even the beauty of a race or of a family, the charm and perfection of all its movements, is attained with pains: like genius it is the final result of the accumulated work of generations. Great sacrifices must have been made on the altar of good taste, for its sake many things must have been done, and much must have been left undone – the seventeenth century in France is admirable for both of these things – in this century there must have been a principle of selection in respect to company, locality, clothing, the gratification of the instinct of sex; beauty must have been preferred to profit, to habit, to opinion and to indolence. The first rule of all: nobody must 'let himself go', not even when he is alone. – Good things are exceedingly costly: and in all cases the law obtains that he who possesses them is a different person from him who is *acquiring* them. Everything good is an inheritance: that which is not inherited is imperfect, it is simply a beginning. In Athens at the time of Cicero – who expresses his surprise at the fact – the men and youths were by far superior in beauty to the women: but what hard work and exertions the male sex had for centuries imposed upon itself in the service of beauty! We must not be mistaken in regard to the method employed here: the mere discipline of feelings and thoughts is little better than nil (it is in this that the great error of German culture, which is quite illusory, lies): the *body* must be persuaded first. The strict maintenance of a distinguished and tasteful demeanour, the oblig-ation of frequenting only those who do not 'let themselves go', is amply sufficient to render one distinguished and tasteful: in two or three generations everything has already *taken deep root*. The fate of a people and of humanity is decided according to whether they begin culture at the *right place* – not at the 'soul' (as the fatal superstition of the priests and half-priests would have it): the right place is the body, demeanour, diet, physiology – the rest follows as

* Clothilde de Veaux. – TR.

the night the day . . . That is why the Greeks remain the *first event in culture* – they knew and they *did* what was needful. Christianity with its contempt of the body is the greatest mishap that has ever befallen mankind.

48

Progress in my sense. – I also speak of a 'return to nature', although it is not a process of going back but of going up – up into lofty, free and even terrible nature and naturalness; such a nature as can play with great tasks and *may* play with them . . . To speak in a *parable*, Napoleon was an example of a 'return to nature', as I understand it (for instance *in rebus tacticis*, and still more, as military experts know, in strategy). But Rousseau – whither did he want to return? Rousseau this first modern man, idealist and *canaille* in one person; who was in need of moral 'dignity', in order even to endure the sight of his own person – ill with unbridled vanity and wanton self-contempt; this abortion, who planted his tent on the threshold of modernity, also wanted a 'return to nature'; but, I ask once more, whither did he wish to return? I hate Rousseau, even *in* the Revolution itself: the latter was the historical expression of this hybrid of idealist and *canaille*. The bloody farce which this Revolution ultimately became, its 'immorality', concerns me but slightly; what I loathe however is its Rousseauesque *morality* – the so-called 'truths' of the Revolution, by means of which it still exercises power and draws all flat and mediocre things over to its side. The doctrine of equality! . . . But there is no more deadly poison than this; for it *seems* to proceed from the very lips of justice, whereas in reality it draws the curtain down on all justice . . . 'To equals equality, to unequals inequality' – that would be the real speech of justice and that which follows from it. 'Never make unequal things equal.' The fact that so much horror and blood are associated with this doctrine of equality has lent this 'modern idea' *par excellence* such a halo of fire and glory, that the Revolution as a drama has misled even the most noble minds. – That after all is no reason for honouring it the more. – I can see only one who regarded it as it should be regarded – that is to say, with *loathing*; I speak of Goethe.

49

Goethe. – No mere German, but a European event: a magnificent attempt to overcome the eighteenth century by means of a return to nature, by means of an ascent to the naturalness of the Renaissance, a kind of self-overcoming on the part of the century in question. – He bore the strongest instincts of this century in his breast: its sentimentality, and idolatry of nature, its anti-historic, idealistic, unreal, and revolutionary spirit (the latter is only a form of the unreal). He enlisted history, natural science, antiquity, as well as Spinoza, and above all practical activity, in his service. He drew a host of very definite horizons around him; far from liberating himself from life, he plunged right into it; he did not give in; he took as much as he could on his own shoulders, and into his heart. That to which he aspired was *totality*; he was opposed to the sundering of reason, sensuality, feeling and will (as preached with most repulsive scholasticism by Kant, the antipodes of Goethe); he disciplined himself into a harmonious whole, he *created* himself. Goethe in the midst of an age of unreal sentiment, was a convinced realist: he said yea to everything that was like him in this regard – there was no greater event in his life than that *ens realissimum*, surnamed Napoleon. Goethe conceived a strong, highly-cultured man, skilful in all bodily accomplishments, able to keep himself in check, having a feeling of reverence for himself, and so constituted as to be able to risk the full enjoyment of naturalness in all its rich profusion and be strong enough for this freedom; a man of tolerance, not out of weakness but out of strength, because he knows how to turn to his own profit that which would ruin the mediocre nature; a man unto whom nothing is any longer forbidden, unless it be weakness either as a vice or as a virtue. Such a spirit, *become free*, appears in the middle of the universe with a feeling of cheerful and confident fatalism; he believes that only individual things are bad, and that as a whole the universe justifies and affirms itself – *He no longer denies* . . . But such a faith is the highest of all faiths: I christened it with the name of Dionysus.

50

It might be said that, in a certain sense, the nineteenth century also strove after all that Goethe himself aspired to: catholicity in understanding, in approving; a certain reserve towards everything, daring realism, and a reverence for every fact. How is it that the total result of this is not a Goethe, but a state of chaos, a nihilistic groan, an inability to discover where one is, an instinct of fatigue which *in praxi* is persistently driving Europe *to hark back to the eighteenth century*? (for instance in the form of maudlin romanticism, altruism, hyper-sentimentality, pessimism in taste, and socialism in politics). Is not the nineteenth century, at least in its closing years, merely an accentuated, brutalised eighteenth century – that is to say a century of decadence? And has not Goethe been – not alone for Germany, but also for the whole of Europe – merely an episode, a beautiful 'in vain'? But great men are misunderstood when they are regarded from the wretched standpoint of public utility. The fact that no advantage can be derived from them – *this in itself may perhaps be peculiar to greatness*.

51

Goethe is the last German whom I respect: he had understood three things as I understand them. We also agree as to the 'cross'. People often ask me why on earth I write in *German:* nowhere am I less read than in the Fatherland. But who knows whether I even *desire* to be read at present? – To create things on which time may try its teeth in vain; to be concerned both in the form and the substance of my writing, about a certain degree of immortality – never have I been modest enough to demand less of myself. The aphorism, the sentence, in both of which I, as the first among Germans, am a master, are the forms of 'eternity'; it is my ambition to say in ten sentences what everyone else says in a whole book – what everyone else does *not* say in a whole book.

I have given mankind the deepest book it possesses, my *Zara-thustra*; before long I shall give it the most independent one.

I

In conclusion I will just say a word concerning that world to which I have sought new means of access, to which I may perhaps have found a new passage – the ancient world. My taste, which is perhaps the reverse of tolerant, is very far from saying yea through and through even to this world: on the whole it is not over eager to say *yea*, it would prefer to say *nay*, and better still nothing whatever . . . This is true of whole cultures; it is true of books – it is also true of places and of landscapes. Truth to tell, the number of ancient books that count for something in my life is but small; and the most famous are not of that number. My sense of style, for the epigram as style, was awakened almost spontaneously upon my acquaintance with Sallust. I have not forgotten the astonishment of my respected teacher Corssen, when he was forced to give his worst Latin pupil the highest marks – at one stroke I had learned all there was to learn. Condensed, severe, with as much substance as possible in the background, and with cold but roguish hostility towards all 'beautiful words' and 'beautiful feelings' – in these things I found my own particular bent. In my writings up to my *Zarathustra*, there will be found a very earnest ambition to attain to the *Roman* style, to the '*aere perennius*' in style. – The same thing happened on my first acquaintance with Horace. Up to the present no poet has given me the same artistic raptures as those which from the first I received from an Horatian ode. In certain languages it would be absurd even to aspire to what is accomplished by this poet. This mosaic of words, in which every unit spreads its power to the left and to the right over the whole, by its sound, by its place in the sentence, and by its meaning, this *minimum* in the compass and number of the signs, and the *maximum* of energy in the signs which is thereby achieved – all this is Roman, and, if you will believe me, noble *par excellence*. By the side of this all the rest of poetry becomes something popular – nothing more than senseless sentimental twaddle.

2

I am not indebted to the Greeks for anything like such strong impressions; and, to speak frankly, they cannot be to us what the Romans are. One cannot *learn* from the Greeks – their style is too strange, it is also too fluid, to be imperative or to have the effect of a classic. Who would ever have learnt writing from a Greek! Who would ever have learned it without the Romans! . . . Do not let anyone suggest Plato to me. In regard to Plato I am a thorough sceptic, and have never been able to agree to the admiration of Plato the *artist*, which is traditional among scholars. And after all, in this matter, the most refined judges of taste in antiquity are on my side. In my opinion Plato bundles all the forms of style pell-mell together, in this respect he is one of the first decadents of style: he has something similar on his conscience to that which the Cynics had who invented the *satura Menippea*. For the Platonic dialogue – this revoltingly self-complacent and childish kind of dialectics – to exercise any charm over you, you must never have read any good French authors – Fontenelle for instance. Plato is boring. In reality my distrust of Plato is fundamental. I find him so very much astray from all the deepest instincts of the Hellenes, so steeped in moral prejudices, so pre-existently Christian – the concept 'good' is already the highest value with him – that rather than use any other expression I would prefer to designate the whole phenomenon Plato with the hard word 'superior bunkum', or, if you would like it better, 'idealism'. Humanity has had to pay dearly for this Athenian having gone to school among the Egyptians (or among the Jews in Egypt? . . .). In the great fatality of Christianity, Plato is that double-faced fascination called the 'ideal', which made it possible for the more noble natures of antiquity to misunderstand themselves and to tread the *bridge* which led to the 'cross'. And what an amount of Plato is still to be found in the concept 'church', and in the construction, the system and the practice of the church! – My recreation, my predilection, my cure, after all Platonism, has always been Thucydides. Thucydides and perhaps Machiavelli's *principe* are most closely related to me owing to the absolute determination which they show of refusing to deceive themselves and of seeing reason in *reality* – not in 'rationality', and still less in 'morality'. There is no more radical cure than Thucydides for the lamentably rose-coloured idealisation of the Greeks which the 'classically-cultured' stripling bears with him into life, as a reward for his public-school training. His writings must be carefully studied line by line, and his unuttered thoughts must be read as distinctly as what he actually says. There are few thinkers so rich in unuttered thoughts. In him the culture 'of the Sophists' – that is to say, the culture of realism – receives its most perfect expression: this inestimable movement in the midst of the moral and idealistic knavery of the Socratic schools which was then breaking out in all directions. Greek philosophy is the decadence of the Greek instinct: Thucydides is the great summing up, the final manifestation of that strong, severe positivism which lay in the instincts of the ancient Hellene. After all, it is courage in the face of reality that distinguishes such natures as Thucydides from Plato: Plato is a coward in the face of reality – consequently he takes refuge in the ideal: Thucydides is master of himself – consequently he is able to master life.

3

To rout up cases of 'beautiful souls', 'golden means' and other perfections among the Greeks, to admire, say, their calm grandeur, their ideal attitude of mind, their exalted simplicity – from this 'exalted simplicity', which after all is a piece of *niaiserie allemande*, I was preserved by the psychologist within me. I saw their strongest instinct, the Will to Power, I saw them quivering with the fierce violence of this instinct – I saw all their institutions grow out of measures of security calculated to preserve each member of their society from the inner *explosive material* that lay in his neighbour's breast. This enormous internal tension thus discharged itself in terrible and reckless hostility outside the state: the various states mutually tore each other to bits, in order that each individual state could remain at peace with itself. It was then necessary to be strong; for danger lay close at hand – it lurked in ambush everywhere. The superb suppleness of their bodies, the daring realism and immorality which is peculiar to the Hellenes, was a necessity not an inherent quality. It was a result, it had not been there from the beginning. Even their festivals and their arts were but means in producing a feeling of superiority, and of showing it: they are measures of self-glorification; and in certain circumstances of making one's self terrible . . . Fancy judging the Greeks in the German style, from their philosophers; fancy using the suburban respectability of the Socratic schools as a key to what is fundamentally Hellenic! . . . The philosophers are of course the decadents of Hellas, the counter-movement directed against the old and noble taste (against the agonal instinct, against the *polis*, against the value of the race, against the authority of tradition). Socratic virtues were preached to the Greeks *because* the Greeks had lost virtue: irritable, cowardly, unsteady, and all turned to play-actors, they had more than sufficient reason to submit to having morality preached to them. Not that it helped them in any way; but great words and attitudes are so becoming to decadents.

4

I was the first who, in order to understand the ancient, still rich and even superabundant Hellenic instinct, took that marvellous phenomenon, which bears the name of Dionysus, seriously: it can be explained only as a manifestation of excessive energy. Whoever had studied the Greeks, as that most profound of modern connoisseurs of their culture, Jakob Burckhardt of Basle, had done, knew at once that something had been achieved by means of this interpretation. And in his *Cultur der Griechen*, Burckhardt inserted a special chapter on the phenomenon in question. If you would like a glimpse of the other side, you have only to refer to the almost laughable poverty of instinct among German philologists when they approach the Dionysian question. The celebrated Lobeck, especially, who with the venerable assurance of a worm dried up between books, crawled into this world of mysterious states, succeeded in convincing himself that he was scientific, whereas he was simply revoltingly superficial and childish – Lobeck, with all the pomp of profound erudition, gave us to understand that, as a matter of fact, there was nothing at all in all these curiosities. Truth to tell, the priests may well have communicated not a few things of value to the participators in such orgies; for instance, the fact that wine provokes desire, that man in certain circumstances lives on fruit, that plants bloom in the spring and fade in the autumn. As regards the astounding wealth of rites,

symbols and myths which take their origin in the orgy, and with
which the world of antiquity is literally smothered, Lobeck finds
that it prompts him to a feat of even greater ingenuity than the
foregoing phenomenon did. 'The Greeks', he says (*Aglaophamus*, i.
p. 672), 'when they had nothing better to do, laughed, sprang and
romped about, or, inasmuch as men also like a change at times,
they would sit down, weep and bewail their lot. Others then came
up who tried to discover some reason for this strange behaviour;
and thus, as an explanation of these habits, there arose an incalculable number of festivals, legends, and myths. On the other hand it
was believed that the *farcical performances* which then perchance
began to take place on festival days, necessarily formed part of the
celebrations, and they were retained as an indispensable part of the
ritual.' – This is contemptible nonsense, and no-one will take a
man like Lobeck seriously for a moment. We are very differently
affected when we examine the notion 'Hellenic', as Winckelmann
and Goethe conceived it, and find it incompatible with that
element out of which Dionysian art springs – I speak of orgiasm.
In reality I do not doubt that Goethe would have completely
excluded any such thing from the potentialities of the Greek soul.
Consequently Goethe did not understand the Greeks. For it is only in
the Dionysian mysteries, in the psychology of the Dionysian state,
that the *fundamental fact* of the Hellenic instinct – its 'will to life' –
is expressed. What did the Hellene secure himself with these
mysteries? *Eternal* life, the eternal recurrence of life; the future
promised and hallowed in the past; the triumphant Yea to life
despite death and change; real life conceived as the collective
prolongation of life through procreation, through the mysteries
of sexuality. To the Greeks, the symbol of sex was the most
venerated of symbols, the really deep significance of all the piety of
antiquity. All the details of the act of procreation, pregnancy and
birth gave rise to the loftiest and most solemn feelings. In the
doctrine of mysteries, *pain* was pronounced holy: the 'pains of
childbirth' sanctify pain in general – all becoming and all growth,
everything that guarantees the future *involves* pain . . . In order
that there may be eternal joy in creating, in order that the will to
life may say Yea to itself in all eternity, the 'pains of childbirth'
must also be eternal. All this is what the word Dionysus signifies: I
know of no higher symbolism than this Greek symbolism, this

symbolism of the Dionysian phenomenon. In it the profoundest instinct of life, the instinct that guarantees the future of life and life eternal, is understood religiously – the road to life itself, procreation, is pronounced *holy* . . . It was only Christianity which, with its fundamental resentment against life, made something impure out of sexuality: it flung *filth* at the very basis, the very first condition of our life.

5

The psychology of orgiasm conceived as the feeling of a superabundance of vitality and strength, within the scope of which even pain acts as a *stimulus*, gave me the key to the concept *tragic* feeling, which has been misunderstood not only by Aristotle, but also even more by our pessimists. Tragedy is so far from proving anything in regard to the pessimism of the Greeks, as Schopenhauer maintains, that it ought rather to be considered as the categorical repudiation and *condemnation* thereof. The saying of yea to life, including even its most strange and most terrible problems, the will to life rejoicing over its own inexhaustibleness in the *sacrifice* of its highest types – this is what I called Dionysian, this is what I divined as the bridge leading to the psychology of the *tragic* poet. Not in order to escape from terror and pity, not to purify one's self of a dangerous passion by discharging it with vehemence – this is how Aristotle understood it – but to be far beyond terror and pity and to be the eternal lust of Becoming itself – that lust which also involves the *lust of destruction*. And with this I once more come into touch with the spot from which I once set out – the *Birth of Tragedy* was my first transvaluation of all values: with this I again take my stand upon the soil from out of which my will and my capacity spring – I, the last disciple of the philosopher Dionysus – I, the prophet of eternal recurrence.

THE END

THE HAMMER SPEAKETH

'Why so hard!' – said the diamond once unto the charcoal; 'are we then not next of kin?'

'Why so soft? O my brethren; this is my question to you. For are ye not – my brothers?

'Why so soft, so servile and yielding? Why are your hearts so fond of denial and self-denial? How is it that so little fate looketh out from your eyes?

'And if ye will not be men of fate and inexorable, how can ye hope one day to conquer with me?

'And if your hardness will not sparkle, cut and divide, how can ye hope one day to create with me?

'For all creators are hard. And it must seem to you blessed to stamp your hand upon millenniums as upon wax –

– Blessed to write upon the will of millenniums as upon brass – harder than brass, nobler than brass. – Hard through and through is only the noblest.

'This new table of values, O my brethren, I set over your heads: Become hard.'

Thus Spake Zarathustra, iii, 29

THE ANTICHRIST

*An Attempted Criticism
of Christianity*

PREFACE

This book belongs to the very few. Maybe not one of them is yet alive; unless he be of those who understand my Zarathustra. How *can* I confound myself with those who today already find a hearing? – Only the day after tomorrow belongs to me. Some are born posthumously.

I am only too well aware of the conditions under which a man understands me, and then *necessarily* understands. He must be intellectually upright to the point of hardness, in order even to endure my seriousness and my passion. He must be used to living on mountain-tops – and to feeling the wretched gabble of politics and national egotism *beneath* him. He must have become indifferent; he must never inquire whether truth is profitable or whether it may prove fatal . . . Possessing from strength a predilection for questions for which no-one has enough courage nowadays; the courage for the *forbidden;* his predestination must be the labyrinth. The experience of seven solitudes. New ears for new music. New eyes for the most remote things. A new conscience for truths which hitherto have remained dumb. And the will to economy on a large scale: to husband his strength and his enthusiasm . . . He must honour himself, he must love himself; he must be absolutely free with regard to himself . . . Very well then! Such men alone are my readers, my proper readers, my preordained readers: of what account are the rest? – The rest are simply – humanity. – One must be superior to humanity in power, in loftiness of soul – in contempt.

FRIEDRICH NIETZSCHE

Let us look each other in the face. We are hyperboreans – we know well enough how far outside the crowd we stand. 'Thou wilt find the way to the Hyperboreans neither by land nor by water': Pindar already knew this much about us. Beyond the north, the ice, and death – *our life, our happiness* . . . We discovered happiness; we know the way; we found the way out of thousands of years of labyrinth. Who *else* would have found it? – Not the modern man, surely? – 'I do not know where I am or what I am to do; I am everything that knows not where it is or what to do,' – sighs the modern man. We were made quite ill by *this* modernity – with its indolent peace, its cowardly compromise, and the whole of the virtuous filth of its yea and nay. This tolerance and *largeur de coeur* which 'forgives' everything because it 'understands' everything, is a sirocco for us. We prefer to live amid ice than to be breathed upon by modern virtues and other southerly winds! . . . We were brave enough; we spared neither ourselves nor others: but we were very far from knowing whither to direct our bravery. We were becoming gloomy; people called us fatalists. *Our* fate – it was the abundance, the tension and the storing up of power. We thirsted for thunder-bolts and great deeds; we kept at the most respectful distance from the joy of the weakling, from 'resignation' . . . Thunder was in our air, that part of nature which we are became overcast – *for we had no direction*. The formula of our happiness: a yea, a nay, a straight line, a goal.

2

What is good? All that enhances the feeling of power, the Will to Power, and power itself in man. What is bad? – All that proceeds from weakness. What is happiness? – The feeling that power is *increasing* – that resistance has been overcome.

Not contentment, but more power; not peace at any price, but war; not virtue, but efficiency* (virtue in the Renaissance sense, *virtù*, free from all moralic acid). The weak and the botched shall perish: first principle of our humanity. And they ought even to be helped to perish.

What is more harmful than any vice? – Practical sympathy with all the botched and the weak – Christianity.

3

The problem I set in this work is not what will replace mankind in the order of living beings (man is an *end*); but what type of man must be *reared*, must be *willed*, as having the highest value, as being the most worthy of life and the surest guarantee of the future.

This more valuable type has appeared often enough already: but as a happy accident, as an exception, never as *willed*. He has rather been precisely the most feared; hitherto he has been almost the terrible in itself; and from out the very fear he provoked there arose the will to rear the type which has now been reared, *attained*: the domestic animal, the gregarious animal, the sick animal man – the Christian.

4

Mankind does *not* represent a development towards a better, stronger or higher type, in the sense in which this is supposed to occur today. 'Progress' is merely a modern idea – that is to say, a false idea.† The modern European is still far below the European of the Renaissance in value. The process of evolution does not by any means imply elevation, enhancement and increasing strength.

On the other hand isolated and individual cases are continually succeeding in different places on earth, as the outcome of the most different cultures, and in these a *higher type* certainly manifests itself: something which by the side of mankind in general represents a kind of superman. Such lucky strokes of great success have always been possible and will perhaps always be possible. And even whole races, tribes and nations may in certain circumstances represent such *lucky strokes*.

---

* The German *Tüchtigkeit* has a nobler ring than our word 'efficiency'. – Tr.
† cf. Disraeli: 'But enlightened Europe is not happy. Its existence is a fever which it calls progress. Progress to what?' (*Tancred*, Book 3, chap. 7). – Tr.

5

We must not deck out and adorn Christianity: it has waged a deadly war upon this *higher* type of man, it has set a ban upon all the fundamental instincts of this type, and has distilled evil and the devil himself out of these instincts: the strong man as the typical pariah, the villain. Christianity has sided with everything weak, low, and botched; it has made an ideal out of *antagonism* towards all the self-preservative instincts of strong life: it has corrupted even the reason of the strongest intellects, by teaching that the highest values of intellectuality are sinful, misleading and full of temptations. The most lamentable example of this was the corruption of Pascal, who believed in the perversion of his reason through original sin, whereas it had only been perverted by his Christianity.

6

A painful and ghastly spectacle has just risen before my eyes. I tore down the curtain which concealed mankind's *corruption*. This word in my mouth is at least secure from the suspicion that it contains a moral charge against mankind. It is − I would fain emphasise this again − free from moralic acid: to such an extent is this so, that I am most thoroughly conscious of the corruption in question precisely in those quarters in which hitherto people have aspired with most determination to 'virtue' and to 'godliness'. As you have already surmised, I understand corruption in the sense of *decadence*. What I maintain is this, that all the values upon which mankind builds its highest hopes and desires are *decadent* values.

I call an animal, a species, an individual corrupt, when it loses its instincts, when it selects and *prefers* that which is detrimental to it. A history of the 'higher feelings', of 'human ideals' − and it is not impossible that I shall have to write it − would almost explain why man is so corrupt. Life itself, to my mind, is nothing more nor less than the instinct of growth, of permanence, of accumulating forces, of power: where the will to power is lacking, degeneration sets in. My contention is that all the highest values of mankind *lack* this will − that the values of decline and of *nihilism* are exercising the sovereign power under the cover of the holiest names.

7

Christianity is called the religion of *pity*. – Pity is opposed to
the tonic passions which enhance the energy of the feeling of life:
its action is depressing. A man loses power when he pities. By
means of pity the drain on strength which suffering itself already
introduces into the world is multiplied a thousandfold. Through
pity, suffering itself becomes infectious; in certain circumstances it
may lead to a total loss of life and vital energy, which is absurdly
out of proportion to the magnitude of the cause (the case of the
death of the Nazarene). This is the first standpoint; but there is a
still more important one. Supposing one measures pity according
to the value of the reactions it usually stimulates, its danger to life
appears in a much more telling light. On the whole, pity thwarts
the law of development which is the law of selection. It preserves
that which is ripe for death, it fights in favour of the disinherited
and the condemned of life; thanks to the multitude of abortions
of all kinds which it maintains in life, it lends life itself a sombre
and questionable aspect. People have dared to call pity a virtue (in
every *noble* culture it is considered as a weakness); people went still
further, they exalted it to *the* virtue, the root and origin of all
virtues – but, of course, what must never be forgotten is the fact
that this was done from the standpoint of a philosophy which was
nihilistic, and on whose shield the device *The Denial of Life* was
inscribed. Schopenhauer was right in this respect: by means of
pity, life is denied and made *more worthy of denial* – pity is the *praxis*
of nihilism. I repeat, this depressing and infectious instinct thwarts
those instincts which aim at the preservation and enhancement of
the value life: by *multiplying* misery quite as much as by preserving
all that is miserable, it is the principal agent in promoting decadence – pity exhorts people to nothing, to *nonentity*! But they do
not say '*nonentity*', they say 'Beyond', or 'God', or 'the true life';
or Nirvana, or Salvation, or Blessedness, instead. This innocent
rhetoric, which belongs to the realm of the religio-moral idiosyncrasy, immediately appears to be *very much less innocent* if one
realises what the tendency is which here tries to drape itself in the
mantle of sublime expressions – the tendency of hostility to life.
Schopenhauer was hostile to life: that is why he elevated pity to a
virtue . . . Aristotle, as you know, recognised in pity a morbid and
dangerous state, of which it was wise to rid one's self from time to

time by a purgative: he regarded tragedy as a purgative. For the sake of the instinct of life, it would certainly seem necessary to find some means of lancing any such morbid and dangerous accumulation of pity, as that which possessed Schopenhauer (and unfortunately the whole of our literary and artistic decadence as well, from St Petersburg to Paris, from Tolstoy to Wagner), if only to make it *burst* . . . Nothing is more unhealthy in the midst of our unhealthy modernity than Christian pity. To be doctors *here*, to be inexorable *here*, to wield the knife effectively *here* – all this is our business, all this is *our* kind of love to our fellows, this is what makes *us* philosophers, us hyperboreans! –

8

It is necessary to state whom we regard as our antithesis: the theologians, and all those who have the blood of theologians in their veins – the whole of our philosophy . . . A man must have had his very nose upon this fatality, or better still he must have experienced it in his own soul; he must almost have perished through it, in order to be unable to treat this matter lightly (the free-spiritedness of our friends the naturalists and physiologists is, in my opinion, a *joke* – what they lack in these questions is passion, what they lack is having suffered from these questions). This poisoning extends much further than people think: I unearthed the 'arrogant' instinct of the theologian, wherever nowadays people feel themselves idealists – wherever, thanks to superior antecedents, they claim the right to rise above reality and to regard it with suspicion . . . Like the priest the idealist has every grandiloquent concept in his hand (and not only in his hand!), he wields them all with kindly contempt against the 'understanding', the 'senses', 'honours', 'decent living', 'science'; he regards such things as *beneath* him, as detrimental and seductive forces, upon the face of which 'the Spirit' moves in pure absoluteness: as if humility, chastity, poverty, in a word *holiness*, had not done incalculably more harm to life hitherto, than any sort of horror and vice . . . Pure spirit is pure falsehood . . . As long as the priest, the *professional* denier, calumniator and poisoner of life, is considered as the *highest* kind of man, there can be no answer to the question, what *is* truth? Truth has already been turned topsy-turvy, when the conscious advocate of nonentity and of denial passes as the representative of 'truth'.

9

It is upon this theological instinct that I wage war. I find traces of it
everywhere. Whoever has the blood of theologians in his veins,
stands from the start in a false and dishonest position to all things.
The pathos which grows out of this state, is called *faith*: that is to
say, to shut one's eyes once and for all, in order not to suffer at the
sight of incurable falsity. People convert this faulty view of all
things into a moral, a virtue, a thing of holiness. They endow
their distorted vision with a good conscience – they claim that no
other point of view is any longer of value, once theirs has been
made sacrosanct with the names 'God', 'Salvation', 'Eternity'. I
unearthed the instinct of the theologian everywhere: it is the most
universal, and actually the most subterranean form of falsity on
earth. That which a theologian considers true, *must* of necessity be
false: this furnishes almost the criterion of truth. It is his most
profound self-preservative instinct which forbids reality ever to
attain to honour in any way, or even to raise its voice. Whithersoever the influence of the theologian extends, *valuations* are
topsy-turvy, and the concepts 'true' and 'false' have necessarily
changed places: that which is most deleterious to life, is here called
'true', that which enhances it, elevates it, says yea to it, justifies it
and renders it triumphant, is called 'false'. . . . If it should happen
that theologians, *via* the 'conscience' either of princes or of the
people, stretch out their hand for power, let us not be in any doubt
as to what results there-from each time, namely: the will to the
end, the *nihilistic* will to power . . .

10

Among Germans I am immediately understood when I say that
philosophy is ruined by the blood of theologians. The Protestant
minister is the grandfather of German philosophy, Protestantism
itself is the latter's *peccatum originale*. Definition of Protestantism:
the partial paralysis of Christianity – and of reason . . . One needs
only to pronounce the words 'Tübingen Seminary' in order to
understand what German philosophy really is at bottom, i.e. –
theology *in disguise* . . . The Swabians are the best liars in Germany,
they lie innocently . . . Whence came all the rejoicing with which
the appearance of Kant was greeted by the scholastic world of
Germany, three-quarters of which consist of clergymen's and

schoolmasters' sons? Whence came the German conviction, which finds an echo even now, that Kant inaugurated a change for the *better*? The theologian's instinct in the German scholar divined what had once again been made possible . . . A back-staircase leading into the old ideal was discovered, the concept 'true world', the concept morality as the *essence* of the world (those two most vicious errors that have ever existed!), were, thanks to a subtle and wily scepticism, once again, if not demonstrable, at least no longer *refutable* . . . Reason, the *prerogative* of reason, does not extend so far . . . Out of reality they had made 'appearance'; and an absolutely false world – that of being – had been declared to be reality. Kant's success is merely a theologian's success. Like Luther, and like Leibniz, Kant was one brake the more upon the already squeaky wheel of German uprightness.

11

One word more against Kant as a *moralist*. A virtue *must* be *our* invention, our most personal defence and need: in every other sense it is merely a danger. That which does not constitute a condition of our life, is merely harmful to it: to possess a virtue merely because one happens to respect the concept 'virtue', as Kant would have us do, is pernicious. 'Virtue', 'Duty', 'Goodness in itself', goodness stamped with the character of impersonality and universal validity – these things are mere mental hallucinations, in which decline the final devitalisation of life and Koenigsbergian Chinadom find expression. The most fundamental laws of preservation and growth demand precisely the reverse, namely: that each should discover *his* own virtue, his own categorical imperative. A nation goes to the dogs when it confounds its concept of duty with the general concept of duty. Nothing is more profoundly, more thoroughly pernicious, than every impersonal feeling of duty, than every sacrifice to the Moloch of abstraction. – Fancy no-one's having thought Kant's categorical imperative *dangerous to life*! . . . The instinct of the theologist alone took it under its wing! – An action stimulated by the instinct of life is proved to be a proper action by the happiness that accompanies it: and that nihilist with the bowels of a Christian dogmatist regarded happiness as an *objection* . . . What is there that destroys a man more speedily than to work, think, feel, as an automaton of 'duty',

without internal promptings, without a profound personal predilection, without joy? This is the recipe *par excellence* of decadence
and even of idiocy . . . Kant became an idiot. – And he was the
contemporary of Goethe! This fatal spider was regarded as *the*
German philosopher – is still regarded as such! . . . I refrain from
saying what I think of the Germans . . . Did Kant not see in the
French Revolution the transition of the state from the inorganic to
the *organic* form? Did he not ask himself whether there was a single
event on record which could be explained otherwise than as a
moral faculty of mankind; so that by means of it, 'mankind's
tendency towards good' might be *proved* once and for all? Kant's
reply: 'that is the Revolution.' Instinct at fault in anything and
everything, hostility to nature as an instinct, German decadence
made into philosophy – *that is Kant!*

12

Except for a few sceptics, the respectable type in the history of
philosophy, the rest do not know the very first prerequisite of
intellectual uprightness. They all behave like females, do these
great enthusiasts and animal prodigies – they regard 'beautiful
feelings' themselves as arguments, the 'heaving breast' as the
bellows of divinity, and conviction as the *criterion* of truth. In the
end, even Kant, with 'Teutonic' innocence, tried to dress this
lack of intellectual conscience up in a scientific garb by means of
the concept 'practical reason'. He deliberately invented a kind of
reason which at times would allow one to dispense with reason,
that is to say when 'morality', when the sublime command 'thou
shalt', makes itself heard. When one remembers that in almost all
nations the philosopher is only a further development of the
priestly type, this heirloom of priesthood, this *fraud towards one's
self*, no longer surprises one. When a man has a holy life-task, as for
instance to improve, save, or deliver mankind, when a man bears
God in his breast, and is the mouthpiece of imperatives from
another world – with such a mission he stands beyond the pale of
all merely reasonable valuations. He is even sanctified by such a
taste, and is already the type of a higher order! What does a priest
care about science! He stands too high for that! – And until now
the priest has *ruled*! – He it was who determined the concept 'true
and false'.

13

Do not let us undervalue the fact that we *ourselves*, we free spirits, are already a 'transvaluation of all values', an incarnate declaration of war against all the old concepts 'true' and 'untrue' and of a triumph over them. The most valuable standpoints are always the last to be found: but the most valuable standpoints are the methods. All the methods and the first principles of our modern scientific procedure had for years to encounter the profoundest contempt: association with them meant exclusion from the society of decent people – one was regarded as an 'enemy of God', as a scoffer at truth and as 'one possessed'. With one's scientific nature, one belonged to the Chandala. We have had the whole feeling of mankind against us; hitherto their notion of that which ought to be truth, of that which ought to serve the purpose of truth: every 'thou shalt', has been directed against us . . . Our objects, our practices, our calm, cautious, distrustful manner – everything about us seemed to them absolutely despicable and beneath contempt. After all, it might be asked with some justice, whether the thing which kept mankind blindfold so long were not an aesthetic taste: what they demanded of truth was a *picturesque* effect, and from the man of science what they expected was that he should make a forcible appeal to their senses. It was our *modesty* which ran counter to their taste so long. . . And oh! how well they guessed this, did these divine turkey-cocks! –

14

We have altered our standpoint. In every respect we have become more modest. We no longer derive man from the 'spirit', and from the 'godhead'; we have thrust him back among the beasts. We regard him as the strongest animal, because he is the craftiest: one of the results thereof is his intellectuality. On the other hand we guard against the vain pretension, which even here would fain assert itself: that man is the great *arrière pensée* of organic evolution! He is by no means the crown of creation, beside him, every other creature stands at the same stage of perfection . . . And even in asserting this we go a little too far; for, relatively speaking, man is the most botched and diseased of animals, and he has wandered furthest from his instincts. Be all this as it may, he is certainly the most *interesting*! As regards animals, Descartes was the first, with really admirable daring, to venture the thought that the beast was *machina*, and the whole of our physiology is endeavouring to prove this proposition. Moreover, logically we do not set man apart, as Descartes did: the extent to which man is understood today goes only so far as he has been understood mechanistically. Formerly man was given 'free will', as his dowry from a higher sphere; nowadays we have robbed him even of will, in view of the fact that no such faculty is any longer known. The only purpose served by the old word 'will' is to designate a result, a sort of individual reaction which necessarily follows upon a host of partly discordant and partly harmonious stimuli: the will no longer 'effects' or 'moves' anything . . . Formerly people thought that man's consciousness, his 'spirit', was a proof of his lofty origin, of his divinity. With the idea of perfecting man, he was conjured to draw his senses inside himself, after the manner of the tortoise, to cut off all relations with terrestrial things, and to divest himself of his mortal shell. Then the most important thing about him, the 'pure spirit', would remain over. Even concerning these things we have improved our standpoint. Consciousness, 'spirit', now seems to us rather a symptom of relative imperfection in the organism, as an experiment, a groping, a misapprehension, an affliction which absorbs an unnecessary quantity of nervous energy. We deny that anything can be done perfectly so long as it is done consciously. 'Pure spirit' is a piece of 'pure stupidity': if we discount the nervous system, the senses and the 'mortal shell', we have miscalculated — that it is all! . . .

15

In Christianity, neither morality nor religion comes in touch at all with reality. Nothing but imaginary *causes* (God, the soul, the ego, spirit, free will — or even non-free will); nothing but imaginary *effects* (sin, salvation, grace, punishment, forgiveness of sins). Imaginary beings are supposed to have intercourse (God, spirits, souls); imaginary natural history (anthropocentric: total lack of the notion 'natural causes'); an imaginary *psychology* (nothing but misunderstandings of self, interpretations of pleasant or unpleasant general feelings; for instance of the states of the *nervus sympathicus*, with the help of the sign language of a religio-moral idiosyncrasy — repentance, pangs of conscience, the temptation of the devil, the presence of God); an imaginary teleology (the kingdom of God, the Last Judgment, everlasting life). – This purely fictitious world distinguishes itself very unfavourably from the world of dreams: the latter *reflects* reality, whereas the former falsifies, depreciates and denies it. Once the concept 'nature' was taken to mean the opposite of the concept God, the word 'natural' had to acquire the meaning of abominable – the whole of that fictitious world takes its root in the hatred of nature (reality!), it is the expression of profound discomfiture in the presence of reality . . . *But this explains everything.* What is the only kind of man who has reasons for wriggling out of reality by lies? The man who suffers from reality. But in order to suffer from reality one must be a bungled portion of it. The preponderance of pain over pleasure is the *cause* of that fictitious morality and religion: but any such preponderance furnishes the formula for decadence.

16

A criticism of the Christian concept of God inevitably leads to the same conclusion. – A nation that still believes in itself, also has its own God. In him it honours the conditions which enable it to remain uppermost – that is to say, its virtues. It projects its joy over itself, its feeling of power, into a being, to whom it can be thankful for such things. He who is rich, will give of his riches: a proud people requires a God unto whom it can *sacrifice* things . . . Religion, when restricted to these principles, is a form of gratitude. A man is grateful for his own existence; for this he must have a God. – Such a God must be able to benefit and to injure him, he must be able to act the friend and the foe. He must be esteemed for his good as well as for his evil qualities. The monstrous castration of a God by making him a God only of goodness would lie beyond the pale of the desires of such a community. The evil God is just as urgently needed as the good God: for a people in such a form of society certainly does not owe its existence to toleration and humaneness . . . What would be the good of a God who knew nothing of anger, revenge, envy, scorn, craft, and violence? – who had perhaps never experienced the rapturous *ardeurs* of victory and of annihilation? No-one would understand such a God: why should one possess him? – Of course, when a people is on the road to ruin; when it feels its belief in a future, its hope of freedom

vanishing for ever; when it becomes conscious of submission as
the most useful quality, and of the virtues of the submissive as
self-preservative measures, then its God must also modify himself.
He then becomes a tremulous and unassuming sneak; he counsels
'peace of the soul', the cessation of all hatred, leniency and 'love'
even towards friend and foe. He is for ever moralising, he crawls
into the heart of every private virtue, becomes a God for everybody,
he retires from active service and becomes a cosmopolitan . . .
Formerly he represented a people, the strength of a people, everything aggressive and desirous of power lying concealed in the heart
of a nation: now he is merely the good God . . . In very truth Gods
have no other alternative, they are *either* the Will to Power – in
which case they are always the Gods of whole nations – or, on
the other hand, the incapacity for power – in which case they
necessarily become good.

17

Wherever the Will to Power, no matter in what form, begins to
decline, a physiological retrogression, decadence, always super-
venes. The godhead of *decadence*, shorn of its masculine virtues and
passions, is perforce converted into the God of the physiologically
degraded, of the weak. Of course they do not call themselves the
weak, they call themselves 'the good'. . . . No hint will be
necessary to help you to understand at what moment in history the
dualistic fiction of a good and an evil God first became possible.
With the same instinct by which the subjugated reduce their God
to 'goodness in itself', they also cancel the good qualities from
their conquerer's God; they avenge themselves on their masters
by diabolising the latter's God. – The *good God* and the devil as
well: – both the abortions of decadence. – How is it possible that
we are still so indulgent towards the simplicity of Christian theologians today, as to declare with them that the evolution of the
concept God, from the 'God of Israel', the God of a people, to the
Christian God, the quintessence of all goodness, marks a *step
forward*? – But even Renan does this. As if Renan had a right to
simplicity! Why, the very contrary stares one in the face. When
the prerequisites of *ascending* life, when everything strong, plucky,
masterful and proud has been eliminated from the concept of God,
and step by step he has sunk down to the symbol of a staff for the

weary, of a last straw for all those who are drowning; when he becomes the pauper's God, the sinner's God, the sick man's God *par excellence*, and the attribute 'Saviour', 'Redeemer', remains *over* as the one essential attribute of divinity: what does such a metamorphosis, such an abasement of the godhead imply? – Undoubtedly, 'the kingdom of God' has thus become larger. Formerly all he had was his people, his 'chosen' people. Since then he has gone travelling over foreign lands, just as his people have done; since then he has never rested anywhere: until one day he felt at home everywhere, the Great Cosmopolitan – until he got the 'greatest number', and half the world on his side. But the God of the 'greatest number', the democrat among gods, did not become a proud heathen god notwithstanding: he remained a Jew, he remained the God of the back streets, the God of all dark corners and hovels, of all the unwholesome quarters of the world! . . . His universal empire is now as ever a netherworld empire, an infirmary, a subterranean empire, a ghetto-empire . . . And he himself is so pale, so weak, so decadent . . . Even the palest of the pale were able to master him – our friends the metaphysicians, those albinos of thought. They spun their webs around him so long that ultimately he was hypnotised by their movements and himself became a spider, a metaphysician. Thenceforward he once more began spinning the world out of his inner being – *sub specie Spinozae* – thenceforward he transfigured himself into something ever thinner and ever more anaemic, became 'ideal', became 'pure spirit', became '*absolutum*', and 'thing-in-itself'. . . . *The decline and fall of a god:* God became the 'thing-in-itself'.

18

The Christian concept of God – God as the deity of the sick, God as a spider, God as spirit – is one of the most corrupt concepts of God that has ever been attained on earth. Maybe it represents the low-water mark in the evolutionary ebb of the godlike type. God degenerated into the *contradiction of life*, instead of being its transfiguration and eternal Yea! With God war is declared on life, nature, and the will to life! God is the formula for every calumny of this world and for every lie concerning a beyond! In God, nonentity is deified, and the will to nonentity is declared holy!

19

The fact that the strong races of northern Europe did not repudiate the Christian God certainly does not do any credit to their
religious power, not to speak of their taste. They ought to have
been able successfully to cope with such a morbid and decrepit
offshoot of decadence. And a curse lies on their heads; because
they were unable to cope with him: they made illness, decrepitude
and contradiction a part of all their instincts – since then they have
not *created* any other God! Two thousand years have passed and
not a single new God! But still there exists, and as if by right – like
an *ultimum* and *maximum* of god-creating power – the *creator spiritus*
in man, this miserable God of Christian monotono-theism! This
hybrid creature of decay, nonentity, concept and contradiction,
in which all the instincts of decadence, all the cowardices and
languors of the soul find their sanction!

20

With my condemnation of Christianity I should not like to have
done an injustice to a religion which is related to it and the number
of whose followers is even greater; I refer to Buddhism. As nihilistic
religions, they are akin – they are religions of decadence – while
each is separated from the other in the most extraordinary fashion.
For being able to compare them at all, the critic of Christianity is
profoundly grateful to Indian scholars. – Buddhism is a hundred
times more realistic than Christianity – it is part of its constitutional
heritage to be able to face problems objectively and coolly, it is the
outcome of centuries of lasting philosophical activity. The concept
'God' was already exploded when it appeared. Buddhism is the
only really *positive* religion to be found in history, even in its
epistemology (which is strict phenomenalism) – it no longer speaks
of the 'struggle with *sin*', but fully recognising the true nature of
reality it speaks of the 'struggle with *pain*'. It already has – and this
distinguishes it fundamentally from Christianity – the self-deception
of moral concepts beneath it – to use my own phraseology, it stands
Beyond Good and Evil. The two physiological facts upon which it
rests and upon which it bestows its attention are: in the first place
excessive irritability of feeling, which manifests itself as a refined
susceptibility to pain, *and also* as super-spiritualisation, an all-too-
lengthy sojourn amid concepts and logical procedures, under the

influence of which the personal instinct has suffered in favour of the 'impersonal'. (Both of these states will be known to a few of my readers, the objective ones, who, like myself, will know them from experience.) Thanks to these physiological conditions, a state of depression set in, which Buddha sought to combat by means of hygiene. Against it, he prescribes life in the open, a life of travel; moderation and careful choice in food; caution in regard to all intoxicating liquor, as also in regard to all the passions which tend to create bile and to heat the blood; and he deprecates care either on one's own or on other people's account. He recommends ideas that bring one either peace or good cheer – he invents means whereby the habit of contrary ideas may be lost. He understands goodness – being good – as promoting health. *Prayer* is out of the question, as is also *asceticism*; there is neither a categorical imperative nor any discipline whatsoever, even within the walls of a monastery (it is always possible to leave it if one wants to). All these things would have been only a means of accentuating the excessive irritability already referred to. Precisely on this account he does not exhort his followers to wage war upon those who do not share their views; nothing is more abhorred in his doctrine than the feeling of revenge, of aversion, and of resentment ('not through hostility doth hostility end': the touching refrain of the whole of Buddhism). And in this he was right; for it is precisely these passions which are thoroughly unhealthy in view of the principal dietetic object. The mental fatigue which he finds already existent and which expresses itself in excessive 'objectivity' (i.e., the enfeeblement of the individual's interest – loss of ballast and of 'egoism'), he combats by leading the spiritual interests as well imperatively back to the individual. In Buddha's doctrine egoism is a duty: the thing which is above all necessary, i.e., 'how canst thou be rid of suffering' regulates and defines the whole of the spiritual diet (let anyone but think of that Athenian who also declared war upon pure 'scientificality', Socrates, who made a morality out of personal egoism even in the realm of problems).

21

The prerequisites for Buddhism are a very mild climate, great gentleness and liberality in the customs of a people and *no* militarism. The movement must also originate among the higher and even learned classes. Cheerfulness, peace and absence of desire, are the highest of inspirations, and they are *realised*. Buddhism is not a religion in which perfection is merely aspired to: perfection is the normal case. In Christianity all the instincts of the subjugated and oppressed come to the fore: it is the lowest classes who seek their salvation in this religion. Here the pastime, the manner of killing time is to practise the casuistry of sin, self-criticism, and conscience inquisition. Here the ecstasy in the presence of a *powerful being*, called 'god', is constantly maintained by means of prayer; while the highest thing is regarded as unattainable, as a gift, as an act of 'grace'. Here plain dealing is also entirely lacking: concealment and the darkened room are Christian. Here the body is despised, hygiene is repudiated as sensual; the church repudiates even cleanliness (the first Christian measure after the banishment of the Moors was the closing of the public baths, of which Cordova alone possessed 270). A certain spirit of cruelty towards one's self and others is also Christian: hatred of all those who do not share one's views; the will to persecute. Sombre and exciting ideas are in the foreground; the most coveted states and those which are endowed with the finest names are really epileptic in their nature; diet is selected in such a way as to favour morbid symptoms and to over-excite the nerves. Christian, too, is the mortal hatred of the earth's rulers – the 'noble' – and at the same time a sort of concealed and secret competition with them (the subjugated leave the 'body' to their master – all they want is the 'soul'). Christian is the hatred of the intellect, of pride, of courage, freedom, intellectual *libertinage*; Christian is the hatred of the *senses*, of the joys of the senses, of joy in general.

22

When Christianity departed from its native soil, which consisted of the lowest classes, the *submerged masses* of the ancient world, and set forth in quest of power among barbaric nations, it no longer met with exhausted men but inwardly savage and self-lacerating men – the strong but bungled men. Here, dissatisfaction with one's self, suffering through one's self, is not as in the case of Buddhism, excessive irritability and susceptibility to pain, but rather, conversely, it is an inordinate desire for inflicting pain, for a discharge of the inner tension in hostile deeds and ideas.

Christianity was in need of *barbaric* ideas and values, in order to be able to master barbarians: such are for instance, the sacrifice of the first-born, the drinking of blood at communion, the contempt of the intellect and of culture; torture in all its forms, sensual and non-sensual; the great pomp of the cult. Buddhism is a religion for *senile* men, for races which have become kind, gentle, and over-spiritual, and which feel pain too easily (Europe is not nearly ripe for it yet); it calls them back to peace and cheerfulness, to a regimen for the intellect, to a certain hardening of the body. Christianity aims at mastering *beasts of prey*; its expedient is to make them *ill* – to render feeble is the Christian recipe for taming, for 'civilisation'. Buddhism is a religion for the close and ex-haustion of civilisation; Christianity does not even find civilisation at hand when it appears, in certain circumstances it lays the foundation of civilisation.

23

Buddhism, I repeat, is a hundred times colder, more truthful, more objective. It no longer requires to justify pain and its susceptibility to suffering by the interpretation of sin – it simply says what it thinks, 'I suffer'. To the barbarian, on the other hand, suffering in itself is not a respectable thing: in order to acknowledge to himself that he suffers, what he requires, in the first place, is an explanation (his instinct directs him more readily to deny his suffering, or to endure it in silence). In his case, the word 'devil' was a blessing: man had an almighty and terrible enemy – he had no reason to be ashamed of suffering at the hands of such an enemy. –

At bottom there are in Christianity one or two subtleties which belong to the Orient. In the first place it knows that it is a matter of indifference whether a thing be true or not; but that it is of the highest importance that it should be believed to be true. Truth and the belief that something is true: two totally separate worlds of interest, almost *opposite worlds*, the road to the one and the road to the other lie absolutely apart. To be initiated into this fact almost constitutes one a sage in the Orient: the Brahmins understood it thus, so did Plato, and so does every disciple of esoteric wisdom. If for example it give anyone pleasure to believe himself delivered from sin, it is *not* a necessary prerequisite thereto that he should be sinful, but only that he should *feel* sinful. If, however, *faith* is above all necessary, then reason, knowledge, and scientific research must be brought into evil repute: the road to truth becomes the *forbidden* road. – Strong *hope* is a much greater stimulant of life than any single realised joy could be. Sufferers must be sustained by a hope which no actuality can contradict – and which cannot ever be realised: the hope of another world. (Precisely on account of this power that hope has of making the unhappy linger on, the Greeks regarded it as the evil of evils, as the most *mischievous* evil: it remained behind in Pandora's box.) In order that *love* may be possible, God must be a person. In order that the lowest instincts may also make their voices heard God must be young. For the ardour of the women a beautiful saint, and for the ardour of the men a Virgin Mary has to be pressed into the foreground. All this on condition that Christianity wishes to rule over a certain soil, on which Aphrodisiac or Adonis cults had already determined the *notion* of a cult. To insist upon *chastity* only intensifies the vehemence and profundity of the religious instinct – it makes the cult warmer, more enthusiastic, more soulful. – Love is the state in which man sees things most widely different from what they are. The force of illusion reaches its zenith here, as likewise the sweetening and transfiguring power. When a man is in love he endures more than at other times; he submits to everything. The thing was to discover a religion in which it was possible to love: by this means the worst in life is overcome – it is no longer even seen. – So much for three Christian virtues Faith, Hope, and Charity: I call them the three Christian *precautionary measures*. – Buddhism is too full of aged wisdom, too positivistic to be shrewd in this way.

24

Here I only touch upon the problem of the origin of Christianity. The first principle of its solution reads: Christianity can be understood only in relation to the soil out of which it grew – it is not a counter-movement against the Jewish instinct, it is the rational outcome of the latter, one step further in its appalling logic. In the formula of the Saviour: 'for salvation is of the Jews'. – The second principle is: the psychological type of the Galilean is still recognisable, but it was only in a state of utter degeneration (which is at once a distortion and an overloading with foreign features) that he

was able to serve the purpose for which he has been used –
namely, as the type of a Redeemer of mankind.

The Jews are the most remarkable people in the history of the
world, because when they were confronted with the question of
Being or non-Being, with simply uncanny deliberateness, they
preferred Being *at any price*: this price was the fundamental *falsification* of all nature, all the naturalness and all the reality, of the
inner quite as much as of the outer world. They hedged themselves in behind all those conditions under which hitherto a
people has been able to live, has been allowed to live; of themselves they created an idea which was the reverse of *natural*
conditions – each in turn, they twisted first religion, then the cult,
then morality, history and psychology, about in a manner so
perfectly hopeless that they were made *to contradict their natural
value*. We meet with the same phenomena again, and exaggerated
to an incalculable degree, although only as a copy: the Christian
Church, as compared with the 'chosen people', lacks all claim to
originality. Precisely on this account the Jews are the most *fatal*
people in the history of the world: their ultimate influence has
falsified mankind to such an extent that even to this day the
Christian can be anti-Semitic in spirit, without comprehending
that he himself is the *final consequence of Judaism*.

It was in my *Genealogy of Morals* that I first gave a psychological
exposition of the idea of the antithesis noble- and *resentment*-
morality, the latter having arisen out of an attitude of negation to
the former: but this is Judaeo-Christian morality heart and soul. In
order to be able to say nay to everything that represents the
ascending movement of life, prosperity, power, beauty, and self-
affirmation on earth, the instinct of resentment, become genius,
had to invent *another* world, from the standpoint of which that
yea-saying to life appeared as *the* most evil and most abominable
thing. From the psychological standpoint the Jewish people are
possessed of the toughest vitality. Transplanted amid impossible
conditions, with profound self-preservative intelligence, it volunt-
arily took the side of all the instincts of decadence – *not* as though
dominated by them, but because it detected a power in them by
means of which it could assert itself *against* 'the world'. The Jews
are the opposite of all *decadents*: they have been forced to represent
them to the point of illusion, and with a *non plus ultra* of histrionic

genius, they have known how to set themselves at the head of all decadent movements (St Paul and Christianity for instance), in order to create something from them which is stronger than every party *saying yea to life*. For the category of men which aspires to power in Judaism and Christianity – that is to say, for the sacerdotal class – decadence is but a *means*: this category of men has a vital interest in making men sick, and in turning the notions 'good' and 'bad', 'true' and 'false', upside down in a manner which is not only dangerous to life, but also slanders it.

25

The history of Israel is invaluable as the typical history of every *denaturalisation* of natural values: let me point to five facts which relate thereto. Originally, and above all in the period of the kings, even Israel's attitude to all things was the *right* one – that is to say, the natural one. Its Jehovah was the expression of its consciousness of power, of its joy over itself, of its hope for itself: victory and salvation were expected from him, through him it was confident that nature would give what a people requires – above all rain. Jehovah is the God of Israel, and *consequently* the God of justice: this is the reasoning of every people which is in the position of power, and which has a good conscience in that position. In the solemn cult both sides of this self-affirmation of a people find expression: it is grateful for the great strokes of fate by means of which it became uppermost; it is grateful for the regularity in the succession of the seasons and for all good fortune in the rearing of cattle and in the tilling of the soil. – This state of affairs remained the ideal for some considerable time, even after it had been swept away in a deplorable manner by anarchy from within and the Assyrians from without. But the people still retained, as their highest desideratum, that vision of a king who was a good soldier and a severe judge; and he who retained it most of all was that typical prophet (that is to say, critic and satirist of the age), Isaiah. – But all hopes remained unrealised. The old God was no longer able to do what he had done formerly. He ought to have been dropped. What happened? The idea of him was changed – the idea of him was denaturalised: this was the price they paid for retaining him. – Jehovah, the God of 'Justice', is no longer one with Israel, no longer the expression of a people's sense of dignity: he is only a god on certain conditions . . . The idea of him becomes a weapon in the hands of priestly agitators who henceforth interpret all happiness as a reward, all unhappiness as a punishment for disobedience to God, for 'sin': that most fraudulent method of interpretation which arrives at a so-called 'moral order of the universe', by means of which the concept 'cause' and 'effect' is turned upside down. Once natural causation has been swept out of the world by reward and punishment, a causation *hostile to nature* becomes necessary; whereupon all the forms of unnaturalness follow. A God who *demands* – in the place of a God who helps, who advises, who is at bottom only a name for every happy inspiration of courage and of self-reliance . . . Morality is no longer the expression of the conditions of life and growth, no longer the most fundamental instinct of life, but it has become abstract, it has become the opposite of life – morality as the fundamental perversion of the imagination, as the 'evil eye' for all things. What is Jewish morality, what is Christian morality? Chance robbed of its innocence; unhappiness polluted with the idea of 'sin'; well-being interpreted as a danger, as a 'temptation'; physiological indisposition poisoned by means of the canker-worm of conscience.

26

The concept of God falsified; the concept of morality falsified: but the Jewish priesthood did not stop at this. No use could be made of the whole *history* of Israel, therefore it must go! These priests accomplished that miracle of falsification, of which the greater part of the Bible is the document: with unparalleled contempt and in the teeth of all tradition and historical facts, they interpreted their own people's past in a religious manner – that is to say, they converted it into a ridiculous mechanical process of salvation, on the principle that all sin against Jehovah led to punishment, and that all pious worship of Jehovah led to reward. We would feel this shameful act of historical falsification far more poignantly if the ecclesiastical interpretation of history through millenniums had not blunted almost all our sense for the demands of uprightness *in historicis*. And the church is seconded by the philosophers: *the lie* of 'a moral order of the universe' permeates the whole development even of more modern philosophy. What does a 'moral order of the universe' mean? That once and for all there is such a thing as a will of God which determines what man has to do and what he has to leave undone; that the value of a people or of an individual is measured according to how much or how little the one or the other obeys the will of God; that in the destinies of a people or of an individual, the will of God shows itself dominant, that is to say it punishes or rewards according to the degree of obedience. In the place of this miserable falsehood, *reality* says: a parasitical type of man, who can flourish only at the cost of all the healthy elements of life, the priest abuses the name of God: he calls that state of affairs in which the priest determines the value of things 'the kingdom of God'; he calls the means whereby such a state of affairs is attained or maintained, 'the will of God'; with cold-blooded cynicism he measures peoples, ages and individuals according to whether they favour or oppose the ascendancy of the priesthood. Watch him at work: in the hands of the Jewish priesthood the Augustan Age in the history of Israel became an age of decline; the exile, the protracted misfortune transformed itself into eternal *punishment* for the Augustan Age – that age in which the priest did not yet exist. Out of the mighty and thoroughly free-born figures of the history of Israel, they made, according to their requirements, either wretched bigots and hypocrites, or 'godless ones': they simplified the psychology of every great event to the idiotic formula 'obedient or disobedient to God'. – A step further: the 'will of God', that is to say the self-preservative measures of the priesthood, must be known – to this end a 'revelation' is necessary. In plain English: a stupendous literary fraud becomes necessary, 'holy scriptures' are discovered – and they are published abroad with all hieratic pomp, with days of penance and lamentations over the long state of 'sin'. The 'will of God' has long stood firm: the whole of the trouble lies in the fact that the 'Holy Scriptures' have been discarded . . . Moses was already the 'will of God' revealed . . . What had happened? With severity and pedantry, the priest had formulated once and for all – even to the largest and smallest contributions that were to be paid to him (not forgetting the daintiest portions of meat; for the priest is a consumer of beefsteaks) – *what he wanted*, 'what the will of God was'. . . . Henceforward everything became so arranged that the priests were *indispensable everywhere*. At all the natural events of life, at birth, at marriage, at the sick-bed, at death – not to speak of the sacrifice ('the meal') – the holy parasite appears in order to denaturalise, or in his language, to 'sanctify', everything . . . For this should be understood: every natural custom, every natural institution (the state, the administration of justice, marriage, the care of the sick and the poor), every demand inspired by the instinct of life, in short everything that has a value in itself, is rendered absolutely worthless and even dangerous through the parasitism of the priest (or of the 'moral order of the universe'): a sanction after the fact is required – a *power which imparts value* is necessary, which in so doing says nay to nature, and which by this means alone *creates* a valuation . . . The priest depreciates and desecrates nature: it is only at this price that he exists at all. – Disobedience to God, that is to say, to the priest, to the 'law', now receives the name of 'sin'; the means of 'reconciling one's self with God' are of course of a nature which render subordination to the priesthood all the more fundamental: the priest alone is able to 'save'. . . . From the psychological standpoint, in every society organised upon a hieratic basis, 'sins' are indispensable: they are the actual weapons of power, the priest *lives* upon sins, it is necessary for him that people should 'sin'. . . . Supreme axiom: 'God forgiveth him that repenteth' – in plain English: *him that submitteth himself to the priest.*

<h2 style="text-align:center">27</h2>

Christianity grew out of an utterly *false* soil, in which all nature, every natural value, every *reality* had the deepest instincts of the ruling class against it; it was a form of deadly hostility to reality which has never been surpassed. The 'holy people' which had retained only priestly values and priestly names for all things, and which, with a logical consistency that is terrifying, had divorced itself from everything still powerful on earth as if it were 'unholy', 'worldly', 'sinful' – this people created a final formula for its instinct which was consistent to the point of self-suppression; as *Christianity* it denied even the last form of reality, the 'holy people', the 'chosen people', *Jewish* reality itself. The case is of supreme interest: the small insurrectionary movement christened with the name of Jesus of Nazareth, is the Jewish instinct *over again* – in other words, it is the sacerdotal instinct which can no longer endure the priest as a fact; it is the discovery of a kind of life even more fantastic than the one previously conceived, a vision of life which is even more unreal than that which the organisation of a church stipulates. Christianity denies the church.*

I fail to see against whom was directed the insurrection of which rightly or *wrongly* Jesus is understood to have been the promoter, if it were not directed against the Jewish church – the word 'church' being used here in precisely the same sense in which it is used today. It was an insurrection against the 'good and the just', against the 'prophets of Israel', against the hierarchy of society – not against the latter's corruption, but against caste, privilege, order, formality. It was the lack of faith in 'higher men', it was a 'nay' uttered against everything that was tinctured with the blood of priests and theologians. But the hierarchy which was set in question if only temporarily by this movement, formed the construction of piles upon which, alone, the Jewish people was able to subsist in the midst of the 'waters'; it was that people's *last* chance of survival wrested from the world at enormous pains, the *residuum* of its political autonomy: to attack this construction was tantamount to attacking the most profound popular instinct, the most tenacious national will to live that has ever existed on earth. This saintly anarchist who called the lowest of the low, the outcasts and 'sinners', the Chandala of Judaism, to revolt against the established order of things (and in language which, if the gospels are to be trusted, would get one sent to Siberia even today) – this man was a political criminal in so far as political criminals were possible in a community so absurdly non-political. This brought him to the cross: the proof of this is the inscription found thereon. He died for *his* sins – and no matter how often the contrary has been asserted there is absolutely nothing to show that he died for the sins of others.

28

As to whether he was conscious of this contrast, or whether he was merely *regarded* as such, is quite another question. And here, alone, do I touch upon the problem of the psychology of the Saviour. – I

---

* It will be seen from this that in spite of Nietzsche's ruthless criticism of the priests, he draws a sharp distinction between Christianity and the Church. As the latter still contained elements of order, it was more to his taste than the denial of authority characteristic of real Christianity. – Tr.

confess there are few books which I have as much difficulty in reading as the gospels. These difficulties are quite different from those which allowed the learned curiosity of the German mind to celebrate one of its most memorable triumphs. Many years have now elapsed since I, like every young scholar, with the sage conscientiousness of a refined philologist, relished the work of the incomparable Strauss. I was then twenty years of age; now I am too serious for that sort of thing. What do I care about the contradictions of 'tradition'? How can saintly legends be called 'tradition' at all! The stories of saints constitute the most ambiguous literature on earth: to apply the scientific method to them, *when there are no other documents to hand*, seems to me to be a fatal procedure from the start – simply learned fooling.

29

The point that concerns me is the psychological type of the Saviour. This type might be contained in the gospels, in spite of the gospels, and however much it may have been mutilated, or overladen with foreign features: just as that of Francis of Assisi is contained in his legends in spite of his legends. It is *not* a question of the truth concerning what he has done, what he has said, and how he actually died; but whether his type may still be conceived in any way, whether it has been handed down to us at all? – The attempts which to my knowledge have been made to read the *history* of a 'soul' out of the gospels, seem to me to point only to disreputable levity in psychological matters. M. Renan, that buffoon *in psychologicis*, has contributed the two most monstrous ideas imaginable to the explanation of the type of Jesus: the idea of the *genius* and the idea of the *hero* ('*héros*'). But if there is anything thoroughly unevangelical surely it is the idea of the hero. It is precisely the reverse of all struggle, of all consciousness of taking part in the fight, that has become instinctive here: the inability to resist is here converted into a morality ('resist not evil', the profoundest sentence in the whole of the gospels, their key in a certain sense), the blessedness of peace, of gentleness, of not *being able* to be an enemy. What is the meaning of 'glad tidings'? – True life, eternal life has been found – it is not promised, it is actually here, it is in *you;* it is life in love, in love free from all selection or exclusion, free from all distance. Everybody is the child of God –

Jesus does not by any means claim anything for himself alone – as the child of God everybody is equal to everybody else . . . Fancy making Jesus a *hero!* – And what a tremendous misunderstanding the word 'genius' is! Our whole idea of 'spirit', which is a civilised idea, could have had no meaning whatever in the world in which Jesus lived. In the strict terms of the physiologist, a very different word ought to be used here . . . We know of a condition of morbid irritability of the sense of *touch*, which recoils shuddering from every kind of contact, and from every attempt at grasping a solid object. Any such physiological *habitus* reduced to its ultimate logical conclusion, becomes an instinctive hatred of all reality, a flight into the 'intangible', into the 'incomprehensible'; a repugnance to all formulae, to every notion of time and space, to everything that is established such as customs, institutions, the church; a feeling at one's ease in a world in which no sign of reality is any longer visible, a merely 'inner' world, a 'true' world, an 'eternal' world . . . 'The Kingdom of God is within you.'. . .

30

The instinctive hatred of reality is the outcome of an extreme susceptibility to pain and to irritation, which can no longer endure to be 'touched' at all, because every sensation strikes too deep.

The instinctive exclusion of all aversion, of all hostility, of all boundaries and distances in feeling, is the outcome of an extreme susceptibility to pain and to irritation, which regards all resistance, all compulsory resistance as insufferable *anguish* (that is to say, as harmful, as *deprecated* by the self-preservative instinct), and which knows blessedness (happiness) only when it is no longer obliged to offer resistance to anybody, either evil or detrimental – love as the only ultimate possibility of life . . .

These are the two *physiological realities* upon which and out of which the doctrine of salvation has grown. I call them a sublime further development of hedonism, upon a thoroughly morbid soil. Epicureanism, the pagan theory of salvation, even though it possessed a large proportion of Greek vitality and nervous energy, remains the most closely related to the above. Epicurus was a *typical* decadent: and I was the first to recognise him as such. – The terror of pain, even of infinitely slight pain – such a state cannot possibly help culminating in a *religion* of love . . .

31

I have given my reply to the problem in advance. The prerequisite thereto was the admission of the fact that the type of the Saviour has reached us only in a very distorted form. This distortion in itself is extremely feasible: for many reasons a type of that kind could not be pure, whole, and free from additions. The environment in which this strange figure moved must have left its mark upon him, and the history, the *destiny* of the first Christian communities must have done so to a still greater degree. Thanks to that destiny, the type must have been enriched retrospectively with features which can be interpreted only as serving the purposes of war and of propaganda. That strange and morbid world into which the gospels lead us – a world which seems to have been drawn from a Russian novel, where the scum and dross of society, diseases of the nerves and 'childish' imbecility seem to have given each other rendezvous – must in any case have *coarsened* the type: the first disciples especially must have translated an existence conceived entirely in symbols and abstractions into their own crudities, in order at least to be able to understand something about it – for them the type existed only after it had been cast in a more familiar mould . . . The prophet, the Messiah, the future judge, the teacher of morals, the thaumaturgist, John the Baptist – all these were but so many opportunities of misunderstanding the type . . . Finally, let us not underrate the *proprium* of all great and especially sectarian veneration: very often it effaces from the venerated object all the original and frequently painfully unfamiliar traits and idiosyncrasies – *it does not even see them*. It is greatly to be deplored that no Dostoevsky lived in the neighbourhood of this most interesting decadent – I mean someone who would have known how to feel the poignant charm of such a mixture of the sublime, the morbid, and the child-like. Finally, the type, as an example of decadence, may actually have been extraordinarily multifarious and contradictory: this, as a possible alternative, is not to be altogether ignored. Albeit, everything seems to point away from it; for, precisely in this case, tradition would necessarily have been particularly true and objective: whereas we have reasons for assuming the reverse. Meanwhile a yawning chasm of contradiction separates the mountain, lake, and pastoral preacher, who strikes us as a Buddha on a soil only very slightly Hindu, from that combative fanatic, the mortal enemy of theologians and priests,

whom Renan's malice has glorified as '*le grand maître en ironie*'. For
my part, I do not doubt but what the greater part of this venom
(and even of *esprit*) was inoculated into the type of the Master only
as the outcome of the agitated condition of Christian propaganda.
For we have ample reasons for knowing the unscrupulousness of
all sectarians when they wish to contrive their own *apology* out of
the person of their master. When the first Christian community
required a discerning, wrangling, quarrelsome, malicious and
hair-splitting theologian, to oppose other theologians, it created
its 'God' according to its needs; just as it did not hesitate to put
upon his lips those utterly unevangelical ideas of 'his second
coming', the 'last judgment' – ideas with which it could not then
dispense – and every kind of expectation and promise which
happened to be current.

32

I can only repeat that I am opposed to the importation of the
fanatic into the type of the Saviour: the word '*impérieux*', which
Renan uses, in itself annuls the type. The 'glad tidings' are simply
that there are no longer any contradictions, that the kingdom of
heaven is for the *children;* the faith which raises its voice here is not
a faith that has been won by a struggle – it is to hand, it was there
from the beginning, it is a sort of spiritual return to childishness.
The case of delayed and undeveloped puberty in the organism as
the result of degeneration is at least familiar to physiologists. A faith
of this sort does not show anger, it does not blame, neither does
it defend itself: it does not bring 'the sword' – it has no inkling
of how it will one day establish feuds between man and man. It
does not demonstrate itself, either by miracles, or by reward and
promises, or yet 'through the scriptures': it is in itself at every
moment its own miracle, its own reward, its own proof, its own
'kingdom of God'. This faith cannot be formulated – it lives, it
guards against formulae. The accident of environment, of speech,
of preparatory culture, certainly determines a particular series of
conceptions: early Christianity deals only in Judaeo-Semitic conceptions (the eating and drinking at the last supper form part of
these – this idea which like everything Jewish has been abused so
maliciously by the church). But one should guard against seeing
anything more than a language of signs, semiotics, an opportunity

for parables in all this. The very fact that no word is to be taken literally is the only condition on which this anti-realist is able to speak at all. Among Indians he would have made use of the ideas of Sankhyam, among Chinese, those of Lao-tze – and would not have been aware of any difference. With a little terminological laxity Jesus might be called a 'free spirit' – he cares not a jot for anything that is established: the word *killeth*, everything fixed *killeth*. The idea, *experience*, 'life' as he alone knows it, is, according to him, opposed to every kind of word, formula, law, faith and dogma. He speaks only of the innermost things: 'life' or 'truth', or 'light', is his expression for the innermost thing – everything else, the whole of reality, the whole of nature, language even, has only the value of a sign, of a simile for him. – It is of paramount importance not to make any mistake at this point, however great may be the temptation thereto that lies in Christian – I mean to say, ecclesiastical – prejudice. Any such essential symbolism stands beyond the pale of all religion, all notions of cult, all history, all natural science, all experience of the world, all knowledge, all politics, all psychology, all books and all art – for his 'wisdom' is precisely the complete ignorance* of the existence of such things. He has not even heard speak of *culture*, he does not require to oppose it – he does not deny it . . . The same holds good of the state, of the whole of civil and social order, of work and of war – he never had any reason to deny the world, he had not the vaguest notion of the ecclesiastical concept 'the world'. . . . Denying is precisely what was quite impossible to him. – Dialectic is also quite absent, as likewise the idea that any faith, any 'truth' can be proved by argument (his proofs are inner 'lights,' inward feelings of happiness and self-affirmation, a host of 'proofs of power'). Neither can such a doctrine contradict, it does not even realise the fact that there are or can be other doctrines, it is absolutely incapable of imagining a contrary judgment . . . Wherever it encounters such things, from a feeling of profound sympathy it bemoans such 'blindness' – for it sees the 'light' – but it raises no objections.

33

The whole psychology of the 'gospels' lacks the concept of guilt and punishment, as also that of reward. 'Sin', any sort of aloofness

* *'reine Thorheit'* in the German text, referring once again to Parsifal. – Tr.

between God and man, is done away with – *this is precisely what constitutes the 'glad tidings'*. Eternal bliss is not promised, it is not bound up with certain conditions; it is the only reality – the rest consists only of signs wherewith to speak about it . . .

The results of such a state project themselves into a new practice of life, the actual evangelical practice. It is not a 'faith' which distinguishes the Christians: the Christian acts, he distinguishes himself by means of a *different* mode of action. He does not resist his enemy either by words or in his heart. He draws no distinction between foreigners and natives, between Jews and Gentiles ('the neighbour' really means the co-religionist, the Jew). He is angry with no-one, he despises no-one. He neither shows himself at the tribunals nor does he acknowledge any of their claims ('Swear not at all'). He never under any circumstances divorces his wife, even when her infidelity has been proved. – All this is at bottom one principle, it is all the outcome of one instinct. –

The life of the Saviour was naught else than this practice – neither was his death. He no longer required any formulae, any rites for his relations with God – not even prayer. He has done with all the Jewish teaching of repentance and of atonement; he alone knows the *mode* of life which makes one feel 'divine', 'saved', 'evangelical', and at all times a 'child of God'. *Not* 'repentance', *not* 'prayer and forgiveness' are the roads to God: the *evangelical mode of life alone* leads to God, it *is* 'God'. – That which the gospels abolished was the Judaism of the concepts 'sin', 'forgiveness of sin', 'faith', 'salvation through faith' – the whole doctrine of the Jewish church was denied by the 'glad tidings'.

The profound instinct of how one must live in order to feel 'in Heaven', in order to feel 'eternal', while in every other respect one feels by *no* means 'in Heaven': this alone is the psychological reality of 'Salvation'. – A new life and *not* a new faith . . .

34

If I understand anything at all about this great symbolist, it is this, that he regarded only *inner* facts as facts, as 'truths' – that he understood the rest, everything natural, temporal, material and historical, only as signs, as opportunities for parables. The concept 'the Son of Man' is not a concrete personality belonging to history, anything individual and isolated, but an 'eternal' fact, a psychological symbol divorced from the concept of time. The same is true, and in the highest degree, of the *God* of this typical symbolist, of the 'Kingdom of God', of the 'Kingdom of Heaven', and of the 'Sonship of God'. Nothing is more un-Christlike than the *ecclesiastical crudity* of a personal God, of a kingdom of God that is coming, of a 'kingdom of heaven' beyond, of a 'Son of God' as the second person of the Trinity. All this, if I may be forgiven the expression, is as fitting as a square peg in a round hole – and oh! what a hole! – the gospels: a *world-historic* cynicism in the scorn of symbols . . . But what is meant by the signs 'Father' and 'Son' is of course obvious – not to everybody, I admit: with the word 'Son', *entrance* into the feeling of the general transfiguration of all things (beatitude) is expressed, with the word 'Father', *this feeling itself*, the feeling of eternity and of perfection. – I blush to have to remind you of what the Church has done with this symbolism: has it not set an Amphitryon story at the threshold of the Christian 'faith'? And a dogma of immaculate conception into the bargain? . . . *But by so doing it defiled conception*. –

The 'kingdom of heaven' is a state of the heart – not something which exists 'beyond this earth' or comes to you 'after death'. The whole idea of natural death is lacking in the gospels. Death is not a bridge, not a means of access: it is absent because it belongs to quite a different and merely apparent world the only use of which is to furnish signs, similes. The 'hour of death' is not a Christian idea – the 'hour', time in general, physical life and its crises do not exist for the messenger of 'glad tidings'. . . . The 'kingdom of God' is not something that is expected; it has no yesterday nor any day after tomorrow, it is not going to come in a 'thousand years' – it is an experience of a human heart; it is everywhere, it is nowhere . . .

35

This 'messenger of glad tidings' died as he lived and as he taught – *not* in order 'to save mankind', but in order to show how one ought to live. It was a mode of life that he bequeathed to mankind: his behaviour before his judges, his attitude towards his executioners, his accusers, and all kinds of calumny and scorn – his demeanour on the *cross*. He offers no resistance; he does not defend his rights; he takes no step to ward off the most extreme consequences, he does more – he provokes them. And he prays,

suffers and loves with those, in those, who treat him ill . . . *Not*
to defend one's self, *not* to show anger, not to hold anyone
responsible . . . But to refrain from resisting even the evil one –
to *love* him . . .

36

Only we spirits that have *become free* possess the necessary condition for understanding something which nineteen centuries
have misunderstood – that honesty which has become an instinct
and a passion in us, and which wages war upon the 'holy lie' with
even more vigour than upon every other lie . . . Mankind was
unspeakably far from our beneficent and cautious neutrality, from
that discipline of the mind, which alone renders the solution of
such strange and subtle things possible: at all times, with shameless
egoism, all that people sought was their *own* advantage in these
matters, the Church was built up out of contradiction to the
gospel . . .

Whoever might seek for signs pointing to the guiding fingers of
an ironical deity behind the great comedy of existence, would find
no small argument in the *huge note of interrogation* that is called
Christianity. The fact that mankind is on its knees before the
reverse of that which formed the origin, the meaning and the *rights*
of the gospel; the fact that, in the idea 'Church', precisely that is
pronounced holy which the 'messenger of glad tidings' regarded as
beneath him, as *behind* him – one might seek in vain for a more
egregious example of *world-historic* irony. –

37

Our age is proud of its historical sense: how could it allow itself
to be convinced of the nonsensical idea that at the beginning
Christianity consisted only of the *clumsy fable of the thaumaturgist
and of the Saviour*, and that all its spiritual and symbolic side was
only developed later? On the contrary: the history of Christianity
– from the death on the cross onwards – is the history of a gradual
and ever coarser misunderstanding of an original symbolism. With
every extension of Christianity over ever larger and ruder masses,
who were ever less able to grasp its first principles, the need of
vulgarising and barbarising it increased proportionately – it absorbed
the teachings and rites of all the *subterranean* cults of the *imperium*

Romanum, as well as the nonsense of every kind of morbid reasoning. The fatal feature of Christianity lies in the necessary fact that its faith had to become as morbid, base and vulgar as the needs to which it had to minister were morbid, base and vulgar. *Morbid barbarism* at last braces itself together for power in the form of the Church – the Church, this deadly hostility to all honesty, to all loftiness of the soul, to all discipline of the mind, to all frank and kindly humanity. – *Christian* and *noble* values: only we spirits *who have become free* have re-established this contrast in values which is the greatest that has ever existed on earth! –

38

I cannot, at this point, stifle a sigh. There are days when I am visited by a feeling blacker than the blackest melancholy – the *contempt of man*. And in order that I may leave you in no doubt as to what I despise, *whom* I despise: I declare that it is the man of today, the man with whom I am fatally contemporaneous. The man of today, I am asphyxiated by his foul breath . . . Towards the past, like all knights of knowledge, I am profoundly tolerant – that is to say, I exercise a sort of *generous* self-control: with gloomy caution I pass through whole millennia of this madhouse world, and whether it be called 'Christianity', 'Christian faith', or 'Christian church', I take care not to hold mankind responsible for its mental disorders. But my feeling suddenly changes, and vents itself the moment I enter the modern age, *our* age. Our age *knows* . . . That which formerly was merely morbid is now positively indecent. It is indecent nowadays to be a Christian. *And it is here that my loathing begins.* I look about me: not a word of what was formerly known as 'truth' has remained standing; we can no longer endure to hear a priest even pronounce the word 'truth'. Even he who makes but the most modest claims upon truth, *must* know at present, that a theologian, a priest, or a pope, not only errs but actually *lies*, with every word that he utters – and that he is no longer able to lie from 'innocence', from 'ignorance'. Even the priest knows quite as well as everybody else does that there is no longer any 'God', any 'sinner' or any 'Saviour', and that 'free will', and 'a moral order of the universe' are *lies*. Seriousness, the profound self-conquest of the spirit no longer allows anyone to be *ignorant* about this . . . All the concepts of the Church have been revealed in their true colours – that is to say, as the most vicious frauds on earth, calculated to *depreciate* nature and all natural values. The priest himself has been recognised as what he is – that is to say, as the most dangerous kind of parasite, as the actual venomous spider of existence . . . At present we know, our *conscience* knows, the real value of the gruesome inventions which the priests and the Church have made, *and what end they served*. By means of them that state of self-profanation on the part of man has been attained, the sight of which makes one heave. The concepts 'Beyond', 'Last Judgment', 'immortality of the soul', the 'soul' itself, are merely so many instruments of torture, so many systems of cruelty, on the strength of which the priest became and remained master . . . Everybody knows this, *and nevertheless everything remains as it was*. Whither has the last shred of decency, of self-respect gone, if nowadays even our statesmen – a body of men who are otherwise so unembarrassed, and such thorough anti-Christians in deed – still declare themselves Christians and still flock to communion?* . . . Fancy a prince at the head of his legions, magnificent as the expression of the egoism and self-exaltation of his people – but *shameless* enough to acknowledge himself a Christian! . . . What then does Christianity deny? What does it call 'world'? 'The world' to Christianity means that a man is a soldier, a judge, a patriot, that he defends himself, that he values his honour, that he desires his own advantage, that he is *proud* . . . The conduct of every moment, every instinct, every valuation that leads to a deed, is at present anti-Christian: what an *abortion of falsehood* modern man must be, in order to be able *without a blush* still to call himself a Christian! –

39

I will retrace my steps, and will tell you the *genuine* history of Christianity. – The very word 'Christianity' is a misunderstanding – truth to tell, there never was more than one Christian, and he *died* on the cross. The 'gospel' *died* on the cross. That which thenceforward was called 'gospel' was the reverse of that 'gospel' that Christ had lived: it was 'evil tidings', a *dysangel*. It is false to the point of nonsense to see in 'faith', in the faith in salvation through

* This applies apparently to Bismarck, the forger of the Ems telegram and a sincere Christian. – TR.

Christ, the distinguishing trait of the Christian: the only thing that is Christian is the Christian mode of existence, a life such as he led who died on the cross . . . To this day a life of this kind is still possible; for certain men, it is even necessary: genuine, primitive Christianity will be possible in all ages . . . *Not* a faith, but a course of action, above all a course of inaction, non-interference, and a different life . . . States of consciousness, any sort of faith, a holding of certain things for true, as every psychologist knows, are indeed of absolutely no consequence, and are only of fifth-rate importance compared with the value of the instincts: more exactly, the whole concept of intellectual causality is false. To reduce the fact of being a Christian, or of Christianity, to a holding of something for true, to a mere phenomenon of consciousness, is tantamount to denying Christianity. *In fact there have never been any Christians.* The 'Christian', he who for two thousand years has been called a Christian, is merely a psychological misunderstanding of self. Looked at more closely, there ruled in him, *notwithstanding* all his faith, only instincts – and *what instincts! –* 'Faith' in all ages, as for instance in the case of Luther, has always been merely a cloak, a pretext, a *screen*, behind which the instincts played their game – a prudent form of *blindness* in regard to the dominion of *certain* instincts . . . 'Faith' I have already characterised as a piece of really Christian cleverness; for people have always spoken of 'faith' and acted according to their instincts . . . In the Christian's world of ideas there is nothing which even touches reality: but I have already recognised in the instinctive hatred of reality the actual motive force, the only driving power at the root of Christianity. What follows therefrom? That here, even *in psychologicis*, error is fundamental – that is to say capable of determining the spirit of things – that is to say, *substance*. Take one idea away from the whole, and put one realistic fact in its stead – and the whole of Christianity tumbles into nonentity! – Surveyed from above, this strangest of all facts – a religion not only dependent upon error, but inventive and showing signs of genius only in those errors which are dangerous and which poison life and the human heart – remains a *spectacle for gods*, for those gods who are at the same time philosophers and whom I met for instance in those celebrated dialogues on the island of Naxos. At the moment when they get rid of their *loathing* (*and we do as well!*), they will be thankful for the spectacle the Christians have offered: the wretched little planet called Earth perhaps deserves on account of *this* curious case alone, a divine glance, and divine interest . . . Let us not therefore underestimate the Christians: the Christian, false *to the point of innocence in falsity*, is far above the apes – in regard to the Christians a certain well-known theory of Descent becomes a mere good-natured compliment.

40

The fate of the gospel was decided at the moment of the death – it hung on the 'cross'. . . . It was only death, this unexpected and ignominious death; it was only the cross which as a rule was reserved simply for the *canaille* – only this appalling paradox which confronted the disciples with the actual riddle: *Who was that? what was that?* – The state produced by the excited and profoundly wounded feelings of these men, the suspicion that such a death might imply the *refutation* of their cause, and the terrible note of interrogation: 'why precisely thus?' will be understood only too well. In this case everything *must* be necessary, everything must have meaning, a reason, the highest reason. The love of a disciple admits of no such thing as accident. Only then did the chasm yawn: 'who has killed him?' 'who was his natural enemy?' – this question rent the firmament like a flash of lightning. Reply: *dominant* Judaism, its ruling class. Thenceforward the disciple felt himself in revolt *against* established order; he understood Jesus, after the fact, as one in *revolt against established order.* Heretofore this warlike, this nay-saying and nay-doing feature in Christ had been lacking; nay more, he was its contradiction. The small primitive community had obviously understood *nothing* of the principal factor of all, which was the example of freedom and of superiority to every form of *resentment* which lay in this way of dying. And this shows how little they understood him altogether! At bottom Jesus could not have desired anything else by his death than to give the strongest public *example* and *proof* of his doctrine . . . But his disciples were very far from *forgiving* this death – though if they had done so it would have been in the highest sense evangelical on their part – neither were they prepared, with a gentle and serene calmness of heart, to *offer* themselves for a similar death . . . Precisely the most unevangelical feeling, *revenge*, became once

more ascendant. It was impossible for the cause to end with this
death: 'compensation' and 'judgment' were required (and forsooth,
what could be more unevangelical than 'compensation', 'punishment', 'judgment'!) The popular expectation of a Messiah once
more became prominent; attention was fixed upon one historical
moment: the 'kingdom of God' descends to sit in judgment upon
his enemies. But this proves that everything was misunderstood:
the 'kingdom of God' regarded as the last scene of the last act, as a
promise! But the gospel had clearly been the living, the fulfilment,
the *reality* of this 'kingdom of God'. It was precisely a death such as
Christ's that was this 'kingdom of God'. It was only now that all
the contempt for the Pharisees and the theologians, and all bitter
feelings towards them, were introduced into the character of the
Master – and by this means he himself was converted into a
Pharisee and a theologian! On the other hand, the savage veneration of these completely unhinged souls could no longer endure
that evangelical right of every man to be the child of God, which
Jesus had taught: their revenge consisted in *elevating* Jesus in a
manner devoid of all reason, and in separating him from themselves: just as, formerly, the Jews, with the view of revenging
themselves on their enemies, separated themselves from their God,
and placed him high above them. The Only God, and the Only
Son of God: both were products of resentment.

41

And from this time forward an absurd problem rose into prominence: 'how *could* God allow it to happen?' To this question the
disordered minds of the small community found a reply which in
its absurdity was literally terrifying: God gave his Son as a *sacrifice*
for the forgiveness of sins. Alas! how prompt and sudden was the
end of the gospel! Expiatory sacrifice for guilt, and indeed in its
most repulsive and barbaric form – the sacrifice of the *innocent* for
the sins of the guilty! What appalling paganism! – For Jesus himself
had done away with the concept 'guilt' – he denied any gulf
between God and man, he *lived* this unity between God and man,
it was this that constituted *his* 'glad tidings'. . . . And he did *not*
teach it as a privilege! – Thenceforward there was gradually
imported into the type of the Saviour the doctrine of the Last
Judgment, and of the 'second coming', the doctrine of sacrificial

death, and the doctrine of *resurrection*, by means of which the whole concept 'blessedness', the entire and only reality of the gospel, is conjured away – in favour of a state *after* death! . . . St Paul, with that rabbinic impudence which characterises all his doings, rationalised this conception, this prostitution of a conception, as follows: 'if Christ did not rise from the dead, our faith is vain.' – And, in a trice, the most contemptible of all unrealisable promises, the *impudent* doctrine of personal immortality, was woven out of the gospel . . . St Paul even preached this immortality as a reward.

42

You now realise what it was that came to an end with the death on the cross: a new and thoroughly original effort towards a Buddhistic movement of peace, towards real and *not* merely promised *happiness on earth*. For, as I have already pointed out, this remains the fundamental difference between the two religions of *decadence*: Buddhism promises little but fulfils more, Christianity promises everything but fulfils nothing. – The 'glad tidings' were followed closely by the absolutely *worst* tidings – those of St Paul. Paul is the incarnation of a type which is the reverse of that of the Saviour; he is the genius in hatred, in the standpoint of hatred, and in the relentless logic of hatred. And alas what did this dysangelist not sacrifice to his hatred! Above all the Saviour himself: he nailed him to *his* cross. Christ's life, his example, his doctrine and death, the sense and the right of the gospel – not a vestige of all this was left, once this forger, prompted by his hatred, had understood in it only that which could serve his purpose. *Not* reality: *not* historical truth! . . . And once more, the sacerdotal instinct of the Jew perpetrated the same great crime against history – he simply cancelled the yesterday, and the day before that, out of Christianity; he *contrived of his own accord a history of the birth of Christianity*. He did more: he once more falsified the history of Israel, so as to make it appear as a prologue to *his* mission: all the prophets had referred to *his* 'Saviour'. . . . Later on the Church even distorted the history of mankind so as to convert it into a prelude to Christianity . . . The type of the Saviour, his teaching, his life, his death, the meaning of his death, even the sequel to his death – nothing remained untouched, nothing was left which even remotely resembled reality. St Paul simply transferred the centre of gravity of the whole of that great life, to a place *behind* this life – in the *lie* of the 'resuscitated' Christ. At bottom, he had no possible use for the life of the Saviour – he needed the death on the cross, *and* something more. To regard as honest a man like St Paul (a man whose home was the very headquarters of Stoical enlightenment) when he devises a proof of the continued existence of the Saviour out of a hallucination; or even to believe him when he declares that he had this hallucination, would amount to foolishness on the part of a psychologist: St Paul desired the end, consequently he also desired the means . . . Even what he himself did not believe, was believed in by the idiots among whom he spread *his* doctrine. – What he wanted was power; with St Paul the priest again aspired to power – he could make use only of concepts, doctrines, symbols with which masses may be tyrannised over, and with which herds are formed. What was the only part of Christianity which was subsequently borrowed by Muhamed? St Paul's invention, his expedient for priestly tyranny and to the formation of herds: the belief in immortality – *that is to say, the doctrine of the 'Last Judgment'* . . .

43

When the centre of gravity of life is laid, *not* in life, but in a beyond – *in nonentity* – life is utterly robbed of its balance. The great lie of personal immortality destroys all reason, all nature in the instincts – everything in the instincts that is beneficent, that promotes life and that is a guarantee of the future, henceforward arouses suspicion. The very meaning of life is now construed as the effort to live in such a way that life no longer has any point . . . Why show any public spirit? Why be grateful for one's origin and one's forebears? Why collaborate with one's fellows, and be confident? Why be concerned about the general weal or strive after it? . . . All these things are merely so many 'temptations', so many deviations from the 'straight path'. 'One thing only is necessary'. . . That everybody, as an 'immortal soul', should have equal rank, that in the totality of beings, the 'salvation' of each individual may lay claim to eternal importance, that insignificant bigots and three-quarter-lunatics may have the right to suppose that the laws of nature may be persistently *broken* on their account – any such magnification of every kind of selfishness to infinity, to *insolence*, cannot be branded with sufficient contempt. And yet it is to this miserable flattery of personal vanity that Christianity owes its *triumph* – by this means it lured all the bungled and the botched, all revolting and revolted people, all abortions, the whole of the refuse and offal of humanity, over to its side. The 'salvation of the soul' – in plain English: 'the world revolves around me.'. . . The poison of the doctrine '*equal* rights for all' – has been dispensed with the greatest thoroughness by Christianity: Christianity, prompted by the most secret recesses of bad instincts, has waged a deadly war upon all feeling of reverence and distance between man and man – that is to say, the *prerequisite* of all elevation, of every growth in culture; out of the resentment of the masses it wrought its *principal weapons* against us, against everything noble, joyful, exalted on earth, against our happiness on earth . . . To grant 'immortality' to every St Peter and St Paul, was the greatest, the most vicious outrage upon *noble* humanity that has ever been perpetrated. – And do not let us underestimate the fatal influence which, springing from Christianity, has insinuated itself even into politics! Nowadays no-one has the courage of special rights, of rights of dominion, of a feeling of self-respect and of respect for his equals – of *pathos of distance*. Our politics are diseased with this lack of courage! – The aristocratic attitude of mind has been most thoroughly undermined by the lie of the equality of souls; and if the belief in the 'privilege of the greatest number' creates and will continue *to create revolutions* – it is Christianity, let there be no doubt about it, and Christian values, which convert every revolution into blood and crime! Christianity is the revolt of all things that crawl on their bellies against everything that is lofty: the gospel of the 'lowly' *lowers* . . .

44

The Gospels are invaluable as a testimony of the corruption which was already persistent *within* the first Christian communities. That which St Paul, with the logician's cynicism of a rabbi, carried to its logical conclusion, was nevertheless merely the process of decay which began with the death of the Saviour. – These gospels cannot be read too cautiously; difficulties lurk behind every word they contain. I confess, and people will not take this amiss, that they are precisely on that account a joy of the first rank for a psychologist – as the reverse of all naïve perversity, as refinement *par excellence*, as a masterpiece of art in psychological corruption. The gospels stand alone. Altogether the Bible allows of no comparison. The *first* thing to be remembered if we do not wish to lose the scent here, is, that we are among Jews. The dissembling of holiness which, here, literally amounts to genius, and which has never been even approximately achieved elsewhere either by books or by men, this fraud in word and pose which in this book is elevated to an *Art*, is not the accident of any individual gift, of any exceptional nature. These qualities are a matter of *race*. With Christianity, the art of telling holy lies, which constitutes the whole of Judaism, reaches its final mastership, thanks to many centuries of Jewish and most thoroughly serious training and practice. The Christian, this *ultima ratio* of falsehood, is the Jew over again – he is even three times a Jew . . . The fundamental will only to make use of concepts, symbols and poses, which are demonstrated by the practice of the priests, the instinctive repudiation of every other kind of practice, every other standpoint of valuation and of utility – all this is not only tradition, it is *hereditary:* only as an inheritance is it able to work like nature. The whole of mankind, the best brains, and even the best ages – (one man only excepted who is perhaps only a monster) – have allowed themselves to be deceived. The gospels were read as the *book of innocence*. . . this is no insignificant sign of the virtuosity with which deception has been practised here. – Of course, if we could only succeed in seeing all these amazing bigots and pretended saints, even for a moment, all would be at an end – and it is precisely because *I* can read no single word of theirs without seeing their pretentious poses, *that I have made an end of them* . . . I cannot endure a certain way they have of casting their eyes heaven-wards. – Fortunately for Christianity, books are for the greatest number merely *literature*. We must not let ourselves be led away: 'judge not!' they say, but they dispatch all those to hell who stand in their way. Inasmuch as they let God do the judging, they themselves judge; inasmuch as they glorify God, they glorify themselves; inasmuch as they *exact* those virtues of which they themselves happen to be capable – nay more, of which they are in need in order to be able to remain on top at all – they assume the grand airs of struggling for virtue, of struggling for the dominion of virtue. 'We live, we die, we sacrifice ourselves for the good' ('the Truth', 'the Light', 'the kingdom of God'): as a matter of fact they do only what they cannot help doing. Like sneaks they have to play a humble part; sit away in corners, and remain obscurely in the shade, and they make all this appear a *duty*: their humble life now appears as a duty, and their humility is one proof the more of their piety . . . Oh, what a humble, chaste and compassionate kind of falsity! 'Virtue itself shall bear us testimony.'. . . Only read the gospels as books calculated to seduce by means of morality: morality is appropriated by these petty people – they know what morality can do! The best way of leading mankind by the nose is with morality! The fact is that the most conscious *conceit* of people who believe themselves to be *chosen* here simulates modesty: in this way they, the Christian community, the 'good and the just' place themselves once and for all on a certain side, the side 'of truth' – and the rest of mankind, 'the world' on the other . . . This was the most fatal kind of megalomania that had ever yet existed on earth: insignificant little abortions of bigots and liars began to lay sole claim to the concepts 'God', 'Truth', 'Light', 'Spirit', 'Love', 'Wisdom', 'Life', as if these things were, so to speak, synonyms of themselves, in order to fence themselves off from 'the world'; little ultra-Jews, ripe for every kind of madhouse, twisted values round in order to suit themselves, just as if the Christian, alone, were the meaning, the salt, the standard and even the '*ultimate tribunal*' of all the rest of mankind . . . The whole fatality was rendered possible only because a kind of megalo-mania, akin to this one and allied to it in race – the Jewish kind – was already to hand in the world: the very moment the gulf between Jews and Judaeo-Christians was opened, the latter had no alternative left, but to adopt the same self-preservative measures as the Jewish instinct suggested, even *against* the Jews themselves, whereas the Jews, theretofore, had employed these same measures only against the Gentiles. The Christian is nothing more than an anarchical Jew.

45

Let me give you a few examples of what these paltry people have stuffed into their heads, what they have laid *on the lips of their Master*: quite a host of confessions from 'beautiful souls'. –

'And whosoever shall not receive you, nor hear you, when ye depart thence, shake off the dust under your feet for a testimony against them. Verily I say unto you, It shall be more tolerable for Sodom and Gomorrah in the day of judgment, than for that city.' (Mark vi. 11) – *How evangelical!* . . .

'And whosoever shall offend one of these little ones that believe in me, it is better for him that a millstone were hanged about his neck, and he were cast into the sea.' (Mark ix. 42) – How *evangelical!* . . .

'And if thine eye offend thee, pluck it out: it is better for thee to enter into the kingdom of God with one eye, than having two eyes to be cast into hell fire: where their worm dieth not, and the fire is not quenched.' (Mark ix. 47, 48) – The eye is not precisely what is meant in this passage . . .

'Verily I say unto you, That there be some of them that stand here, which shall not taste of death, till they have seen the kingdom of God come with power.' (Mark ix. 1) – Well *lied*, lion!* . . .

'Whosoever will come after me, let him deny himself, and take up his cross, and follow me. *For* . . .' (*A psychologist's comment.* Christian morality is refuted by its 'For's': its 'reasons' refute – this is Christian.) (Mark viii. 34)

'Judge not, that ye be not judged. For with what judgment ye judge, ye shall be judged.' (Matthew vii. 1, 2) – What a strange notion of justice on the part of a 'just' judge! . . .

'For if ye love them which love you, what reward have ye? Do not even the publicans the same? And if ye salute your brethren only, what do ye more *than others*? Do not even the publicans so?' (Matthew v. 46, 47) The principle of 'Christian love': it insists upon being *well paid* . . .

'But if ye forgive not men their trespasses neither will your Father forgive your trespasses.' (Matthew vi. 15) – Very compromising for the 'Father' in question.

'But seek ye first the kingdom of God, and his righteousness; and all these things shall be added unto you.' (Matthew vi. 33) – 'All these things' – that is to say, food, clothing, all the necessities of

---

* An adaptation of Shakespeare's 'Well roared, lion' (*Midsummer Night's Dream*, Act 5, sc. i) – the lion, as is well known, being the symbol for St Mark in Christian literature and art. – TR.

life. To use a moderate expression, this is an *error* . . . Shortly before this God appears as a tailor, at least in certain cases . . .

'Rejoice ye in that day, and leap for joy: for behold, your reward *is* great in heaven: for in the like manner did their fathers unto the prophets.' (Luke vi. 23) – *Impudent* rabble! They dare to compare themselves with the prophets . . .

'Know ye not that ye are the temple of God and *that* the Spirit of God dwelleth in you? If any man defile the temple of God, *him shall God destroy*; for the temple of God is holy, which *temple ye are*.' (St Paul, 1 Corinthians iii. 16, 17) – One cannot have too much contempt for this sort of thing . . .

'Do ye not know that the saints shall judge the world? And if the world shall be judged by you, are ye unworthy to judge the smallest matters?' (St Paul, 1 Corinthians vi. 2) – Unfortunately this is not merely the speech of a lunatic . . . This *appalling impostor* proceeds thus: 'Know ye not that we shall judge angels? How much more things that pertain to this life?'

'Hath not God made foolish the wisdom of this world? For after that in the wisdom of God, the world by wisdom knew not God, it pleased God by the foolishness of preaching to save them that believe . . . not many wise men after the flesh, not many mighty, not many noble *are called*: But God hath chosen the foolish things of the world to confound the wise; and God hath chosen the weak things of the world to confound the things which are mighty; and base things of the world, and things which are despised, hath God chosen; *yea*, and things which are not, to bring to nought things that are: That no flesh should glory in his presence.' (St Paul, 1 Corinthians i. 20 *et seq.*) – In order to *understand* this passage, which is of the highest importance as an example of the psychology of every Chandala morality, the reader should refer to my *Genealogy of Morals:* in this book, the contrast between a *noble* and a Chandala morality born of *resentment* and impotent revengefulness, is brought to light for the first time. St Paul was the greatest of all the apostles of revenge . . .

46

What follows from this? That one does well to put on one's gloves when reading the New Testament. The proximity of so much pitch almost defiles one. We should feel just as little inclined to hobnob with 'the first Christians' as with Polish Jews: not that we need explain our objections . . . They simply smell bad. – In vain have I sought for a single sympathetic feature in the New Testament; there is not a trace of freedom, kindliness, open-heartedness and honesty to be found in it. Humaneness has not even made a start in this book, while *cleanly* instincts are entirely absent from it . . . Only evil instincts are to be found in the New Testament, it shows no sign of courage, these people lack even the courage of their evil instincts. All is cowardice, all is a closing of one's eyes and self-deception. Every book becomes clean, after one has just read the New Testament: for instance, immediately after laying down St Paul, I read with particular delight that most charming and most wanton of scoffers, Petronius, of whom some-one might say what Domenico Boccaccio wrote to the Duke of Parma about Caesar Borgia: '*è tutto festo*' – immortally healthy, immortally cheerful and well-constituted . . . These petty bigots err in their calculations and in the most important thing of all. They certainly attack; but everything they assail is, by that very fact alone, *distinguished*. He whom a 'primitive Christian' attacks, is *not* thereby sullied . . . Conversely it is an honour to be opposed by 'primitive Christians'. One cannot read the New Testament without feeling a preference for everything in it which is the subject of abuse – not to speak of the 'wisdom of this world', which an impudent windbag tries in vain to confound 'by the foolishness of preaching'. Even the Pharisees and the Scribes derive advantage from such opposition: they must certainly have been worth something in order to have been hated in such a disreputable way. Hypocrisy – as if this were a reproach which the 'first Christians' *were at liberty* to make! – After all the Scribes and Pharisees were the *privileged ones*: this was quite enough, the hatred of the Chandala requires no other reasons. I very much fear that the 'first Christian' – as also the '*last Christian*' *whom I may yet be able to meet* – is in his deepest instincts a rebel against every-thing privileged; he lives and struggles unremittingly for 'equal rights'! . . . Regarded more closely, he has no alternative . . . If one's desire be personally to represent 'one of the chosen of God' – or a 'temple of God', or 'a judge of angels' – then every *other* principle of selection, for instance that based upon a standard of honesty, intellect, manliness and pride, or upon beauty and

freedom of heart, becomes the 'world' – *evil in itself*. Moral: every
word on the lips of a 'first Christian' is a lie, every action he does is
an instinctive falsehood – all his values, all his aims are pernicious;
but the man he hates, *the thing* he hates, *has value* . . . The Christian,
more particularly the Christian priest, is a *criterion of values*. – Do
I require to add that in the whole of the New Testament only
one figure appears which we cannot help respecting? Pilate, the
Roman Governor. To take a Jewish quarrel *seriously* was a thing he
could not get himself to do. One Jew more or less – what did it
matter? . . . The noble scorn of a Roman, in whose presence the
word 'truth' had been shamelessly abused, has enriched the
New Testament with the only saying which *is of value* – and this
saying is not only the criticism, but actually the shattering of that
Testament: 'What is truth!' . . .

47

That which separates us from other people is not the fact that we
can discover no God, either in history, or in nature, or behind
nature – but that we regard what has been revered as 'God', not as
'divine', but as wretched, absurd, pernicious; not as an error, but as
a *crime against life* . . . We deny God as God . . . If the existence of
this Christian God were *proved* to us, we should feel even less able
to believe in him. – In a formula: *deus qualem Paulus creavit, dei
negatio*. – A religion such as Christianity which never once comes
in touch with reality, and which collapses the very moment reality
asserts its rights even on one single point, must naturally be a
mortal enemy of the 'wisdom of this world' – that is to say, *science*.
It will call all those means good with which mental discipline,
lucidity and severity in intellectual matters, nobility and freedom
of the intellect may be poisoned, calumniated and *decried*. 'Faith' as
an imperative is a *veto* against science – *in praxi*, it means lies at any
price. St Paul *understood* that falsehood – that 'faith' was necessary;
subsequently the Church understood St Paul. – That 'God' which
St Paul invented for himself, a God who 'confounds' the 'wisdom
of this world' (in a narrower sense, the two great opponents of all
superstition, philology and medicine), means, in very truth, simply
St Paul's firm *resolve* to do so: to call his own will 'God', *thora*, that
is arch-Jewish. St Paul insists upon confounding the 'wisdom of
this world': his enemies are the *good old* philologists and doctors of

the Alexandrine schools; it is on them that he wages war. As a matter of fact no-one is either a philologist or a doctor, who is not also an *Antichrist*. As a philologist, for instance, a man sees *behind* the 'holy books', as a doctor he sees *behind* the physiological rottenness of the typical Christian. The doctor says 'incurable', the philologist says 'forgery'.

48

Has anybody ever really understood the celebrated story which stands at the beginning of the Bible – concerning God's deadly panic over *science*? . . . Nobody has understood it. This essentially sacerdotal book naturally begins with the great inner difficulty of the priest: *he* knows only one great danger, *consequently* 'God' has only one great danger. –

The old God, entirely 'spirit', a high-priest through and through, and wholly perfect, is wandering in a leisurely fashion round his garden; but he is bored. Against boredom even the gods themselves struggle in vain.* What does he do? He invents man – man is entertaining . . . But, behold, even man begins to be bored. God's compassion for the only form of misery which is peculiar to all paradises exceeds all bounds: so forthwith he creates yet other animals. God's *first* mistake: man did not think animals entertaining – he dominated them, he did not even wish to be an 'animal'. Consequently God created woman. And boredom did indeed cease from that moment – but many other things ceased as well! Woman was God's *second* mistake. – 'Woman in her innermost nature is a serpent, Heva' – every priest knows this: 'all evil came into this world through woman' – every priest knows this too. '*Consequently science* also comes from woman.'. . . Only through woman did man learn to taste of the tree of knowledge. – What had happened? Panic had seized the old God. Man himself had been his *greatest* mistake, he had created a rival for himself, science makes you *equal to God* – it is all up with priests and gods when man becomes scientific! – Moral: science is the most prohibited thing of all – it alone is forbidden. Science is the *first*, the germ of all sins, the original sin. *This alone is morality.* – 'Thou shalt

* A parody of a line in Schiller's *Jungfrau von Orleans* (Act 3, sc. vi): '*Mit der Dummheit kämpfen Götter selbst vergebens*' ('With stupidity even the gods themselves struggle in vain'). – Tʀ.

not know': the rest follows as a matter of course. God's panic did not deprive him of his intelligence. How can one *guard* against science? For ages this was his principal problem. Reply: man must be kicked out of paradise! Happiness, leisure leads to thinking – all thoughts are bad thoughts . . . Man *must* not think. – And the 'priest-per-se' proceeds to invent distress, death, the vital danger of pregnancy, every kind of misery, decrepitude, and affliction, and above all *disease* – all these are but weapons employed in the struggle with science! Trouble prevents man from thinking . . . And notwithstanding all these precautions! oh, horror! the work of science towers aloft, it storms heaven itself, it rings the death-knell of the gods – what's to be done? – The old God invents *war*; he separates the nations, and contrives to make men destroy each other mutually (the priests have always been in need of war). War, among other things, is a great disturber of science! – Incredible! Knowledge, *the rejection of the sacerdotal yoke*, nevertheless increases. – So the old God arrives at this final decision: 'Man has become scientific – *there is no help for it, he must be drowned!*' . . .

49

You have understood me. The beginning of the Bible contains the whole psychology of the priest. – The priest knows only one great danger, and that is science – the healthy concept of cause and effect. But, on the whole, science flourishes only under happy conditions – a man must have time, he must also have superfluous mental energy in order to 'pursue knowledge'. . . . '*Consequently* man must be made unhappy', – this has been the argument of the priest of all ages. – You have already divined what, in accordance with such a manner of arguing, must first have come into the world: 'sin'. . . . The notion of guilt and punishment, the whole 'moral order of the universe', was invented against science – against the deliverance of man from the priest . . . Man must *not* cast his glance upon the outer world, he must turn it inwards into himself; he must not as a learner look cleverly and cautiously *into* things; he must not see at all: he must *suffer* . . . And he must suffer, so that he may be in need of the priest every minute. – Away with doctors! What is needed is a Saviour! – The notion of guilt and punishment, including the doctrine of 'grace', of 'salvation' and of 'forgiveness' – all *lies* through and through without a shred of psychological reality – were invented in order to destroy man's *sense of causality*: they are an attack on the concept of cause and effect! – And *not* an attack with the fist, with the knife, with honesty in hate and love! But one actuated by the most cowardly, most crafty, and most ignoble instincts! A *priest's* attack! A *parasite's* attack! A vampyrism of pale subterranean leeches! – When the natural consequences of an act are no longer 'natural', but are thought to be conjured up by phantom concepts of superstition, by 'God', by 'spirits', and by 'souls', as merely moral consequences, in the form of rewards, punishments, hints, and educational means – then the whole basis of knowledge is destroyed – *then the greatest crime against man has been perpetrated.* – Sin, I repeat, this form of self-pollution *par excellence* on the part of man, was invented in order to make science, culture and every elevation and noble trait in man quite impossible; by means of the invention of sin the priest is able to *rule*.

50

I cannot here dispense with a psychology of 'faith' and of the 'faithful', which will naturally be to the advantage of the 'faithful'. If today there are still many who do not know how very *indecent* it is to be a 'believer' – *or* to what extent such a state is the sign of decadence, and of the broken will to life – they will know it no later than tomorrow. My voice can make even those hear who are hard of hearing. – If perchance my ears have not deceived me, it seems that among Christians there is such a thing as a kind of criterion of truth, which is called 'the proof of power'. 'Faith saveth; *therefore* it is true.' – It might be objected here that it is precisely salvation which is not proved but only *promised:* salvation is bound up with the condition 'faith' – one *shall* be saved, *because* one has faith . . . But how prove *that* that which the priest promises to the faithful really will take place, to wit: the 'Beyond' which defies all demonstration? – The assumed 'proof of power' is at bottom once again only a belief in the fact that the effect which faith promises will not fail to take place. In a formula: 'I believe that faith saveth; – *consequently* it is true.' – But with this we are at the end of our tether. This 'consequently' would be the *absurdum* itself as a criterion of truth. – Let us be indulgent enough to assume, however, that salvation is proved by faith (*not* only desired, and *not* merely promised by the somewhat suspicious lips of a priest): could salvation – or, in technical terminology, *happiness* – ever be a proof of truth? So little is it so that, when pleasurable sensations make their influence felt in replying to the question 'what is true', they furnish almost the contradiction of truth, or at any rate they make it in the highest degree suspicious. The proof through 'happiness' is a proof of happiness – and nothing else; why in the world should we take it for granted that *true* judgments cause more pleasure than false ones, and that in accordance with a pre-established harmony, they necessarily bring pleasant feelings in their wake? – The experience of all strict and profound minds teaches the *reverse*. Every inch of truth has been conquered only after a struggle, almost everything to which our heart, our love and our trust in life cleaves, has had to be sacrificed for it. Greatness of soul is necessary for this: the service of truth is the hardest of all services. – What then is meant by honesty in things intellectual? It means that a man is severe towards his own heart, that he scorns 'beautiful feelings', and that he makes a matter of conscience out of every yea and nay! – Faith saveth: *consequently* it lies . . .

51

The fact that faith may in certain circumstances save, the fact that salvation as the result of an *idée fixe* does not constitute a true idea, the fact that faith moves *no* mountains, but may very readily raise them where previously they did not exist – all these things are made sufficiently clear by a mere casual stroll through a *lunatic asylum*. Of course *no* priest would find this sufficient: for he instinctively denies that illness is illness or that lunatic asylums are lunatic asylums. Christianity is in *need* of illness, just as ancient Greece was in need of a superabundance of health. The actual ulterior motive of the whole of the Church's system of salvation is to *make people ill*. And is not the Church itself the Catholic madhouse as an ultimate ideal? – The earth as a whole converted into a madhouse? – The kind of religious man which the Church aims at producing is a typical *decadent*. The moment of time at which a religious crisis attains the ascendancy over a people, is always characterised by nerve-epidemics; the 'inner world' of the religious man is ridiculously like the 'inner world' of over-irritable and exhausted people; the 'highest' states which Christianity holds up to mankind as the value of values, are epileptic in character – the Church has pronounced only madmen *or* great swindlers *in majorem dei honorem* holy. Once I ventured to characterise the whole of the Christian training of penance and salvation (which nowadays is best studied in England) as a *folie circulaire* methodically generated upon a soil which, of course, is already prepared for it – that is to say, which is thoroughly morbid. Not every one who likes can be a Christian: no man is 'converted' to Christianity – he must be sick enough for it . . . We others who possess enough courage both for health and for contempt, how rightly *we* may despise a religion which taught men to misunderstand the body! which would not rid itself of the superstitions of the soul! which made a virtue of taking inadequate nourishment! which in health combats a sort of enemy, devil, temptation! which persuaded itself that it was possible to bear a perfect soul about in a cadaverous body, and which, to this end, had to make up for itself a new concept of 'perfection', a pale, sickly, idiotically gushing ideal – so-called 'holiness' – holiness, which in itself is simply a symptom of an impoverished, enervated and incurably deteriorated body! . . . The movement of Christianity, as a European movement, was from first to last a general accumulation of the ruck and scum of all sorts and kinds (and these, by means of Christianity, aspire to power). It does *not* express the downfall of a race, it is rather a conglomerate assembly of all the decadent elements from everywhere which seek each other and crowd together. It was not, as some believe, the corruption of antiquity, of *noble* antiquity, which made Christianity possible: the learned idiocy which nowadays tries to support such a notion cannot be too severely contradicted. At the time when the morbid and corrupted Chandala classes became Christianised in the whole of the *imperium*, the very *contrary type*, nobility, was extant in its finest and maturest forms. The greatest number became master; the democracy of Christian instincts triumphed . . . Christianity was not 'national', it was not determined by race – it appealed to all the disinherited forms of life, it had its allies everywhere. Christianity is built upon the rancour of the sick; its instinct is directed *against* the sound, against health. Everything well-constituted, proud, high-spirited, and beautiful is offensive to its ears and eyes. Again I remind you of St Paul's priceless words: 'And God hath chosen the *weak* things of the world, the *foolish* things of the world; and *base* things of the world, and things which are *despised*': this was the formula, *in hoc signo* decadence triumphed. – *God on the cross* – does no-one yet understand the terrible ulterior motive of this symbol? – Everything that suffers, everything that hangs on the cross, is *divine* . . . All of us hang on the cross, consequently we are *divine* . . . We alone are divine . . . Christianity was a victory; a *nobler* type of character perished through it – Christianity has been humanity's greatest misfortune hitherto. –

52

Christianity also stands opposed to everything happily constituted in the *mind* – it can make use only of morbid reason as Christian reason; it takes the side of everything idiotic, it utters a curse upon 'intellect', upon the *superbia* of the healthy intellect. Since illness belongs to the essence of Christianity, the typically Christian state, 'faith', *must* also be a form of illness, and all straight, honest and scientific roads to knowledge must be repudiated by the Church as forbidden . . . Doubt in itself is already a sin . . . The total lack of psychological cleanliness in the priest, which reveals itself in his look, is a *result* of decadence. Hysterical women, as also children with scrofulous constitutions, should be observed as a proof of how invariably instinctive falsity, the love of lying for the sake of lying, and the inability either to look or to walk straight, are the expression of decadence. 'Faith' simply means the refusal to know what is true. The pious person, the priest of both sexes, is false because he is ill: his instinct *demands* that truth should not assert its right anywhere. 'That which makes ill is good: that which proceeds from abundance, from super-abundance and from power, is evil': that is the view of the faithful. The *constraint to lie* – that is the sign by which I recognise every predetermined theologian. – Another characteristic of the theologian is his lack of *capacity* for *philology*. What I mean here by the word philology is in a general sense to be understood as the art of reading well, of being able to take account of facts *without* falsifying them by interpretation, without losing either caution, patience or subtlety owing to one's desire to understand. Philology as *ephexis*[*] in interpretation, whether one be dealing with books, newspaper reports, human destinies or meteorological records – not to speak of the 'salvation of the soul' . . . The manner in which a theologian, whether in Berlin or in Rome, interprets a verse from the 'Scriptures', or an experience, or the triumph of his nation's army for instance, under the superior guiding light of David's Psalms, is always so exceedingly *daring*, that it is enough to make a philologist's hair stand on end. And what is he to do, when pietists and other cows from Swabia explain their miserable everyday lives in their smoky hovels by means of the 'finger of God', a miracle of 'grace', of 'Providence', of experiences of 'salvation'! The most modest effort of the intellect, not to speak of decent feeling, ought at least to lead these interpreters to convince themselves of the absolute childishness and unworthiness of any such abuse of the dexterity of God's fingers. However small an amount of loving piety we might possess, a god who cured us in time of a cold in the nose, or who arranged for us to enter a carriage just at the moment when a cloud burst over our heads, would be such an absurd God that he would have to be abolished, even if he existed. God as a domestic servant, as a postman, as a general provider – in short, merely a word for the most foolish kind of accidents . . . 'Divine Providence', as it is believed in today by almost every third man in 'cultured Germany', would be an argument against God, in fact it would be the strongest argument against God that could be imagined. And in any case it is an argument against the Germans.

53

The notion that martyrs prove anything at all in favour of a thing, is so exceedingly doubtful, that I would fain deny that there has ever yet existed a martyr who had anything to do with truth. In the very manner in which a martyr flings his little parcel of truth at the head of the world, such a low degree of intellectual honesty and such obtuseness in regard to the question 'truth' makes itself felt, that one never requires to refute a martyr. Truth is not a thing

* *ephexis* = Lat. *retentio, inhibitio* (Stephanus, *Thesaurus Graecae Linguae*); therefore: reserve, caution. The Greek Sceptics were also called Ephectics owing to their caution in judging and in concluding from facts. – Tr.

which one might have and another be without: only peasants or peasant-apostles, after the style of Luther, can think like this about truth. You may be quite sure that the greater a man's degree of conscientiousness may be in matters intellectual, the more modest he will show himself on this point. To *know* about five things, and with a subtle wave of the hand to refuse to know *others* . . . 'Truth' as it is understood by every prophet, every sectarian, every free thinker, every socialist and every church-man, is an absolute proof of the fact that these people haven't even begun that discipline of the mind and that process of self-mastery, which is necessary for the discovery of any small, even exceedingly small truth. – Incidentally, the deaths of martyrs have been a great misfortune in the history of the world: they led people astray . . . The conclusion which all idiots, women and common people come to, that there must be something in a cause for which someone lays down his life (or which, as in the case of primitive Christianity, provokes an epidemic of sacrifices) – this conclusion put a tremendous check upon all investigation, upon the spirit of investigation and of caution. Martyrs have *harmed* the cause of truth . . . Even to this day it only requires the crude fact of persecution in order to create an honourable name for any obscure sect who does not matter in the least. What? is a cause actually changed in any way by the fact that someone has laid down his life for it? An error which becomes honourable, is simply an error that possesses one seductive charm the more: do you suppose, dear theologians, that we shall give you the chance of acting the martyrs for your lies? – A thing is refuted by being laid respectfully on ice, and theologians are refuted in the same way. This was precisely the world-historic foolishness of all persecutors; they lent the thing they combated a semblance of honour by conferring the fascination of martyrdom upon it . . . Women still lie prostrate before an error today, because they have been told that someone died on the cross for it. *Is the cross then an argument?* – But concerning all these things, one person alone has said what mankind has been in need of for thousands of years – *Zarathustra.*

> Letters of blood did they write on the way they went, and their folly taught that truth is proved by blood.

But blood is the very worst testimony of truth; blood poisoneth
even the purest teaching, and turneth it into delusion and into
blood feuds.

And when a man goeth through fire for his teaching – what does that
prove? Verily, it is more when out of one's own burning springeth
one's own teaching. *

54

Do not allow yourselves to be deceived: great minds are sceptical.
Zarathustra is a sceptic. Strength and the *freedom* which proceeds
from the power and excessive power of the mind, *manifests* itself
through scepticism. Men of conviction are of no account whatever
in regard to any principles of value or of non-value. Convictions are
prisons. They never see far enough, they do not look down from a
sufficient height: but in order to have any say in questions of value
and non-value, a man must see five hundred convictions *beneath*
him – *behind* him . . . A spirit who desires great things, and who
also desires the means thereto, is necessarily a sceptic. Freedom
from every kind of conviction *belongs* to strength, to the *ability* to
open one's eyes freely . . . The great passion of a sceptic, the basis
and power of his being, which is more enlightened and more
despotic than he is himself, enlists all his intellect into its service;
it makes him unscrupulous; it even gives him the courage to
employ unholy means; in certain circumstances it even allows him
convictions. Conviction as a *means:* much is achieved merely by
means of a conviction. Great passion makes use of and consumes
convictions, it does not submit to them – it knows that it is a
sovereign power. Conversely; the need of faith, of anything either
absolutely affirmative or negative, Carlylism (if I may be allowed
this expression), is the need of *weakness*. The man of beliefs, the
'believer' of every sort and condition, is necessarily a dependent
man; – he is one who cannot regard *himself* as an aim, who cannot postulate aims from the promptings of his own heart. The
'believer' does not belong to himself, he can be only a means, he
must be *used up*, he is in need of someone who uses him up.
His instinct accords the highest honour to a morality of self-
abnegation: everything in him, his prudence, his experience, his

* *Thus Spake Zarathustra*, 'The Priests'. – TR.

vanity, persuade him to adopt this morality. Every sort of belief is
in itself an expression of self-denial, of self-estrangement . . . If one
considers how necessary a regulating code of conduct is to the
majority of people, a code of conduct which constrains them and
fixes them from outside; and how control, or in a higher sense,
slavery, is the only and ultimate condition under which the weak-
willed man, and especially woman, flourish; one also understands
conviction, 'faith'. The man of conviction finds in the latter
his *backbone*. To be *blind* to many things, to be impartial about
nothing, to belong always to a particular side, to hold a strict and
necessary point of view in all matters of values – these are the only
conditions under which such a man can survive at all. But all this is
the reverse of, the *antagonist* of, the truthful man – of truth . . .
The believer is not at liberty to have a conscience for the question
'true' and 'untrue': to be upright on *this* point would mean his
immediate downfall. The pathological limitations of his standpoint
convert the convinced man into the fanatic – Savonarola, Luther,
Rousseau, Robespierre, Saint-Simon – these are the reverse type
of the strong spirit that has become *free*. But the grandiose poses
of these *morbid* spirits, of these epileptics of ideas, exercise an
influence over the masses – fanatics are picturesque, mankind
prefers to look at poses than to listen to reason.

55

One step further in the psychology of conviction, of 'faith'. It is
already some time since I first thought of considering whether
convictions were not perhaps more dangerous enemies of truth
than lies (*Human All-too-Human*, Part I, Aphs. 54 and 483). Now I
would fain put the decisive question: is there any difference at all
between a lie and a conviction? – All the world believes that there
is, but what in Heaven's name does not all the world believe!
Every conviction has its history, its preliminary stages, its period of
groping and of mistakes: it becomes a conviction only after it has
not been one for a long time, only after it has *scarcely* been one for
a long time. What? might not falsehood be the embryonic form of
conviction? – At times all that is required is a change of personality: very often what was a lie in the father becomes a conviction
in the son. – I call a lie, to refuse to see something that one sees, to
refuse to see it exactly *as* one sees it: whether a lie is perpetrated

before witnesses or not is beside the point. – The most common sort of lie is the one uttered to one's self; to lie to others is relatively exceptional. Now this refusal to see what one sees, this refusal to see a thing exactly as one sees it, is almost the first condition for all those who belong to a *party* in any sense whatsoever: the man who belongs to a party perforce becomes a liar. German historians, for instance, are convinced that Rome stood for despotism, whereas the Teutons introduced the spirit of freedom into the world: what difference is there between this conviction and a lie? After this is it to be wondered at that all parties, including German historians, instinctively adopt the grandiloquent phraseology of morality – that morality almost owes its *survival* to the fact that the man who belongs to a party, no matter what it may be, is in need of morality every moment? – 'This is our conviction: we confess it to the whole world, we live and die for it – let us respect everything that has a conviction!' – I have actually heard anti-semites speak in this way. On the contrary, my dear sirs! An anti-semite does not become the least bit more respectable because he lies on principle . . . Priests, who in such matters are more subtle, and who perfectly understand the objection to which the idea of a conviction lies open – that is to say of a falsehood which is perpetrated on principle *because* it serves a purpose – borrowed from the Jews the prudent measure of setting the concept 'God', 'will of God', 'revelation of God', at this place. Kant, too, with his categorical imperative, was on the same road: this was his *practical* reason. – There are some questions in which it is *not* given to man to decide between true and false; all the principal questions, all the principal problems of value, stand beyond human reason . . . To comprehend the limits of reason – this alone is genuine philosophy. For what purpose did God give man revelation? Would God have done anything superfluous? Man cannot of his own accord know what is good and what is evil, that is why God taught man his will . . . Moral: the priest does *not* lie, such questions as 'truth' or 'falseness' have nothing to do with the things concerning which the priest speaks; such things do not allow of lying. For, in order to lie, it would be necessary to know *what* is true in this respect. But that is precisely what man cannot know: hence the priest is only the mouthpiece of God. – This sort of sacerdotal syllogism is by no means exclusively Judaic or Christian;

the right to lie and the *prudent measure* of 'revelation' belongs to
the priestly type, whether of decadent periods or of pagan times
(pagans are all those who say yea to life, and to whom 'God' is the
word for the great yea to all things). The 'law', the 'will of God',
the 'holy book', and inspiration. – All these things are merely
words for the conditions under which the priest attains to power,
and with which he maintains his power – these concepts are to be
found at the base of all sacerdotal organisations, of all priestly or
philosophical and ecclesiastical governments. The 'holy lie', which
is common to Confucius, to the law-book of Manu, to Muhamed,
and to the Christian church, is not even absent in Plato. 'Truth is
here'; this phrase means, wherever it is uttered: *the priest lies* . . .

56

After all, the question is, to what *end* are falsehoods perpetrated?
The fact that, in Christianity, 'holy' ends are entirely absent,
constitutes *my* objection to the means it employs. Its ends are only
bad ends: the poisoning, the calumniation and the denial of life, the
contempt of the body, the degradation and self-pollution of man
by virtue of the concept sin – consequently its means are bad as
well. – My feelings are quite the reverse when I read the law-book
of *Manu*, an incomparably superior and more intellectual work,
which it would be a sin against the *spirit* even to *mention* in the
same breath with the Bible. You will guess immediately why: it
has a genuine philosophy behind it, *in* it, not merely an evil-
smelling Jewish distillation of Rabbinism and superstition – it gives
something to chew even to the most fastidious psychologist. And,
not to forget the most important point of all, it is fundamentally
different from every kind of Bible: by means of it the *noble classes,*
the philosophers and the warriors guard and guide the masses; it is
replete with noble values, it is filled with a feeling of perfection,
with a saying of yea to life, and a triumphant sense of well-being in
regard to itself and to life – the sun shines upon the whole book. –
All those things which Christianity smothers with its bottomless
vulgarity: procreation, woman, marriage, are here treated with
earnestness, with reverence, with love and confidence. How can
one possibly place in the hands of children and women, a book
that contains those vile words: 'to avoid fornication, let every
man have his own wife, and let every woman have her own

husband . . . it is better to marry than to burn.'* And is it decent to
be a Christian so long as the very origin of man is Christianised –
that is to say, befouled – by the idea of the *immaculata conceptio*? . . .
I know of no book in which so many delicate and kindly things are
said to woman, as in the Law-Book of Manu; these old grey-
beards and saints have a manner of being gallant to women which,
perhaps, cannot be surpassed. 'The mouth of a woman,' says Manu
on one occasion, 'the breast of a maiden, the prayer of a child, and
the smoke of the sacrifice, are always pure.' Elsewhere he says:
'there is nothing purer than the light of the sun, the shadow cast by
a cow, air, water, fire and the breath of a maiden.' And finally –
perhaps this is also a holy lie: 'all the openings of the body above
the navel are pure, all those below the navel are impure. Only in a
maiden is the whole body pure.'

57

The unholiness of Christian means is caught *in flagranti*, if only the
end aspired to by Christianity be compared with that of the Law-
Book of Manu; if only these two utterly opposed aims be put
under a strong light. The critic of Christianity simply cannot avoid
making Christianity *contemptible*. – A Law-Book like that of Manu
comes into being like every good law-book: it epitomises the
experience, the precautionary measures, and the experimental
morality of long ages, it settles things definitely, it no longer
creates. The prerequisite for a codification of this kind is the
recognition of the fact that the means which procure authority
for a *truth* to which it has cost both time and great pains to attain,
are fundamentally different from those with which that same
truth would be proved. A law-book never relates the utility, the
reasons, the preliminary casuistry, of a law: for it would be
precisely in this way that it would forfeit its imperative tone, the
'thou shalt', the first condition of its being obeyed. The problem
lies exactly in this. – At a certain stage in the development of
a people, the most far-seeing class within it (that is to say, the
class that sees farthest backwards and forwards), declares the
experience of how its fellow-creatures ought to live – i.e., *can*
live – to be finally settled. Its object is, to reap as rich and as
complete a harvest as possible, in return for the ages of experiment

* 1 Corinthians vii. 2, 9. – TR.

and *terrible* experience it has traversed. Consequently, that which has to be avoided, above all, is any further experimentation, the continuation of the state when values are still fluid, the testing, choosing, and criticising of values *in infinitum*. Against all this a double wall is built up: in the first place, *revelation*, which is the assumption that the rationale of every law is not human in its origin, that it was not sought and found after ages of error, but that it is divine in its origin, completely and utterly without a history, a gift, a miracle, a mere communication . . . And secondly, *tradition*, which is the assumption that the law has obtained since the most primeval times, that it is impious and a crime against one's ancestors to attempt to doubt it. The authority of law is established on the principles: God *gave* it, the ancestors *lived* it. – The superior reason of such a procedure lies in the intention to draw consciousness off step by step from that mode of life which has been recognised as correct (i.e., *proved* after enormous and carefully examined experience), so that perfect automatism of the instincts may be attained – this being the only possible basis of all mastery of every kind of perfection in the art of life. To draw up a law-book like Manu's is tantamount to granting a people mastership for the future, perfection for the future – the right to aspire to the highest art of life. *To that end it must be made unconscious*: this is the object of every holy lie. – *The order of castes*, the highest, the dominating law, is only the sanction of a *natural order*, of a natural legislation of the first rank, over which no arbitrary innovation, no 'modern idea' has any power. Every healthy society falls into three distinct types, which reciprocally condition one another and which gravitate differently in the physiological sense; and each of these has its own hygiene, its own sphere of work, its own special feeling of perfection, and its own mastership. It is nature, not Manu, that separates from the rest those individuals preponderating in intellectual power, those excelling in muscular strength and temperament, and the third class which is distinguished neither in one way nor the other, the mediocre – the latter as the greatest number, the former as the *élite*. The superior caste – I call them the *fewest* – has, as the perfect caste, the privileges of the fewest: it devolves upon them to represent happiness, beauty and goodness on earth. Only the most intellectual men have the right to beauty, to the beautiful: only in them is goodness not weakness. *Pulchrum est paucorum hominum*: goodness is a privilege. On the other hand there is nothing which they should be more strictly forbidden than repulsive manners or a pessimistic look, a look that makes everything *seem ugly* – or even indignation at the general aspect of things. Indignation is the privilege of the Chandala, and so is pessimism. '*The world is perfect*' – that is what the instinct of the most intellectual says, the yea-saying instinct; 'imperfection, every kind of *inferiority* to us, distance, the pathos of distance, even the Chandala belongs to this perfection.' The most intellectual men, as the *strongest*, find their happiness where others meet with their ruin: in the labyrinth, in hardness towards themselves and others, in endeavour; their delight is self-mastery: with them asceticism becomes a second nature, a need, an instinct. They regard a difficult task as their privilege; to play with burdens which crush their fellows is to them a *recreation* . . . Knowledge, a form of asceticism. – They are the most honourable kind of men: but that does not prevent them from being the most cheerful and most gracious. They rule, not because they will, but because they *are*; they are not at liberty to take a second place. – The second in rank are the guardians of the law, the custodians of order and of security, the noble warriors, the king, above all, as the highest formula of the warrior, the judge, and keeper of the law. The second in rank are the executive of the most intellectual, the nearest to them in duty, relieving them of all that is *coarse* in the work of ruling – their retinue, their right hand, their best disciples. In all this, I repeat, there is nothing arbitrary, nothing 'artificial', that which is *otherwise* is artificial – by that which is otherwise, nature is put to shame . . . The order of castes and the order of rank merely formulates the supreme law of life itself; the differentiation of the three types is necessary for the maintenance of society, and for enabling higher and highest types to be reared – the *inequality* of rights is the only condition of there being rights at all. – A right is a privilege. And in his way, each has his privilege. Let us not underestimate the privileges of the *mediocre*. Life always gets harder towards the summit – the cold increases, responsibility increases. A high civilisation is a pyramid: it can stand only upon a broad base, its first prerequisite is a strongly and soundly consolidated mediocrity. Handicraft, commerce, agriculture, science, the greater part of art – in a word, the whole range of professional and business callings, is compatible only with mediocre ability and ambition ; such pursuits would be out of place among exceptions, the instinct pertaining thereto would oppose not only aristocracy but anarchy as well. The fact that one is publicly useful, a wheel, a function, presupposes a certain natural destiny: it is not *society*, but the only kind of *happiness* of which the great majority are capable, that makes them intelligent machines. For the mediocre it is a joy to be mediocre; in them mastery in one thing, a speciality, is a natural instinct. It would be absolutely unworthy of a profound thinker to see any objection in mediocrity *per se*. For in itself it is the first essential condition under which exceptions are possible; a high culture is determined by it. When the exceptional man treats the mediocre with more tender care than he does himself or his equals, this is not mere courtesy of heart on his part – but simply his *duty* . . . Whom do I hate most among the rabble of the present day? The socialistic rabble, the Chandala apostles, who undermine the working man's instinct, his happiness and his feeling of contentedness with his insignificant existence – who make him envious, and who teach him revenge . . . The wrong never lies in unequal rights; it lies in the claim to equal rights. What is *bad*? But I have already replied to this: Everything that proceeds from weakness, envy and *revenge*. – The anarchist and the Christian are offspring of the same womb . . .

58

In point of fact, it matters greatly to what end one lies: whether one preserves or *destroys* by means of falsehood. It is quite justifiable to bracket the *Christian* and the *anarchist* together: their object, their instinct, is concerned only with destruction. The proof of this proposition can be read quite plainly from history: history spells it with appalling distinctness. Whereas we have just seen a religious legislation, whose object was to render the highest possible means of making life *flourish*, and of making a grand organisation of society, eternal – Christianity found its mission in putting an end to such an organisation, *precisely because life flourishes through it*. In the one case, the net profit to the credit of reason, acquired through long ages of experiment and of insecurity, is applied usefully to the most remote ends, and the harvest, which is as large, as rich and as complete as possible, is reaped and garnered: in the other case, on the contrary, the harvest is *blighted* in a single night. That which stood there, *aere perennius*, the *imperium Romanum*, the most magnificent form of organisation, under difficult conditions, that has ever been achieved, and compared with which everything that preceded, and everything which followed it, is mere patchwork, gimcrackery, and dilettantism – those holy anarchists made it their 'piety', to destroy 'the world' – that is to say, the *imperium Romanum*, until no two stones were left standing one on the other – until even the Teutons and other clodhoppers were able to become master of it. The Christian and the anarchist are both decadents; they are both incapable of acting in any other way than disintegratingly, poisonously and witheringly, like *bloodsuckers*; they are both actuated by an instinct of *mortal hatred* of everything that stands erect, that is great, that is lasting, and that is a guarantee of the future . . . Christianity was the vampire of the *imperium Romanum* – in a night it shattered the stupendous achievement of the Romans, which was to acquire the territory for a vast civilisation which could *bide its time*. – Does no-one understand this yet? The *imperium Romanum* that we know, and which the history of the Roman province teaches us to know ever more thoroughly, this most admirable work of art on a grand scale, was the beginning, its construction was calculated *to prove* its worth by millenniums – unto this day nothing has ever again been built in this fashion, nor have men even dreamt since of building on this scale *sub specie aeterni*! – This organisation was sufficiently firm to withstand bad emperors: the accident of personalities must have nothing to do with such matters – the *first* principle of all great architecture. But it was not sufficiently firm to resist the *corruptest* form of corruption, to resist the Christians . . . These stealthy canker-worms, which under the shadow of night, mist and duplicity, insinuated themselves into the company of every individual, and proceeded to drain him of all seriousness for *real* things, of all his instinct for *realities*; this cowardly, effeminate and sugary gang have step by step alienated all 'souls' from this colossal edifice – those valuable, virile and noble natures who felt that the cause of Rome was their own personal cause, their own personal seriousness, their own personal *pride*. The stealth of the bigot, the secrecy of the conventicle, concepts as black as hell such as the sacrifice of the innocent, the *unio mystica* in the drinking of blood, above all the slowly kindled fire of revenge, of Chandala revenge – such things became master of Rome, the same kind of religion on the pre-existent form of which Epicurus had waged war. One has only to read Lucretius in order to understand what Epicurus combated, *not* paganism, but 'Christianity', that is to say the corruption of souls through the concept of guilt, through the concept of punishment and immortality. He combated the *subterranean* cults, the whole of latent Christianity – to deny immortality was at that time a genuine *deliverance*. – And Epicurus had triumphed, every respectable thinker in the Roman Empire was an Epicurean: *then St Paul appeared* . . . St Paul, the Chandala hatred against Rome, against 'the world', the Jew, the eternal Jew *par excellence*, become flesh and genius . . . What he divined was, how, by the help of the small sectarian Christian movement, independent of Judaism, a universal conflagration could be kindled; how, with the symbol of the 'God on the cross', everything submerged, everything secretly insurrectionary, the whole offspring of anarchical intrigues could be gathered together to constitute an enormous power. 'For salvation is of the Jews.' – Christianity is the formula for the supersession *and* epitomising of all kinds of subterranean cults, that of Osiris, of the Great Mother, of Mithras for example: St Paul's genius consisted in his discovery of this. In this matter his instinct was so certain, that, regardless of doing violence to truth, he laid the ideas by means of which those Chandala religions fascinated, upon the very lips of the 'Saviour' he had invented, and not only upon his lips – that he *made* out of him something which even a Mithras priest could understand . . . This was his moment of Damascus: he saw that he had *need* of the belief in immortality in order to depreciate 'the world', that the notion of 'hell' would become master of Rome, that with a 'Beyond' *this life* can be killed . . . Nihilist and Christian – they rhyme in German, and they do not only rhyme.

59

The whole labour of the ancient world *in vain:* I am at a loss for a word which could express my feelings at something so atrocious. – And in view of the fact that its labour was only preparatory, that with adamantine self-consciousness it laid the substructure, alone, to a work which was to last millenniums, the whole *significance* of the ancient world was certainly in vain! . . . What was the use of the Greeks? What was the use of the Romans? – All the prerequisites of a learned culture, all the scientific methods already existed, the great and peerless art of reading well had already been established – that indispensable condition to tradition, to culture and to scientific unity; natural science hand in hand with mathematics and mechanics was on the best possible road – the sense for facts, the last and most valuable of all senses, had its schools, and its tradition was already centuries old! Is this understood? Everything *essential* had been discovered to make it possible for work to be begun: methods, and this cannot be said too often, are the essential thing, also the most difficult thing, while they moreover have to wage the longest war against custom and indolence. That which today we have successfully reconquered for ourselves, by dint of unspeakable self-discipline – for in some way or other all of us still have the bad instincts, the Christian instincts, in our body – the impartial eye for reality, the cautious hand, patience and seriousness in the smallest details, complete *uprightness* in knowledge – all this was already there; it had been there over two thousand years before! And in addition to this there was also that excellent and subtle tact and taste! *Not* in the form of brain drilling! *Not* in the form of 'German' culture with the manners of a boor! But incarnate, manifesting itself in men's bearing and in their instinct – in short constituting reality . . . *All this in vain!* In one night it became merely a memory! – The Greeks! The Romans! Instinctive nobility, instinctive taste, methodic research, the genius of organisation and administration, faith, the *will* to the future of mankind, the great *yea* to all things materialised in the *imperium Romanum*, become visible to all the senses, grand style no longer manifested in mere art, but in reality, in truth, in *life*. – And buried in a night, not by a natural catastrophe! Not stamped to death by Teutons and other heavy-footed vandals! But destroyed by crafty, stealthy, invisible anaemic vampires! Not conquered – but only drained of blood! . . . The concealed lust of revenge, miserable envy become *master*! Everything wretched, inwardly ailing, and full of ignoble feelings, the whole ghetto-world of souls, was in a trice *uppermost*! – One only needs to read any one of the Christian agitators – St Augustine, for instance – in order to realise, in order to *smell*, what filthy fellows came to the top in this movement.

You would deceive yourselves utterly if you supposed that the leaders of the Christian agitation showed any lack of understanding: ah! they were shrewd, shrewd to the point of holiness were these dear old Fathers of the Church! What they lack is something quite different. Nature neglected them – it forgot to give them a modest dowry of decent, of respectable and of *cleanly* instincts . . . Between ourselves, they are not even men. If Islam despises Christianity, it is justified a thousand times over; for Islam presupposes men.

60

Christianity destroyed the harvest we might have reaped from the culture of antiquity, later it also destroyed our harvest of the culture of Islam. The wonderful Moorish world of Spanish culture, which in its essence is more closely related to *us*, and which appeals more to our sense and taste than Rome and Greece, was *trampled to death* (I do not say by what kind of feet), why? – because it owed its origin to noble, to manly instincts, because it said yea to life, even that life so full of the rare and refined luxuries of the Moors! . . . Later on the Crusaders waged war upon something before which it would have been more seemly in them to grovel in the dust – a culture, beside which even our nineteenth century would seem very poor and very 'senile'. – Of course they wanted booty: the Orient was rich . . . For goodness' sake let us forget our prejudices! Crusades – superior piracy, that is all! German nobility – that is to say, a Viking nobility at bottom, was in its element in such wars: the Church was only too well aware of how German nobility is to be won . . . German nobility was always the 'Swiss Guard' of the Church, always at the service of all the bad instincts of the Church; but it was *well paid for it all* . . . Fancy the Church having waged its deadly war upon everything noble on earth, precisely with the help of German swords, German blood and courage! A host of painful *questions* might be raised on this point. German nobility scarcely takes a place in the history of higher culture: the reason of this is obvious. Christianity, alcohol – the two *great* means of corruption. As a matter of fact, choice ought to be just as much out of the question between Islam and Christianity, as between an Arab and a Jew. The decision is already self-evident; nobody is at liberty to exercise a choice in this matter.

A man is either of the Chandala or he is *not* . . . 'War with Rome
to the knife! Peace and friendship with Islam': this is what that
great free spirit, that genius among German emperors – Frederick
the Second – not only felt but also *did*. What? Must a German in
the first place be a genius, a free-spirit, in order to have *decent*
feelings? I cannot understand how a German was ever able to have
Christian feelings.

61

Here it is necessary to revive a memory which will be a hundred
times more painful to Germans. The Germans have destroyed the
last great harvest of culture which was to be garnered for Europe –
it destroyed the *Renaissance*. Does anybody at last understand, *will*
anybody understand what the Renaissance was? *The transvaluation
of Christian values*, the attempt undertaken with all means, all
instincts and all genius to make the *opposite* values, the *noble* values
triumph . . . Hitherto there has been only *this* great war: there has
never yet been a more decisive question than the Renaissance –
my question is the question of the Renaissance: there has never
been a more fundamental, a more direct and a more severe *attack*,
delivered with a whole front upon the centre of the foe. To attack
at the decisive quarter, at the very seat of Christianity, and there to
place *noble* values on the throne – that is to say, to *introduce* them
into the instincts, into the most fundamental needs and desires of
those sitting there . . . I see before me a possibility perfectly magic
in its charm and glorious colouring – it seems to me to scintillate
with all the quivering grandeur of refined beauty, that there is an
art at work within it which is so divine, so infernally divine, that
one might seek through millenniums in vain for another such
possibility; I see a spectacle so rich in meaning and so wonderfully
paradoxical to boot, that it would be enough to make all the
gods of Olympus rock with immortal laughter – *Caesar Borgia as
Pope* . . . Do you understand me? . . . Very well then, this would
have been the triumph which *I* alone am longing for today: this
would have *swept* Christianity *away*! – What happened? A German
monk, Luther, came to Rome. This monk, with all the vindictive
instincts of an abortive priest in his body, foamed with rage over
the Renaissance in Rome . . . Instead of, with the profoundest
gratitude, understanding the vast miracle that had taken place, the

overcoming of Christianity at its *headquarters* – the fire of his hate knew only how to draw fresh fuel from this spectacle. A religious man thinks only of himself. – Luther saw the corruption of the papacy when the very reverse stared him in the face: the old corruption, the *peccatum originale*, Christianity *no longer* sat upon the papal chair! But life! The triumph of life! The great yea to all lofty, beautiful and daring things! . . . And Luther reinstated the Church; he attacked it. The Renaissance thus became an event without meaning, a great *in vain*! – Ah these Germans, what have they not cost us already! In vain – this has always been the achievement of the Germans. – The Reformation, Leibniz, Kant and so-called German philosophy, the Wars of Liberation, the Empire – in each case are in vain for something which had already existed, for something which *cannot be recovered* . . . I confess it, these Germans are my enemies: I despise every sort of uncleanliness in concepts and valuations in them, every kind of cowardice in the face of every honest yea or nay. For almost one thousand years now, they have tangled and confused everything they have laid their hands on; they have on their conscience all the half-measures, all the three-eighth measures of which Europe is sick; they also have the most unclean, the most incurable, and the most irrefutable kind of Christianity – Protestantism – on their conscience . . . If we shall never be able to get rid of Christianity, the *Germans* will be to blame.

62

With this I will now conclude and pronounce my judgment. I *condemn* Christianity and confront it with the most terrible accusation that an accuser has ever had in his mouth. To my mind it is the greatest of all conceivable corruptions, it has had the will to the last imaginable corruption. The Christian Church allowed nothing to escape from its corruption; it converted every value into its opposite, every truth into a lie, and every honest impulse into an ignominy of the soul. Let anyone dare to speak to me of its humanitarian blessings! To *abolish* any sort of distress was opposed to its profoundest interests; its very existence depended on states of distress; it created states of distress in order to make itself immortal . . . The cancer germ of sin, for instance: the Church was the first to enrich mankind with this misery! – The

'equality of souls before God', this falsehood, this *pretext* for the
rancunes of all the base-minded, this anarchist bomb of a concept,
which has ultimately become the revolution, the modern idea,
the principle of decay of the whole of social order – this is
Christian dynamite . . . The 'humanitarian' blessings of Christianity! To breed a self-contradiction, an art of self-profanation,
a will to lie at any price, an aversion, a contempt of all good
and honest instincts out of *humanitas*! Is this what you call the
blessings of Christianity? – Parasitism as the only method of the
Church; sucking all the blood, all the love, all the hope of life out
of mankind with anaemic and sacred ideals. A 'Beyond' as the
will to deny all reality; the cross as the trademark of the most
subterranean form of conspiracy that has ever existed – against
health, beauty, well-constitutedness, bravery, intellect, kindliness
of soul, *against life itself* . . .

This eternal accusation against Christianity I would fain write on
all walls, wherever there are walls – I have letters with which I can
make even the blind see . . . I call Christianity the one great curse,
the one enormous and innermost perversion, the one great instinct
of revenge, for which no means are too venomous, too under-
hand, too underground and too *petty* – I call it the one immortal
blemish of mankind . . .

And *time* is reckoned from the *dies nefastus* upon which this
fatality came into being – from the first day of Christianity! – *why
not rather from its last day? – From today?* – Transvaluation of all
values! . . .

ECCE HOMO

*How one becomes
what one is*

PREFACE

As it is my intention within a very short time to confront my fellow-men with the very greatest demand that has ever yet been made upon them, it seems to me above all necessary to declare here who and what I am. As a matter of fact, this ought to be pretty well known already, for I have not 'held my tongue' about myself. But the disparity which obtains between the greatness of my task and the smallness of my contemporaries is revealed by the fact that people have neither heard me nor yet seen me. I live on my own self-made credit, and it is probably only a prejudice to suppose that I am alive at all. I do but require to speak to any one of the scholars who come to the Ober-Engadine in the summer in order to convince myself that I am *not* alive . . . Under these circumstances, it is a duty – and one against which my customary reserve, and to a still greater degree the pride of my instincts, rebel – to say: *Listen! for I am such and such a person. For Heaven's sake do not confound me with anyone else!*

I am, for instance, in no wise a bogeyman, or moral monster. On the contrary, I am the very opposite in nature to the kind of man that has been honoured hitherto as virtuous. Between ourselves, it seems to me that this is precisely a matter on which I may feel proud. I am a disciple of the philosopher Dionysus, and I would prefer to be even a satyr than a saint. But just read this book! Maybe I have here succeeded in expressing this contrast in a cheerful and at the same time sympathetic manner – maybe this is the only purpose of the present work.

The very last thing I should promise to accomplish would be to 'improve' mankind. I do not set up any new idols; may old idols only learn what it costs to have feet of clay. To overthrow idols (idols is the name I give to all ideals) is much more like my business. In proportion as an ideal world has been falsely assumed, reality has been robbed of its value, its meaning, and its truthfulness . . . The 'true world' and the 'apparent world' – in plain English, the fictitious world and reality . . . Hitherto the *lie* of the ideal has been the curse of reality; by means of it the very source of mankind's instincts has become mendacious and false; so much so that those values have come to be worshipped which are the exact *opposite* of the ones which would ensure man's prosperity, his future, and his great right to a future.

3

He who knows how to breathe in the air of my writings is conscious that it is the air of the heights, that it is bracing. A man must be built for it, otherwise the chances are that it will chill him. The ice is near, the loneliness is terrible – but how serenely everything lies in the sunshine! How freely one can breathe! How much, one feels, lies beneath one! Philosophy, as I have understood it hitherto, is a voluntary retirement into regions of ice and mountain-peaks – the seeking-out of everything strange and questionable in existence, everything upon which, hitherto, morality has set its ban. Through long experience, derived from such wanderings in forbidden country, I acquired an opinion very different from that which may seem generally desirable, of the causes which hitherto have led to men's moralising and idealising. The secret history of philosophers, the psychology of their great names, was revealed to me. How much truth can a certain mind endure; how much truth can it dare? – these questions became for me ever more and more the actual test of values. Error (the belief in the ideal) is not blindness; error is cowardice . . . Every conquest, every step forward in knowledge, is the outcome of courage, of hardness towards one's self, of cleanliness towards one's self. I do not refute ideals; all I do is to draw on my gloves in their presence . . . *Nitimur in vetitum*: with this device my philosophy will one day be victorious; for that which has hitherto been most stringently forbidden is, without exception, truth.

4

In my lifework, my *Zarathustra* holds a place apart. With it, I gave my fellow-men the greatest gift that has ever been bestowed upon them. This book, the voice of which speaks out across the ages, is not only the loftiest book on earth, literally the book of mountain air – the whole phenomenon, mankind, lies at an incalculable distance beneath it – but it is also the deepest book, born of the inmost abundance of truth; an inexhaustible well, into which no pitcher can be lowered without coming up again laden with gold and with goodness. Here it is not a 'prophet' who speaks, one of those gruesome hybrids of sickness and Will to Power, whom men call founders of religions. If a man would not do a sad wrong to his wisdom, he must above all give proper heed to the tones – the halcyonic tones – that fall from the lips of Zarathustra:

> The most silent words are harbingers of the storm; thoughts that come on dove's feet lead the world.
> The figs fall from the trees; they are good and sweet, and when they fall, their red skins are rent.
> A north wind am I unto ripe figs.
> Thus, like figs, do these precepts drop down to you, my friends; now drink their juice and their sweet pulp.
> It is autumn all around, and clear sky, and afternoon.

No fanatic speaks to you here; this is not a 'sermon'; no faith is demanded in these pages. From out an infinite treasure of light and well of joy, drop by drop, my words fall out – a slow and gentle gait is the cadence of these discourses. Such things can reach only the most elect; it is a rare privilege to be a listener here; not everyone who likes can have ears to hear Zarathustra. Is not Zarathustra, because of these things, a *seducer*? . . . But what, indeed, does he himself say, when for the first time he goes back to his solitude? Just the reverse of that which any 'sage', 'saint', 'Saviour of the world', and other decadent would say . . . Not only his words, but he himself is other than they.

> Alone do I now go, my disciples! Get ye also hence, and alone! Thus would I have it.
> Verily, I beseech you: take your leave of me and arm yourselves

against Zarathustra! And better still, be ashamed of him! Maybe he hath deceived you.

The knight of knowledge must be able not only to love his enemies, but also to hate his friends.

The man who remaineth a pupil requiteth his teacher but ill. And why would ye not pluck at my wreath?

Ye honour me; but what if your reverence should one day break down? Take heed, lest a statue crush you.

Ye say ye believe in Zarathustra? But of what account is Zarathustra? Ye are my believers: but of what account are all believers?

Ye had not yet sought yourselves when ye found me. Thus do all believers; therefore is all believing worth so little.

Now I bid you lose me and find yourselves; and only when ye have all denied me will I come back unto you.

FRIEDRICH NIETZSCHE

On this perfect day, when everything is ripening, and not only the grapes are getting brown, a ray of sunshine has fallen on my life: I looked behind me, I looked before me, and never have I seen so many good things all at once. Not in vain have I buried my four-and-fortieth year today; I had the *right* to bury it – that in it which still had life has been saved and is immortal. The first book of the *Transvaluation of all Values*, *The Songs of Zarathustra*, *The Twilight of the Idols*, my attempt to philosophise with the hammer – all these things are the gift of this year, and even of its last quarter. *How could I help being thankful to the whole of my life?*

That is why I am now going to tell myself the story of my life.

ECCE HOMO

How one becomes what one is

WHY I AM SO WISE

I

The happiness of my existence, its unique character perhaps, consists in its fatefulness: to speak in a riddle, as my own father I am already dead, as my own mother I still live and grow old. This double origin, taken as it were from the highest and lowest rungs of the ladder of life, at once a decadent and a beginning, this, if anything, explains that neutrality, that freedom from partisanship in regard to the general problem of existence, which perhaps distinguishes me. To the first indications of ascending or of descending life my nostrils are more sensitive than those of any man that has yet lived. In this domain I am a master to my backbone – I know both sides, for I am both sides. My father died in his six-and-thirtieth year: he was delicate, lovable, and morbid, like one who is preordained to pay simply a flying visit – a gracious reminder of life rather than life itself. In the same year that his life declined mine also declined: in my six-and-thirtieth year I reached the lowest point in my vitality – I still lived, but my eyes could distinguish nothing that lay three paces away from me. At that time – it was the year 1879 – I resigned my professorship at Basle, lived through the summer like a shadow in St. Moritz, and spent the following winter, the most sunless of my life, like a shadow in Naumburg. This was my lowest ebb. During this period I wrote *The Wanderer and His Shadow*. Without a doubt I was conversant with shadows then. The winter that followed, my first winter in Genoa, brought forth that sweetness and spirituality which is almost inseparable from extreme poverty of blood and muscle, in the shape of *The Dawn of Day*. The perfect lucidity and cheerfulness, the intellectual exuberance even, that this work reflects, coincides, in my case, not only with the most profound physiological weakness, but also with an excess of suffering. In the midst of the agony of a headache which lasted three days, accompanied by violent nausea, I was possessed of most singular dialectical clearness, and in absolutely cold blood I then thought out things, for which, in my more healthy moments, I am not enough of a climber, not sufficiently subtle, not sufficiently cold. My readers perhaps know to what extent I consider dialectic a symptom of decadence, as, for instance, in the most famous of all cases – the case of Socrates. All the morbid disturbances of the intellect, even that semi-stupor which accompanies fever, have, unto this day, remained completely unknown to me; and for my first information concerning their nature and frequency, I was obliged to have recourse to the learned works which have been compiled on the subject. My circulation is slow. No-one has ever been able to detect fever in me. A doctor who treated me for some time as a nerve patient finally declared: 'No! there is nothing wrong with your nerves, it is simply I who am nervous.' It has been absolutely impossible to ascertain any local degeneration in me, nor any organic stomach trouble, however much I may have suffered from profound weakness of the gastric system as the result of general exhaustion. Even my eye trouble, which sometimes approached so parlously near to blindness, was only an effect and not a cause; for, whenever my general vital condition improved, my power of vision also increased. Having admitted all this, do I need to say that I am experienced in questions of decadence? I know them inside and out. Even that filigree art of prehension and comprehension in general, that feeling for delicate shades of difference, that psychology of 'seeing through brick walls', and whatever else I may be able to do, was first learnt then, and is the specific gift of that period during which everything in me was subtilised – observation itself, together with all the organs of observation. To look upon healthier concepts and values from the standpoint of the sick, and conversely to look down upon the secret work of the instincts of decadence from the standpoint of him who is laden and self-reliant with the richness of life – this has been my longest exercise, my principal experience. If in anything at all, it was in this that I became a master. Today my hand knows the trick, I now have the knack of reversing perspectives: the first reason perhaps why a *Transvaluation of all Values* has been possible to me alone.

2

For, apart from the fact that I am a decadent, I am also the reverse of such a creature. Among other things my proof of this is, that I always instinctively select the proper remedy when my spiritual or bodily health is low; whereas the decadent, as such, invariably chooses those remedies which are bad for him. As a whole I was sound, but in certain details I was a decadent. That energy with which I sentenced myself to absolute solitude, and to a severance from all those conditions in life to which I had grown accustomed; my discipline of myself, and my refusal to allow myself to be pampered, to be tended hand and foot, and to be doctored – all this betrays the absolute certainty of my instincts respecting what at that time was most needful to me. I placed myself in my own hands, I restored myself to health: the first condition of success in such an undertaking, as every physiologist will admit, is that at bottom a man should be sound. An intrinsically morbid nature cannot become healthy. On the other hand, to an intrinsically sound nature, illness may even constitute a powerful stimulus to life, to a surplus of life. It is in this light that I now regard the long period of illness that I endured: it seemed as if I had discovered life afresh, my own self included. I tasted all good things and even trifles in a way in which it was not easy for others to taste them – out of my Will to Health and to Life I made my philosophy . . . For this should be thoroughly understood; it was during those years in which my vitality reached its lowest point that I ceased from being a pessimist: the instinct of self-recovery forbade my holding to a philosophy of poverty and desperation. Now, by what signs are nature's lucky strokes recognised among men? They are recognised by the fact that any such lucky stroke gladdens our senses; that he is carved from one integral block, which is hard, sweet, and fragrant as well. He enjoys that only which is good for him; his pleasure, his desire, ceases when the limits of that which is good for him are overstepped. He divines remedies for injuries; he knows how to turn serious accidents to his own advantage; that which does not kill him makes him stronger. He instinctively gathers his material from all he sees, hears, and experiences. He is a selective principle; he rejects much. He is always in his own company, whether his intercourse be with books, with men, or with natural scenery; he honours the things he chooses, the things he acknowledges, the things he trusts. He reacts slowly to all kinds of stimuli, with that tardiness which long caution and deliberate pride have bred in him – he tests the approaching stimulus; he would not dream of meeting it half-way. He believes neither in 'ill-luck' nor 'guilt'; he can digest himself and others; he knows how to forget – he is strong enough to make everything turn to his own advantage.

Lo then! I am the very reverse of a decadent, for he whom I have just described is none other than myself.

3

This double thread of experiences, this means of access to two worlds that seem so far asunder, finds in every detail its counterpart in my own nature – I am my own complement: I have a 'second' sight, as well as a first. And perhaps I also have a third sight. By the very nature of my origin I was allowed an outlook beyond all merely local, merely national and limited horizons; it required no effort on my part to be a 'good European'. On the other hand, I am perhaps more German than modern Germans – mere Imperial Germans – can hope to be – I, the last anti-political German. Be this as it may, my ancestors were Polish noblemen: it is owing to them that I have so much race instinct in my blood – who knows? perhaps even the *liberum veto*.* When I think of the number of times in my travels that I have been accosted as a Pole, even by Poles themselves, and how seldom I have been taken for a German, it seems to me as if I belonged to those only who have a sprinkling of German in them. But my mother, Franziska Oehler, is at any rate something very German; as is also my paternal grandmother, Erdmuthe Krause. The latter spent the whole of her youth in good old Weimar, not without coming into contact with Goethe's circle. Her brother, Krause, the Professor of Theology in

* The right which every Polish deputy, whether a great or an inferior nobleman, possessed of forbidding the passing of any measure by the Diet, was called in Poland the *liberum veto* (in Polish *nie pozwalam*), and brought all legislation to a standstill. – TR.

Königsberg, was called to the post of General Superintendent at Weimar after Herder's death. It is not unlikely that her mother, my great-grandmother, is mentioned in young Goethe's diary under the name of 'Muthgen'. She married twice, and her second husband was Superintendent Nietzsche of Eilenburg. In 1813, the year of the great war, when Napoleon with his general staff entered Eilenburg on 10 October, she gave birth to a son. As a daughter of Saxony she was a great admirer of Napoleon, and maybe I am so still. My father, born in 1813, died in 1849. Previous to taking over the pastorship of the parish of Röcken, not far from Lützen, he lived for some years at the Castle of Altenburg, where he had charge of the education of the four princesses. His pupils were the Queen of Hanover, the Grand-Duchess Constantine, the Grand-Duchess of Oldenburg, and the Princess Theresa of Saxe-Altenburg. He was full of loyal respect for the Prussian King, Frederick William the Fourth, from whom he obtained his living at Röcken; the events of 1848 saddened him extremely. As I was born on 15 October, the birthday of the king above mentioned, I naturally received the Hohenzollern names of Frederick William. There was at all events one advantage in the choice of this day: my birthday throughout the whole of my childhood was a day of public rejoicing. I regard it as a great privilege to have had such a father: it even seems to me that this embraces all that I can claim in the matter of privileges – life, the great yea to life, excepted. What I owe to him above all is this, that I do not need any special intention, but merely a little patience, in order involuntarily to enter a world of higher and more delicate things. There I am at home, there alone does my inmost passion become free. The fact that I had to pay for this privilege almost with my life, certainly does not make it a bad bargain. In order to understand even a little of my *Zarathustra*, perhaps a man must be situated and constituted very much as I am myself – with one foot beyond the realm of the living.

4

I have never understood the art of arousing ill-feeling against myself – this is also something for which I have to thank my incomparable father – even when it seemed to me highly desirable to do so. However un-Christian it may seem, I do not even bear any ill-feeling towards myself. Turn my life about as you may, you will find but seldom – perhaps indeed only once – any trace of someone's having shown me ill-will. You might perhaps discover, however, too many traces of *good*-will . . . My experiences even with those on whom every other man has burnt his fingers, speak without exception in their favour; I tame every bear, I can make even clowns behave decently. During the seven years in which I taught Greek to the sixth form of the College at Basle, I never had occasion to administer a punishment; the laziest youths were diligent in my class. The unexpected has always found me equal to it; I must be unprepared in order to keep my self-command. Whatever the instrument was, even if it were as out of tune as the instrument 'man' can possibly be – it was only when I was ill that I could not succeed in making it express something that was worth hearing. And how often have I not been told by the 'instruments' themselves, that they had never before heard their voices express such beautiful things . . . This was said to me most delightfully perhaps by that young fellow Heinrich von Stein, who died at such an unpardonably early age, and who, after having consider-ately asked leave to do so, once appeared in Sils-Maria for a three days' sojourn, telling everybody there that it was *not* for the Engadine that he had come. This excellent person, who with all the impetuous simplicity of a young Prussian nobleman had waded deep into the swamp of Wagnerism (and into that of Dühringism* into the bargain!), seemed almost transformed during these three days by a hurricane of freedom, like one who has been suddenly raised to his full height and given wings. Again and again I said to him that this was all owing to the splendid air; everybody felt the same – one could not stand 6000 feet above Bayreuth for nothing – but he would not believe me . . . Be this as it may, if I have been the victim of many a small or even great offence, it was not 'will', and least of all *ill*-will that actuated the offenders; but rather, as I have already suggested, it was goodwill, the cause of no small amount of mischief in my life, about which I had to complain. My experience gave me a right to feel suspicious in regard to all so-called 'unselfish' instincts, in regard to the whole of

---

* Eugen Dühring is a philosopher and political economist whose general doctrine might be characterised as a sort of abstract Materialism with an optimistic colouring. – Tr.

'neighbourly love' which is ever ready and waiting with deeds or with advice. To me it seems that these instincts are a sign of weakness, they are an example of the inability to withstand a stimulus – it is only among decadents that this *pity* is called a virtue. What I reproach the pitiful with is that they are too ready to forget shame, reverence, and the delicacy of feeling which knows how to keep at a distance; they do not remember that this gushing pity stinks of the mob, and that it is next of kin to bad manners – that pitiful hands may be thrust with results fatally destructive into a great destiny, into a lonely and wounded retirement, and into the privileges with which great guilt endows one. The overcoming of pity I reckon among the noble virtues. In the 'Temptation of Zarathustra' I have imagined a case, in which a great cry of distress reaches his ears, in which pity swoops down upon him like a last sin, and would make him break faith with himself. To remain one's own master in such circumstances, to keep the sublimity of one's mission pure in such cases – pure from the many ignoble and more short-sighted impulses which come into play in so-called unselfish actions – this is the rub, the last test perhaps which a Zarathustra has to undergo – the actual proof of his power.

5

In yet another respect I am no more than my father over again, and as it were the continuation of his life after an all-too-early death. Like every man who has never been able to meet his equal, and to whom the concept 'retaliation' is just as incomprehensible as the notion of 'equal rights', I have forbidden myself the use of any sort of measure of security or protection – and also, of course, of defence and 'justification' – in all cases in which I have been made the victim either of trifling or even *very great* foolishness. My form of retaliation consists in this: as soon as possible to set a piece of cleverness at the heels of an act of stupidity; by this means perhaps it may still be possible to overtake it. To speak in a parable: I dispatch a pot of jam in order to get rid of a bitter experience . . . Let anybody only give me offence, I shall 'retaliate', he can be quite sure of that: before long I discover an opportunity of expressing my thanks to the 'offender' (among other things even for the offence) – or of *asking* him for something, which can be more courteous even than giving. It also seems to me that the rudest word, the rudest letter, is more good-natured, more straightforward, than silence. Those who keep silent are almost always lacking in subtlety and refinement of heart; silence is an objection, to swallow a grievance must necessarily produce a bad temper – it even upsets the stomach. All silent people are dyspeptic. You perceive that I should not like to see rudeness undervalued; it is by far the most *humane* form of contradiction, and, in the midst of modern effeminacy, it is one of our first virtues. If one is sufficiently rich for it, it may even be a joy to be wrong. If a god were to descend to this earth, he would have to do nothing but wrong – to take *guilt*, not punishment, on one's shoulders, is the first proof of divinity.

6

Freedom from resentment and the understanding of the nature of resentment – who knows how very much after all I am indebted to my long illness for these two things? The problem is not exactly simple: a man must have experienced both through his strength and through his weakness. If illness and weakness are to be charged with anything at all, it is with the fact that when they prevail, the very instinct of recovery, which is the instinct of defence and of war in man, becomes decayed. He knows not how to get rid of anything, how to come to terms with anything, and how to cast anything behind him. Everything wounds him. People and things draw importunately near, all experiences strike deep, memory is a gathering wound. To be ill is a sort of resentment in itself. Against this resentment the invalid has only one great remedy – I call it *Russian fatalism*, that fatalism which is free from revolt, and with which the Russian soldier, to whom a campaign proves unbearable, ultimately lays himself down in the snow. To accept nothing more, to undertake nothing more, to absorb nothing more – to cease entirely from reacting . . . The tremendous sagacity of this fatalism, which does not always imply merely the courage for death, but which in the most dangerous cases may actually constitute a self-preservative measure, amounts to a reduction of activity in the vital functions, the slackening down of which is like a sort of will to hibernate. A few steps farther in this direction we find the fakir, who will sleep for weeks in a tomb . . . Owing to the fact that one would be used up too quickly if one reacted, one no longer reacts at all: this is the principle. And nothing on earth consumes a man more quickly than the passion of resentment. Mortification, morbid susceptibility, the inability to wreak revenge, the desire and thirst for revenge, the concoction of every sort of poison – this is surely the most injurious manner of reacting which could possibly be conceived by exhausted men. It involves a rapid wasting away of nervous energy, an abnormal increase of detrimental secretions, as, for instance, that of bile into the stomach. To the sick man resentment ought to be more strictly forbidden than anything else – it is *his* special danger: unfortunately, however, it is also his most natural propensity. This was fully grasped by that profound physiologist Buddha. His 'religion', which it would be better to call a system of hygiene, in order to avoid confounding it with a creed so wretched as Christianity, depended for its effect upon the triumph over resentment: to make the soul free therefrom was considered the first step towards recovery. 'Not through hostility is hostility put to flight; through friendship does hostility end': this stands at the beginning of Buddha's teaching – this is not a precept of morality, but of physiology. Resentment born of weakness is not more deleterious to anybody than it is to the weak man himself – conversely, in the case of that man whose nature is fundamentally a rich one, resentment is a superfluous feeling, a feeling to remain master of which is almost a proof of riches. Those of my readers who know the earnestness with which my philosophy wages war against the feelings of revenge and rancour, even to the extent of attacking the doctrine of 'free will' (my conflict with Christianity is only a particular instance of it), will understand why I wish to focus attention upon my own personal attitude and the certainty of my practical instincts precisely in this matter. In my moments of decadence I forbade myself the indulgence of the above feelings, because they were harmful; as soon as my life recovered enough riches and pride, however, I regarded them again as forbidden, but this time because they were *beneath* me. That 'Russian fatalism' of which I have spoken manifested itself in me in such a way that for years I held tenaciously to almost insufferable conditions, places, habitations, and companions, once chance had placed them on my path – it was better than changing them, than feeling that they could be changed, than revolting against them . . . He who stirred me from this fatalism, he who violently tried to shake me into consciousness, seemed to me then a mortal enemy — in point of fact, there was danger of death each time this was done. To regard one's self as a destiny, not to wish one's self 'different' — this, in such circumstances, is sagacity itself.

7

War, on the other hand, is something different. At heart I am a warrior. Attacking belongs to my instincts. To *be able to be* an enemy, to *be* an enemy — maybe these things presuppose a strong nature; in any case all strong natures involve these things. Such natures need resistance, consequently they go in search of obstacles: the pathos of aggression belongs of necessity to strength as much as the feelings of revenge and of rancour belong to weakness. Woman, for instance, is revengeful; her weakness involves this passion, just as it involves her susceptibility in the presence of other people's suffering. The strength of the aggressor can be measured by the opposition which he needs; every increase of growth betrays itself by a seeking out of more formidable opponents — or problems: for a philosopher who is combative challenges even problems to a duel. The task is not to overcome opponents in general, but only those opponents against whom one has to summon all one's strength, one's skill, and one's swordsmanship — in fact, opponents who are one's equals . . . To be one's enemy's equal — this is the first condition of an honourable duel. Where one despises, one cannot wage war. Where one commands, where one sees something *beneath* one, one *ought* not to wage war. My war tactics can be reduced to four principles: First, I attack only things that are triumphant — if necessary I wait until they become triumphant. Secondly, I attack only those things against which I find no allies, against which I stand alone — against which I compromise nobody but myself . . . I have not yet taken one single step before the public eye, which did not compromise me: that is *my* criterion of a proper mode of action. Thirdly, I never make personal attacks — I use a personality merely as a magnifying-glass, by means of which I render a general, but elusive and scarcely noticeable evil, more apparent. In this way I attacked David Strauss, or rather the success given to a senile book by the cultured classes of Germany — by this means I caught German culture red-handed. In this way I attacked Wagner, or rather the falsity or mongrel instincts of our 'culture' which confounds the super-refined with the strong, and the effete with the great. Fourthly, I attack only those things from which all personal differences are excluded, in which any such thing as a background of disagreeable experiences is lacking. On the contrary, attacking is to me a proof of goodwill and, in certain circumstances, of gratitude. By means of it, I do honour to a thing, I distinguish a thing; whether I associate my name with that of an institution or a person, by being *against* or *for* either, is all the same to me. If I wage war against Christianity, I feel justified in doing so, because in that quarter I have met with no fatal experiences and difficulties – the most earnest Christians have always been kindly disposed to me. I, personally, the most essential opponent of Christianity, am far from holding the individual responsible for what is the fatality of long ages.

8

May I be allowed to hazard a suggestion concerning one last trait in my character, which in my intercourse with other men has led me into some difficulties? I am gifted with a sense of cleanliness the keenness of which is phenomenal; so much so, that I can ascertain physiologically – that is to say, smell – the proximity, nay, the inmost core, the 'entrails' of every human soul . . . This sensitiveness of mine is furnished with psychological antennae, wherewith I feel and grasp every secret: the quality of concealed filth lying at the base of many a human character which may be the inevitable outcome of base blood, and which education may have veneered, is revealed to me at the first glance. If my observation has been correct, such people, whom my sense of cleanliness rejects, also become conscious, on their part, of the cautiousness to which my loathing prompts me: and this does not make them any more fragrant . . . In keeping with a custom which I have long observed – pure habits and honesty towards myself are among the first conditions of my existence, I would die in unclean surroundings – I swim, bathe, and splash about, as it were, incessantly in water, in any kind of perfectly transparent and shining element. That is why my relations with my fellows try my patience to no small extent; my humanity does not consist in the fact that I understand the feelings of my fellows, but that I can endure to understand . . . My humanity is a perpetual process of self-mastery. But I need solitude – that is to say, recovery, return to myself, the breathing of free, crisp, bracing air . . . The whole of my *Zarathustra* is a dithyramb in honour of solitude, or, if I have been understood, in honour of purity. Thank Heaven, it is not in honour of 'pure foolery'!* He who has an eye for colour will call him a diamond. The loathing of mankind, of the rabble, was always my greatest danger . . . Would you hearken to the words spoken by Zarathustra concerning deliverance from loathing?

What forsooth hath come unto me? How did I deliver myself from loathing? Who hath made mine eye younger? How did I soar to the height, where there are no more rabble sitting about the well?

Did my very loathing forge me wings and the strength to scent fountains afar off? Verily to the loftiest heights did I need to fly, to find once more the spring of joyfulness.

Oh, I found it, my brethren! Up here, on the loftiest height, the spring of joyfulness gusheth forth for me. And there is a life at the well of which no rabble can drink with you.

Almost too fiercely dost thou rush, for me, thou spring of joyfulness! And ofttimes dost thou empty the pitcher again in trying to fill it.

And yet must I learn to draw near thee more humbly. Far too eagerly doth my heart jump to meet thee.

My heart, whereon my summer burneth, my short, hot, melancholy, over-blessed summer: how my summer heart yearneth for thy coolness!

Farewell, the lingering affliction of my spring! Past is the wickedness of my snowflakes in June! Summer have I become entirely, and summer noontide!

A summer in the loftiest heights, with cold springs and blessed stillness: oh come, my friends, that the stillness may wax even more blessed!

For this is our height and our home: too high and steep is our dwelling for all the unclean and their appetites.

Do but cast your pure eyes into the well of my joyfulness, my friends! How could it thus become muddy! It will laugh back at you with its purity.

---

* This, of course, is a reference to Wagner's *Parsifal*.

On the tree called Future do we build our nest: eagles shall bring food in their beaks unto us lonely ones!

Verily not the food whereof the unclean might partake. They would think they ate fire and would burn their mouths!

Verily, no abodes for the unclean do we here hold in readiness! To their bodies our happiness would seem an ice-cavern, and to their spirits also!

And like strong winds will we live above them, neighbours to the eagles, companions of the snow, and playmates of the sun: thus do strong winds live.

And like a wind shall I one day blow amidst them, and take away their soul's breath with my spirit: thus my future willeth it.

Verily, a strong wind is Zarathustra to all low lands; and this is his counsel to his foes and to all those who spit and spew: 'Beware of spitting against the wind!'

I

Why do I know more things than other people? Why, in fact, am I so clever? I have never pondered over questions that are not questions. I have never squandered my strength. Of actual religious difficulties, for instance, I have no experience. I have never known what it is to feel 'sinful'. In the same way I completely lack any reliable criterion for ascertaining what constitutes a prick of conscience: from all accounts a prick of conscience does not seem to be a very estimable thing . . . Once it was done I should hate to leave an action of mine in the lurch; I should prefer completely to omit the evil outcome, the consequences, from the problem concerning the value of an action. In the face of evil consequences one is too ready to lose the proper standpoint from which one's deed ought to be considered. A prick of conscience strikes me as a sort of 'evil eye'. Something that has failed should be honoured all the more jealously, precisely because it has failed – this is much more in keeping with my morality. – 'God', 'the immortality of the soul', 'salvation', a 'beyond' – to all these notions, even as a child, I never paid any attention whatsoever, nor did I waste any time upon them – maybe I was never naive enough for that? – I am quite unacquainted with atheism as a result, and still less as an event in my life: in me it is inborn, instinctive. I am too inquisitive, too incredulous, too high-spirited, to be satisfied with such a palpably clumsy solution of things. God is a too palpably clumsy solution of things; a solution which shows a lack of delicacy towards us thinkers – at bottom He is really no more than a coarse and rude *prohibition* of us: ye shall not think! . . . I am much more interested in another question – a question upon which the 'salvation of humanity' depends to a far greater degree than it does upon any piece of theological curiosity: I refer to nutrition. For ordinary purposes, it may be formulated as follows: 'How precisely must *thou* feed thyself in order to attain to thy maximum of power, or *virtù* in the Renaissance style – of virtue free from moralic acid?' My experiences in regard to this matter have been as bad as they possibly could be; I am surprised that I set myself this question so late in life, and that it took me so long to draw 'rational' conclusions from my experiences. Only the absolute worthlessness of German culture – its 'idealism' – can to some extent explain how it was that precisely in this matter I was so backward that my ignorance was almost saintly. This 'culture', which from first to last teaches one to lose sight of actual things and to hunt after thoroughly problematic and so-called ideal aims, as, for instance, 'classical culture' – as if it were not hopeless from the start to try to unite 'classical' and 'German' in one concept. It is even a little comical – try and imagine a 'classically cultured' citizen of Leipzig! – Indeed, I can say, that up to a very mature age, my food was entirely bad – expressed morally, it was 'impersonal', 'selfless', 'altruistic', to the glory of cooks and all other fellow-Christians. It was through the cooking in vogue at Leipzig, for instance, together with my first study of Schopenhauer (1865), that I earnestly renounced my 'will to live'. To spoil one's stomach by absorbing insufficient nourishment – this problem seemed to my mind solved with admirable felicity by the above-mentioned cookery. (It is said that in the year 1866 changes were introduced into this department.) But as to German cookery in general – what has it not got on its conscience! Soup *before* the meal (still called *alla tedesca* in the Venetian cookery books of the sixteenth century); meat boiled to shreds, vegetables cooked with fat and flour; the degeneration of pastries into paper-weights! And, if you add thereto the absolutely bestial post-prandial drinking habits of the *ancients*, and not alone of the ancient Germans, you will understand where German intellect took its origin – that is to say, in sadly disordered intestines . . . German intellect is indigestion; it can assimilate nothing. But even English diet, which in comparison with German, and indeed with French alimentation, seems to me to constitute a 'return to nature' – that is to say, to cannibalism – is profoundly opposed to my own instincts. It seems to me to give the intellect heavy feet, in fact, Englishwomen's feet . . . The best cooking is that of Piedmont. Alcoholic drinks do not agree with me; a single glass of wine or beer a day is amply sufficient to turn life into a valley of tears for me; in Munich live my antipodes. Although I admit that this knowledge came to me somewhat late, it already formed part of my experience even as a child. As a boy I believed that the drinking of wine and the smoking of tobacco were at first but the vanities of youths, and later merely bad habits. Maybe the poor wine of Naumburg was partly responsible for this poor opinion of wine in general. In order to believe that wine was exhilarating, I should have had to be a Christian – in other words, I should have had to believe in what, to my mind, is an absurdity. Strange to say, whereas small quantities of alcohol, taken with plenty of water, succeed in making me feel out of sorts, large quantities turn me almost into a rollicking tar. Even as a boy I showed my bravado in this respect. To compose a long Latin essay in one night, to revise and recopy it, to aspire with my pen to emulating the exactitude and the terseness of my model, Sallust, and to pour a few very strong grogs over it all – this mode of procedure, while I was a pupil at the venerable old school of Pforta, was not in the least out of keeping with my physiology, nor perhaps with that of Sallust, however much it may have been alien to dignified Pforta. Later on, towards the middle of my life, I grew more and more opposed to alcoholic drinks: I, an opponent of vegetarianism, who have experienced what vegetarianism is – just as Wagner, who converted me back to meat, experienced it – cannot with sufficient earnestness advise all more spiritual natures to abstain absolutely from alcohol. Water answers the purpose . . . I have a predilection in favour of those places where in all directions one has opportunities of drinking from running brooks (Nice, Turin, Sils). In vino veritas: it seems that here once more I am at variance with the rest of the world about the concept 'truth' – with me spirit moves on the face of the waters . . . Here are a few more indications as to my morality. A heavy meal is digested more easily than an inadequate one. The first principle of a good digestion is that the stomach should become active as a whole. A man ought, therefore, to know the size of his stomach. For the same reasons all those interminable meals, which I call interrupted sacrificial feasts, and which are to be had at any table d'hôte, are strongly to be deprecated. Nothing should be eaten between meals, coffee should be given up – coffee makes one gloomy. Tea is beneficial only in the morning. It should be taken in small quantities, but very strong. It may be very harmful, and indispose you for the whole day, if it be taken the least bit too weak. Everybody has his own standard in this matter, often between the narrowest and most delicate limits. In an enervating climate tea is not a good beverage with which to start the day: an hour before taking it an excellent thing is to drink a cup of thick cocoa, freed from oil. Remain seated as little as possible, put no trust in any thought that is not born in the open, to the accompaniment of free bodily motion – nor in one in which even the muscles do not celebrate a feast. All prejudices take their origin in the intestines. A sedentary life, as I have already said elsewhere, is the real sin against the Holy Spirit.

2

To the question of nutrition, that of locality and climate is next of kin. Nobody is so constituted as to be able to live everywhere and anywhere; and he who has great duties to perform, which lay claim to all his strength, has in this respect a very limited choice. The influence of climate upon the bodily functions, affecting their acceleration or retardation, extends so far, that a blunder in the choice of locality and climate is able not only to alienate a man from his actual duty, but also to withhold it from him altogether, so that he never even comes face to face with it. Animal vigour never acquires enough strength in him in order to reach that pitch of artistic freedom which makes his own soul whisper to him: I, alone, can do that . . . Ever so slight a tendency to laziness in the intestines, once it has become a habit, is quite sufficient to make something mediocre, something 'German' out of a genius; the climate of Germany, alone, is enough to discourage the strongest and most heroically disposed intestines. The tempo of the body's functions is closely bound up with the agility or the clumsiness of the spirit's feet; spirit itself is indeed only a form of these organic functions. Let anybody make a list of the places in which men of great intellect have been found, and are still found; where wit, subtlety, and malice constitute happiness; where genius is almost necessarily at home: all of them rejoice in exceptionally dry air. Paris, Provence, Florence, Jerusalem, Athens – these names prove something, namely: that genius is conditioned by dry air, by a pure sky – that is to say, by rapid organic functions, by the constant and ever-present possibility of procuring for one's self great and even enormous quantities of strength. I have a certain case in mind in which a man of remarkable intellect and independent spirit became a narrow, craven specialist and a grumpy old crank, simply owing to a lack of subtlety in his instinct for climate. And I myself might have been an example of the same thing, if illness had not compelled me to reason, and to reflect upon reason realistically. Now that I have learnt through long practice to read the effects of climatic and meteorological influences, from my own body, as though from a very delicate and reliable instrument, and that I am able to calculate the change in degrees of atmospheric moisture by means of physiological observations upon myself, even on so short a journey as that from Turin to Milan; I think with horror of the ghastly fact that my whole life, until the last ten years – the most perilous years – has always been spent in the wrong, and what to me ought to have been the most forbidden, places. Naumburg, Pforta, Thuringia in general, Leipzig, Basle, Venice – so many ill-starred places for a constitution like mine. If I cannot recall one single happy reminiscence of my childhood and youth, it is nonsense to suppose that so-called 'moral' causes could account for this – as, for instance, the incontestable fact that I lacked companions that could have satisfied me; for this fact is the same today as it ever was, and it does not prevent me from being cheerful and brave. But it was ignorance in physiological matters – that confounded 'Idealism' – that was the real curse of my life. This was the superfluous and foolish element in my existence; something from which nothing could spring, and for which there can be no settlement and no compensation. As the outcome of this 'Idealism' I regard all the blunders, the great aberrations of instinct, and the 'modest specialisations' which drew me aside from the task of my life; as, for instance, the fact that I became a philologist – why not at least a medical man or anything else which might have opened my eyes? My days at Basle, the whole of my intellectual routine, including my daily timetable, was an absolutely senseless abuse of extraordinary powers, without the slightest compensation for the strength that I spent, without even a thought of what I was squandering and how its place might be filled. I lacked all subtlety in egoism, all the fostering care of an imperative instinct; I was in a state in which one is ready to regard one's self as anybody's equal, a state of 'disinterestedness', a forgetting of one's distance from others – something, in short, for which I can never forgive myself. When I had well-nigh reached the end of my tether, simply because I had almost reached my end, I began to reflect upon the fundamental absurdity of my life – 'Idealism'. It was *illness* that first brought me to reason.

3

After the choice of nutrition, the choice of climate and locality, the third matter concerning which one must not on any account make a blunder is the choice of the manner in which one *recuperates one's strength*. Here, again, according to the extent to which a spirit is *sui generis*, the limits of that which he can allow himself – in other words, the limits of that which is beneficial to him – become more and more confined. As far as I in particular am concerned, *reading* in general belongs to my means of recuperation; consequently it belongs to that which rids me of myself, to that which enables me to wander in strange sciences and strange souls – to that, in fact, about which I am no longer in earnest. Indeed, it is while reading that I recover from *my* earnestness. During the time that I am deeply absorbed in my work, no books are found within my reach; it would never occur to me to allow anyone to speak or even to think in my presence. For that is what reading would mean . . . Has anyone ever actually noticed, that, during the period of profound tension to which the state of pregnancy condemns not only the mind, but also, at bottom, the whole organism, accident and every kind of external stimulus acts too acutely and strikes too deep? Accident and external stimuli must, as far as possible, be avoided: a sort of walling-of-one's-self-in is one of the primary instinctive precautions of spiritual pregnancy. Shall I allow a strange thought to steal secretly over the wall? For that is what reading would mean . . . The periods of work and fruitfulness are followed by periods of recuperation: come hither, ye delightful, intellectual, intelligent books! Shall I read German books? . . . I must go back six months to catch myself with a book in my hand. What was it? An excellent study by Victor Brochard upon the Greek sceptics, in which my Laertiana* was used to advantage.

* Nietzsche, as is well known, devoted much time when a student at Leipzig to the study of three Greek philosophers, Theognis, Diogenes Laertius, and Democritus. This study first bore fruit in the case of a paper, *Zur Geschichte der Theognideischen Spruchsammlung*, which was subsequently published by the most influential journal of classical philology in Germany. Later, however, it enabled Nietzsche to enter for the prize offered by the University of Leipzig for an essay,

The sceptics! – the only *honourable* types among that double-faced and sometimes quintuple-faced throng, the philosophers! . . . Otherwise I almost always take refuge in the same books: altogether their number is small; they are books which are precisely my proper fare. It is not perhaps in my nature to read much, and of all sorts: a library makes me ill. Neither is it my nature to love much or many kinds of things. Suspicion or even hostility towards new books is much more akin to my instinctive feeling than 'toleration,' *largeur de coeur*, and other forms of 'neighbour-love'. . . . It is to a small number of old French authors that I always return again and again; I believe only in French culture, and regard everything else in Europe which calls itself 'culture' as a misunderstanding. I do not even take the German kind into consideration . . . The few instances of higher culture with which I have met in Germany were all French in their origin. The most striking example of this was Madame Cosima Wagner, by far the most decisive voice in matters of taste that I have ever heard. If I do not read, but literally love Pascal, as the most instinctive sacrifice to Christianity, killing himself inch by inch, first bodily, then spiritually, according to the terrible consistency of this most appalling form of inhuman cruelty; if I have something of Montaigne's mischievousness in my soul, and – who knows? – perhaps also in my body; if my artist's taste endeavours to defend the names of Molière, Corneille, and Racine, and not without bitterness, against such a wild genius as Shakespeare – all this does not prevent me from regarding even the latter-day Frenchmen also as charming companions. I can think of absolutely no century in history, in which a netful of more inquisitive and at the same time more subtle psychologists could be drawn up together than in the Paris of the present day. Let me mention a few at random – for their number is by no means small – Paul Bourget, Pierre Loti, Gyp, Meilhac, Anatole France, Jules Lemaître; or, to point to one of strong race, a genuine Latin, of whom I am particularly fond, Guy de Maupassant. Between ourselves, I prefer this generation even to its masters, all of whom were corrupted by German

---

De fontibus Diogenis Laertii. He was successful in gaining the prize, and the treatise was afterwards published in the *Rheinisches Museum*, and is still quoted as an authority. It is to this essay, written when he was twenty-three years of age, that he here refers. – Tr.

philosophy (Taine, for instance, by Hegel, whom he has to thank for his misunderstanding of great men and great periods). Wherever Germany extends her sway, she *ruins* culture. It was the war which first saved the spirit of France . . . Stendhal is one of the happiest accidents of my life – for everything that marks an epoch in it has been brought to me by accident and never by means of a recommendation. He is quite priceless, with his psychologist's eye, quick at forestalling and anticipating; with his grasp of facts, which is reminiscent of the same art in the greatest of all masters of facts (*ex ungue Napoleonem*); and, last but not least, as an honest atheist – a specimen which is both rare and difficult to discover in France – all honour to Prosper Mérimée! . . . Maybe that I am even envious of Stendhal? He robbed me of the best atheistic joke, which I of all people could have perpetrated: 'God's only excuse is that He does not exist.' . . . I myself have said somewhere – What has been the greatest objection to life hitherto? – God . . .

4

It was Heinrich Heine who gave me the most perfect idea of what a lyrical poet could be. In vain do I search through all the king-doms of antiquity or of modern times for anything to resemble his sweet and passionate music. He possessed that divine wickedness, without which perfection itself becomes unthinkable to me – I estimate the value of men, of races, according to the extent to which they are unable to conceive of a god who has not a dash of the satyr in him. And with what mastery he wields his native tongue! One day it will be said of Heine and me that we were by far the greatest artists of the German language that have ever existed, and that we left all the efforts that mere Germans made in this language an incalculable distance behind us. I must be profoundly related to Byron's *Manfred*: of all the dark abysses in this work I found the counterparts in my own soul – at the age of thirteen I was ripe for this book. Words fail me, I have only a look, for those who dare to utter the name of *Faust* in the presence of *Manfred*. The Germans are *incapable* of conceiving anything sublime: for a proof of this, look at Schumann! Out of anger for this mawkish Saxon, I once deliberately composed a counter-overture to *Manfred*, of which Hans von Bülow declared he had never seen the like before on paper: such compositions amounted

to a violation of Euterpe. When I cast about me for my highest
formula of Shakespeare, I find invariably but this one: that he
conceived the type of Caesar. Such things a man cannot guess –
he either is the thing, or he is not. The great poet draws his
creations only from out of his own reality. This is so to such an
extent, that often after a lapse of time he can no longer endure his
own work . . . After casting a glance between the pages of my
Zarathustra, I pace my room to and fro for half an hour at a time,
unable to overcome an insufferable fit of tears. I know of no more
heartrending reading than Shakespeare: how a man must have
suffered to be so much in need of playing the clown! Is Hamlet
understood? It is not doubt, but certitude that drives one mad . . .
But in order to feel this, one must be profound, one must be an
abyss, a philosopher . . . We all fear the truth . . . And, to make a
confession; I feel instinctively certain and convinced that Lord
Bacon is the originator, the self-torturer, of this most sinister kind
of literature: what do I care about the miserable gabble of American
muddlers and blockheads? But the power for the greatest realism in
vision is not only compatible with the greatest realism in deeds,
with the monstrous in deeds, with crime – *it actually presupposes the
latter* . . . We do not know half enough about Lord Bacon – the
first realist in all the highest acceptation of this word – to be sure
of everything he did, everything he willed, and everything he
experienced in his inmost soul . . . Let the critics go to hell!
Suppose I had christened my *Zarathustra* with a name not my
own – let us say with Richard Wagner's name – the acumen of two
thousand years would not have sufficed to guess that the author of
Human, all-too-Human was the visionary of *Zarathustra*.

5

As I am speaking here of the recreations of my life, I feel I must
express a word or two of gratitude for that which has refreshed me
by far the most heartily and most profoundly. This, without the
slightest doubt, was my intimate relationship with Richard Wagner.
All my other relationships with men I treat quite lightly; but I would
not have the days I spent at Tribschen – those days of confidence, of
cheerfulness, of sublime flashes, and of profound moments – blotted
from my life at any price. I know not what Wagner may have been
for others; but no cloud ever darkened *our* sky. And this brings me

back again to France – I have no arguments against Wagnerites, and *hoc genus omne*, who believe that they do honour to Wagner by believing him to be like themselves; for such people I have only a contemptuous curl of my lip. With a nature like mine, which is so strange to everything Teutonic that even the presence of a German retards my digestion, my first meeting with Wagner was the first moment in my life in which I breathed freely: I felt him, I honoured him, as a foreigner, as the opposite and the incarnate contradiction of all 'German virtues'. We who as children breathed the marshy atmosphere of the fifties, are necessarily pessimists in regard to the concept 'German'; we cannot be anything else than revolution- aries – we can assent to no state of affairs which allows the canting bigot to be at the top. I care not a jot whether this canting bigot acts in different colours today, whether he dresses in scarlet or dons the uniform of a hussar.* Very well, then! Wagner was a revolutionary – he fled from the Germans . . . As an artist, a man has no home in Europe save in Paris; that subtlety of all the five senses which Wagner's art presupposes, those fingers that can detect slight grad- ations, psychological morbidity – all these things can be found only in Paris. Nowhere else can you meet with this passion for questions of form, this earnestness in matters of *mise-en-scène*, which is the Parisian earnestness *par excellence*. In Germany no-one has any idea of the tremendous ambition that fills the heart of a Parisian artist. The German is a good fellow. Wagner was by no means a good fellow . . . But I have already said quite enough on the subject of Wagner's real nature (see *Beyond Good and Evil*, Aphorism 269), and about those to whom he is most closely related. He is one of the late French romanticists, that high-soaring and heaven-aspiring band of artists, like Delacroix and Berlioz, who in their inmost natures are sick and incurable, and who are all fanatics of *expression*, and virtuosos through and through . . . Who, in sooth, was the first intelligent follower of Wagner? Charles Baudelaire, the very man who first understood Delacroix – that typical decadent, in whom a whole generation of artists saw their reflection; he was perhaps the last of them too . . . What is it that I have never forgiven Wagner? The fact that he condescended to the Germans – that he became a German Imperialist . . . Wherever Germany spreads, she *ruins* culture.

* The favourite uniform of the German Emperor, William II. – Tr.

6

Taking everything into consideration, I could never have survived
my youth without Wagnerian music. For I was condemned to the
society of Germans. If a man wish to get rid of a feeling of
insufferable oppression, he has to take to hashish. Well, I had to
take to Wagner. Wagner is the counter-poison to everything
essentially German – the fact that he is a poison too, I do not deny.
From the moment that *Tristan* was arranged for the piano – all
honour to you, Herr von Bülow! – I was a Wagnerite. Wagner's
previous works seemed beneath me – they were too common-
place, too 'German'. . . . But to this day I am still seeking for a
work which would be a match to *Tristan* in dangerous fascination,
and possess the same gruesome and dulcet quality of infinity; I seek
among all the arts in vain. All the quaint features of Leonardo da
Vinci's work lose their charm at the sound of the first bar in
Tristan. This work is without question Wagner's *non plus ultra*;
after its creation, the composition of the *Mastersingers* and of the
Ring was a relaxation to him. To become more healthy – this in a
nature like Wagner's amounts to going backwards. The curiosity
of the psychologist is so great in me, that I regard it as quite a
special privilege to have lived at the right time, and to have lived
precisely among Germans, in order to be ripe for this work. The
world must indeed be empty for him who has never been unhealthy enough for this 'infernal voluptuousness': it is allowable, it
is even imperative, to employ a mystic formula for this purpose. I
suppose I know better than anyone the prodigious feats of which
Wagner was capable, the fifty worlds of strange ecstasies to which
no-one else had wings to soar; and as I am alive today and strong
enough to turn even the most suspicious and most dangerous
things to my own advantage, and thus to grow stronger, I declare
Wagner to have been the greatest benefactor of my life. The bond
which unites us is the fact that we have suffered greater agony,
even at each other's hands, than most men are able to bear
nowadays, and this will always keep our names associated in the
minds of men. For, just as Wagner is merely a misunderstanding
among Germans, so in truth am I, and ever will be. Ye lack two
centuries of psychological and artistic discipline, my dear country-
men! . . . But ye can never recover the time lost.

7

To the most exceptional of my readers I should like to say just one word about what I really exact from music. It must be cheerful and yet profound, like an October afternoon. It must be original, exuberant, and tender, and like a dainty, soft woman in roguishness and grace . . . I shall never admit that a German *can* understand what music is. Those musicians who are called German, the greatest and most famous foremost, are all foreigners, either Slavs, Croats, Italians, Dutchmen – or Jews; or else, like Heinrich Schütz, Bach, and Händel, they are Germans of a strong race which is now extinct. For my own part, I have still enough of the Pole left in me to let all other music go, if only I can keep Chopin. For three reasons I would except Wagner's *Siegfried Idyll*, and perhaps also one or two things of Liszt, who excelled all other musicians in the noble tone of his orchestration; and finally everything that has been produced beyond the Alps – *this side* of the Alps.* I could not possibly dispense with Rossini, and still less with my Southern soul in music, the work of my Venetian maestro, Pietro Gasti. And when I say beyond the Alps, all I really mean is Venice. If I try to find a new word for music, I can never find any other than Venice. I know not how to draw any distinction between tears and music. I do not know how to think either of joy, or of the south, without a shudder of fear.

> On the bridge I stood
> Lately, in gloomy night.
> Came a distant song:
> In golden drops it rolled
> Over the glittering rim away.
> Music, gondolas, lights –
> Drunk, swam far forth in the gloom . . .
>
> A stringed instrument, my soul,
> Sang, imperceptibly moved,
> A gondola song by stealth,
> Gleaming for gaudy blessedness.
> – Hearkened any thereto?

* In the latter years of his life, Nietzsche practically made Italy his home. – TR.

8

In all these things – in the choice of food, place, climate, and recreation – the instinct of self-preservation is dominant, and this instinct manifests itself with least ambiguity when it acts as an instinct of defence. To close one's eyes to much, to seal one's ears to much, to keep certain things at a distance – this is the first principle of prudence, the first proof of the fact that a man is not an accident but a necessity. The popular word for this instinct of defence is *taste*. A man's imperative command is not only to say 'no' in cases where 'yes' would be a sign of 'disinterestedness', but also to say 'no' *as seldom as possible*. One must part with all that which compels one to repeat 'no' with ever greater frequency. The rationale of this principle is that all discharges of defensive forces, however slight they may be, involve enormous and absolutely superfluous losses when they become regular and habitual. Our greatest expenditure of strength is made up of those small and most frequent discharges of it. The act of keeping things off, of holding them at a distance, amounts to a discharge of strength – do not deceive yourselves on this point! – and an expenditure of energy directed at purely negative ends. Simply by being compelled to keep constantly on his guard, a man may grow so weak as to be unable any longer to defend himself. Suppose I were to step out of my house, and, instead of the quiet and aristocratic city of Turin, I were to find a German provincial town, my instinct would have to brace itself together in order to repel all that which would pour in upon it from this crushed-down and cowardly world. Or suppose I were to find a large German city – that structure of vice in which nothing grows, but where every single thing, whether good or bad, is squeezed in from outside. In such circumstances should I not be compelled to become a hedgehog? But to have prickles amounts to a squandering of strength; they even constitute a twofold luxury, when, if we only chose to do so, we could dispense with them and open our hands instead . . .

Another form of prudence and self-defence consists in trying to react as seldom as possible, and to keep one's self aloof from those circumstances and conditions wherein one would be condemned, as it were, to suspend one's 'liberty' and one's initiative, and become a mere reacting medium. As an example of this I point to the intercourse with books. The scholar who, in sooth, does little else than handle books – with the philologist of average attainments their number may amount to two hundred a day – ultimately forgets entirely and completely the capacity of thinking for himself. When he has not a book between his fingers he cannot think. When he thinks, he responds to a stimulus (a thought he has read) – finally all he does is to react. The scholar exhausts his whole strength in saying either 'yes' or 'no' to matter which has already been thought out, or in criticising it – he is no longer capable of thought on his own account . . . In him the instinct of self-defence has decayed, otherwise he would defend himself against books. The scholar is a decadent. With my own eyes I have seen gifted, richly endowed, and free-spirited natures already 'read to ruins' at thirty, and mere wax vestas that have to be rubbed before they can give off any sparks – or 'thoughts'. To set to early in the morning, at the break of day, in all the fulness and dawn of one's strength, and to read a book – this I call positively vicious!

9

At this point I can no longer evade a direct answer to the question, *how one becomes what one is*. And in giving it, I shall have to touch upon that masterpiece in the art of self-preservation, which is *selfishness* . . . Granting that one's life-task – the determination and the fate of one's life-task – greatly exceeds the average measure of such things, nothing more dangerous could be conceived than to come face to face with one's self by the side of this life-task. The fact that one becomes what one is, presupposes that one has not the remotest suspicion of what one is. From this standpoint even the blunders of one's life have their own meaning and value, the temporary deviations and aberrations, the moments of hesitation and of modesty, the earnestness wasted upon duties which lie outside the actual life-task. In these matters great wisdom, perhaps even the highest wisdom, comes into activity: in these circumstances, in which *nosce teipsum* would be the sure road to ruin, forgetting one's self, misunderstanding one's self, belittling one's self, narrowing one's self, and making one's self mediocre, amount to reason itself. Expressed morally, to love one's neighbour and to live for others and for other things *may* be the means of protection employed to maintain the hardest kind of egoism. This is the exceptional case in which I, contrary to my principle and conviction, take the side of the altruistic instincts; for here they are concerned in subserving selfishness and self-discipline. The whole surface of consciousness − for consciousness *is* a surface − must be kept free from any one of the great imperatives. Beware even of every striking word, of every striking attitude! They are all so many risks which the instinct runs of 'understanding itself' too soon. Meanwhile the organising 'idea', which is destined to become master, grows and continues to grow into the depths − it begins to command, it leads you slowly back from your deviations and aberrations, it prepares individual qualities and capacities, which one day will make themselves felt as indispensable to the whole of your task − step by step it cultivates all the serviceable faculties, before it ever whispers a word concerning the dominant task, the 'goal', the 'object', and the 'meaning' of it all. Looked at from this standpoint my life is simply amazing. For the task of *transvaluing values*, more capacities were needful perhaps than could well be found side by side in one individual; and above all, antagonistic capacities which had to be free from the mutual strife and destruction which they involve. An order of rank among capacities; distance; the art of separating without creating hostility; to refrain from confounding things; to keep from reconciling things; to possess enormous multifariousness and yet to be the reverse of chaos − all this was the first condition, the long secret work, and the artistic mastery of my instinct. Its superior guardianship manifested itself with such exceeding strength, that not once did I ever dream of what was growing within me − until suddenly all my capacities were ripe, and one day burst forth in all the perfection of their highest bloom. I cannot remember ever having exerted myself, I can point to no trace of *struggle* in my life; I am the reverse of a heroic nature. To 'will' something, to 'strive' after something, to have an 'aim' or a 'desire' in my mind − I know none of these things from experience. Even at this moment I look out upon my future − a *broad* future! − as upon a calm sea: no sigh of longing makes a ripple on its surface. I have not the slightest wish that anything should be otherwise than it is: I myself would not be otherwise . . . But in this matter I have always been the same. I have never had a desire. A man who, after his four-and-fortieth year, can say that he has never bothered himself about *honours, women,* or *money*! – not that they did not come his way . . . It was thus that I became one day a university professor – I had never had the remotest idea of such a thing; for I was scarcely four-and-twenty years of age. In the same way, two years previously, I had one day become a philologist, in the sense that my *first* philological work, my start in every way, was expressly obtained by my master Ritschl for publication in his *Rheinisches Museum.** (Ritschl – and I say it in all reverence – was the only genial scholar that I have ever met. He possessed that pleasant kind of depravity which distinguishes us Thuringians, and which makes even a German sympathetic – even in the pursuit of truth we prefer to avail ourselves of roundabout ways. In saying this I do not mean to underestimate in any way my Thuringian brother, the intelligent Leopold von Ranke . . .)

10

You may be wondering why I should actually have related all these trivial and, according to traditional accounts, insignificant details to you; such action can but tell against me, more particularly if I am fated to figure in great causes. To this I reply that these trivial matters – diet, locality, climate, and one's mode of recreation, the whole casuistry of self-love – are inconceivably more important than all that which has hitherto been held in high esteem. It is precisely in this quarter that we must begin to learn afresh. All those things which mankind has valued with such earnestness heretofore are not even real; they are mere creations of fancy, or, more strictly speaking, *lies* born of the evil instincts of diseased and, in the deepest sense, noxious natures – all the concepts, 'God', 'soul', 'virtue', 'sin', 'Beyond', 'truth', 'eternal life' . . . But the greatness of human nature, its 'divinity', was sought for in them . . . All questions of politics, of social order, of education, have been falsified, root and branch, owing to the fact that the most noxious men have been taken for great men, and that people were taught to despise the small things, or rather the fundamental things, of life. If I now choose to compare myself with those creatures who have hitherto been honoured as the first among men, the difference becomes obvious. I do not reckon the

* See note on page 191.

so-called 'first' men even as human beings – for me they are the excrements of mankind, the products of disease and of the instinct of revenge: they are so many monsters laden with rottenness, so many hopeless incurables, who avenge themselves on life . . . I wish to be the opposite of these people: it is my privilege to have the very sharpest discernment for every sign of healthy instincts. There is no such thing as a morbid trait in me; even in times of serious illness I have never grown morbid, and you might seek in vain for a trace of fanaticism in my nature. No-one can point to any moment of my life in which I have assumed either an arrogant or a pathetic attitude. Pathetic attitudes are not in keeping with greatness; he who needs attitudes is false . . . Beware of all picturesque men! Life was easy – in fact easiest – to me, in those periods when it exacted the heaviest duties from me. Whoever could have seen me during the seventy days of this autumn, when, without interruption, I did a host of things of the highest rank – things that no man can do nowadays – with a sense of responsibility for all the ages yet to come, would have noticed no sign of tension in my condition, but rather a state of overflowing freshness and good cheer. Never have I eaten with more pleasant sensations, never has my sleep been better. I know of no other manner of dealing with great tasks, than as *play*: this, as a sign of greatness, is an essential prerequisite. The slightest constraint, a sombre mien, any hard accent in the voice – all these things are objections to a man, but how much more to his work! . . . One must not have nerves . . . Even to *suffer* from solitude is an objection – the only thing I have always suffered from is 'multitude'.*

At an absurdly tender age, in fact when I was seven years old, I already knew that no human speech would ever reach me: did anyone ever see me sad on that account? At present I still possess the same affability towards everybody, I am even full of consideration for the lowest: in all this there is not an atom of haughtiness or of secret contempt. He whom I despise soon guesses that he is despised by me: the very fact of my existence is enough to rouse indignation in all those who have polluted blood in their veins.

* The German words are, *Einsamkeit* and *Vielsamkeit*. The latter was coined by Nietzsche. The English word 'multitude' should, therefore, be understood as signifying multifarious instincts and gifts, which in Nietzsche strove for ascendancy and caused him more suffering than any solitude. – Tr.

My formula for greatness in man is *amor fati*: the fact that a man wishes nothing to be different, either in front of him or behind him, or for all eternity. Not only must the necessary be borne, and on no account concealed – all idealism is falsehood in the face of necessity – but it must also be *loved* . . .

I

I am one thing, my creations are another. Here, before I speak of the books themselves, I shall touch upon the question of the understanding and misunderstanding with which they have met. I shall proceed to do this in as perfunctory a manner as the occasion demands; for the time has by no means come for this question. My time has not yet come either; some are born posthumously. One day institutions will be needed in which men will live and teach, as I understand living and teaching; maybe, also, that by that time, chairs will be founded and endowed for the interpretation of *Zarathustra*. But I should regard it as a complete contradiction of myself, if I expected to find ears and eyes for my truths today: the fact that no-one listens to me, that no-one knows how to receive at my hands today, is not only comprehensible, it seems to me quite the proper thing. I do not wish to be mistaken for another – and to this end I must not mistake myself. To repeat what I have already said, I can point to but few instances of ill-will in my life: and as for literary ill-will, I could mention scarcely a single example of it. On the other hand, I have met with far too much *pure foolery*! . . . It seems to me that to take up one of my books is one of the rarest honours that a man can pay himself – even supposing that he put his shoes from off his feet beforehand, not to mention boots . . . When on one occasion Dr Heinrich von Stein honestly complained that he could not understand a word of my *Zarathustra*, I said to him that this was just as it should be: to have understood six sentences in that book – that is to say, to have lived them – raises a man to a higher level among mortals than 'modern' men can attain. With this feeling of distance how could I even wish to be read by the 'moderns' whom I know! My triumph is just the opposite of what Schopenhauer's was – I say '*Non* legor, *non* legar.' – Not that I should like to underestimate the pleasure I have derived from the innocence with which my works have frequently been contradicted. As late as last summer, at a time when I was attempting, perhaps by means of my weighty, all-too-weighty literature, to throw the rest of literature off its balance, a certain professor of Berlin University kindly gave me to understand that I ought really to make use of a different form: no-one could read such stuff as I wrote. – Finally, it was not Germany but Switzerland that presented me with the two most extreme cases. An essay on *Beyond Good and Evil*, by Dr V. Widmann in the paper called the *Bund*, under the heading 'Nietzsche's Dangerous Book', and a general account of all my works, from the pen of Herr Karl Spitteler, also in the *Bund*, constitute a maximum in my life – I shall not say of what . . . The latter treated my *Zarathustra*, for instance, as '*advanced exercises in style*', and expressed the wish that later on I might try and attend to the question of substance as well; Dr Widmann assured me of his respect for the courage I showed in endeavouring to abolish all decent feeling. Thanks to a little trick of destiny, every sentence in these criticisms seemed, with a consistency that I could but admire, to be an inverted truth. In fact it was most remarkable that all one had to do was to 'transvalue all values', in order to hit the nail on the head with regard to me, instead of striking my head with the nail . . . I am more particularly anxious therefore to discover an explanation. After all, no-one can draw more out of things, books included, than he already knows. A man has no ears for that to which experience has given him no access. To take an extreme case, suppose a book contains simply incidents which lie quite outside the range of general or even rare experience – suppose it to be the *first* language to express a whole series of experiences. In this case nothing it contains will really be heard at all, and, thanks to an acoustic delusion, people will believe that where nothing is heard there is nothing to hear . . . This, at least, has been my usual experience, and proves, if you will, the originality of my experience. He who thought he had understood something in my work, had as a rule adjusted some-thing in it to his own image – not infrequently the very opposite of myself, an 'idealist', for instance. He who understood nothing in my work, would deny that I was worth considering at all. – The word 'Superman', which designates a type of man that would be one of nature's rarest and luckiest strokes, as opposed to 'modern' men, to 'good' men, to Christians and other nihilists – a word which in the mouth of Zarathustra, the annihilator of morality, acquires a very profound meaning – is understood almost everywhere, and with perfect innocence, in the light of those values to which a flat contradiction was made manifest in the figure of Zarathustra – that is to say, as an 'ideal' type, a higher kind of man, half 'saint' and half 'genius'. . . . Other learned cattle have suspected me of Darwinism on account of this word: even the 'hero cult' of that great unconscious and involuntary swindler, Carlyle – a cult which I repudiated with such roguish malice – was recognised in my doctrine. Once, when I whispered to a man that he would do better to seek for the Superman in a Caesar Borgia than in a Parsifal, he could not believe his ears. The fact that I am quite free from curiosity in regard to criticisms of my books, more particularly when they appear in newspapers, will have to be forgiven me. My friends and my publishers know this, and never speak to me of such things. In one particular case, I once saw all the sins that had been committed against a single book – it was *Beyond Good and Evil*; I could tell you a nice story about it. Is it possible that the *National-Zeitung* – a Prussian paper (this comment is for the sake of my foreign readers – for my own part, I beg to state, I read only *Le Journal des Débats*) – really and seriously regarded the book as a 'sign of the times', or a genuine and typical example of Tory philosophy,* for which the *Kreuz-Zeitung* had not sufficient courage? . . .

2

This was said for the benefit of Germans: for everywhere else I have my readers – all of them exceptionally intelligent men, characters that have won their spurs and that have been reared in high offices and superior duties; I have even real geniuses among my readers. In Vienna, in St Petersburg, in Stockholm, in Copenhagen, in Paris, and New York – I have been discovered everywhere: I have not yet been discovered in Europe's flatland – Germany . . . And, to make a confession, I rejoice much more heartily over those who do not

---

* *Junker-Philosophie.* The landed proprietors constituted the dominating class in Prussia, and it was from this class that all officers and higher officials were drawn. The *Kreuz-Zeitung* was the organ of the Junker party. – Tr.

read me, over those who have neither heard of my name nor of the word philosophy. But whithersoever I go, here in Turin, for instance, every face brightens and softens at the sight of me. A thing that has flattered me more than anything else hitherto, is the fact that old market-women cannot rest until they have picked out the sweetest of their grapes for me. To this extent must a man be a philosopher . . . It is not in vain that the Poles are considered as the French among the Slavs. A charming Russian lady will not be mistaken for a single moment concerning my origin. I am not successful at being pompous, the most I can do is to appear embarrassed . . . I can think in German, I can feel in German – I can do most things; but this is beyond my powers . . . My old master Ritschl went so far as to declare that I planned even my philological treatises after the manner of a Parisian novelist – that I made them absurdly thrilling. In Paris itself people are surprised at 'toutes mes audaces et finesses'; – the words are Monsieur Taine's; – I fear that even in the highest forms of the dithyramb, that salt will be found pervading my work which never becomes insipid, which never becomes 'German' – and that is, wit . . . I can do nought else. God help me! Amen. – We all know, some of us even from experience, what a 'long-ears' is. Well then, I venture to assert that I have the smallest ears that have ever been seen. This fact is not without interest to women – it seems to me they feel that I understand them better! . . . I am essentially the anti-ass, and on this account alone a monster in the world's history – in Greek, and not only in Greek, I am the *Antichrist*.

3

I am to a great extent aware of my privileges as a writer: in one or two cases it has even been brought home to me how very much the habitual reading of my works 'spoils' a man's taste. Other books simply cannot be endured after mine, and least of all philosophical ones. It is an incomparable distinction to cross the threshold of this noble and subtle world – in order to do so one must certainly not be a German; it is, in short, a distinction which one must have deserved. He, however, who is related to me through loftiness of will, experiences genuine raptures of understanding in my books: for I swoop down from heights into which no bird has ever soared; I know abysses into which no foot has ever slipped. People have told me that it is impossible to lay down a book of mine – that I disturb even the night's rest . . . There is no prouder or at the same time more subtle kind of books: they sometimes attain to the highest pinnacle of earthly endeavour, cynicism; to capture their thoughts a man must have the tenderest fingers as well as the most intrepid fists. Any kind of spiritual decrepitude utterly excludes all intercourse with them – even any kind of dyspepsia: a man must have no nerves, but he must have a cheerful belly. Not only the poverty of a man's soul and its stuffy air excludes all intercourse with them, but also, and to a much greater degree, cowardice, uncleanliness, and secret intestinal revengefulness; a word from my lips suffices to make the colour of all evil instincts rush into a face. Among my acquaintances I have a number of experimental subjects, in whom I see depicted all the different, and instructively different, reactions which follow upon a perusal of my works. Those who will have nothing to do with the contents of my books, as for instance my so-called friends, assume an 'impersonal' tone concerning them: they wish me luck, and congratulate me for having produced another work; they also declare that my writings show progress, because they exhale a more cheerful spirit . . . The thoroughly vicious people, the 'beautiful souls', the false from top to toe, do not know in the least what to do with my books – consequently, with the beautiful consistency of all beautiful souls, they regard my work as beneath them. The cattle among my acquaintances, the mere Germans, leave me to understand, if you please, that they are not always of my opinion, though here and there they agree with me . . . I have heard this said even about *Zarathustra*. 'Feminism', whether in mankind or in man, is likewise a barrier to my writings; with it, no-one could ever enter into this labyrinth of fearless knowledge. To this end, a man must never have spared himself, he must have been hard in his habits, in order to be good-humoured and merry among a host of inexorable truths. When I try to picture the character of a perfect reader, I always imagine a monster of courage and curiosity, as well as of suppleness, cunning, and prudence – in short, a born adventurer and explorer. After all, I could not describe better than *Zarathustra* has done unto whom I really address myself: unto whom alone would he reveal his riddle?

Unto you, daring explorers and experimenters, and unto all who
  have ever embarked beneath cunning sails upon terrible seas;
Unto you who revel in riddles and in twilight, whose souls are lured
  by flutes unto every treacherous abyss:
For ye care not to grope your way along a thread with craven fingers;
  and where ye are able to *guess*, ye hate to *argue*.

4

I will now pass just one or two general remarks about my *art of style*.
To communicate a state, an inner tension of pathos, by means of
signs, including the tempo of these signs – that is the meaning of
every style; and in view of the fact that the multiplicity of inner
states in me is enormous, I am capable of many kinds of style – in
short, the most multifarious art of style that any man has ever had at
his disposal. Any style is *good* which genuinely communicates an
inner condition, which does not blunder over the signs, over the
tempo of the signs, or over *moods* – all the laws of phrasing are the
outcome of representing moods artistically. Good style, in itself, is a
piece of sheer foolery, mere idealism, like 'beauty in itself', for
instance, or 'goodness in itself', or 'the thing-in-itself'. All this takes
for granted, of course, that there exist ears that can hear, and such
men as are capable and worthy of a like pathos, that those
are not wanting unto whom one may communicate one's self.
Meanwhile my Zarathustra, for instance, is still in quest of such
people – alas! he will have to seek a long while yet! A man must be
worthy of listening to him . . . And, until that time, there will be
no-one who will understand the art that has been squandered in
this book. No-one has ever existed who has had more novel,
more strange, and purposely created art forms to fling to the winds.
The fact that such things were possible in the German language
still awaited proof; formerly, I myself would have denied most
emphatically that it was possible. Before my time people did not
know what could be done with the German language – what could
be done with language in general. The art of grand rhythm, of grand
style in periods, for expressing the tremendous fluctuations of
sublime and superhuman passion, was first discovered by me: with
the dithyramb entitled 'The Seven Seals', which constitutes the last
discourse of the third part of *Zarathustra*, I soared miles above all that
which heretofore has been called poetry.

5

The fact that the voice which speaks in my works is that of a psychologist who has not his peer, is perhaps the first conclusion at which a good reader will arrive — a reader such as I deserve, and one who reads me just as the good old philologists used to read their Horace. Those propositions about which all the world is fundamentally agreed — not to speak of fashionable philosophy, of moralists and other empty-headed and cabbage-brained people — are to me but ingenuous blunders: for instance, the belief that 'altruistic' and 'egoistic' are opposites, while all the time the 'ego' itself is merely a 'supreme swindle', an 'ideal'. . . . There are no such things as egoistic or altruistic actions: both concepts are psychological nonsense. Or the proposition that 'man pursues happiness'; or the proposition that 'happiness is the reward of virtue'. . . . Or the proposition that 'pleasure and pain are opposites'. . . .Morality, the Circe of mankind, has falsified everything psychological, root and branch — it has bemoralised everything, even to the terribly nonsensical point of calling love 'unselfish'. A man must first be firmly poised, he must stand securely on his two legs, otherwise he cannot love at all. This indeed the girls know only too well: they don't care two pins about unselfish and merely objective men . . . May I venture to suggest, incidentally, that I know women? This knowledge is part of my Dionysian patri-mony. Who knows? Maybe I am the first psychologist of the eternally feminine. Women all like me . . . But that's an old story: save, of course, the abortions among them, the emancipated ones, those who lack the wherewithal to have children. Thank goodness I am not willing to let myself be torn to pieces! The perfect woman tears you to pieces when she loves you: I know these amiable Maenads . . . Oh! what a dangerous, creeping, subterranean little beast of prey she is! And so agreeable withal! . . . A little woman, pursuing her vengeance, would force open even the iron gates of Fate itself. Woman is incalculably more wicked than man, she is also cleverer. Goodness in a woman is already a sign of *degeneration*. All cases of 'beautiful souls' in women may be traced to a faulty physiological condition — but I go no further, lest I should become medicynical. The struggle for equal rights is even a symptom of disease; every doctor knows this. The more womanly a woman is, the more she fights tooth and nail against rights in general: the natural order of things, the eternal war between the sexes, assigns to her by far the foremost rank. Have people had ears to hear my definition of love? It is the only definition worthy of a philosopher. Love, in its means, is war; in its foundation, it is the mortal hatred of the sexes. Have you heard my reply to the question how a woman can be cured, 'saved' in fact? – Give her a child! A woman needs children, man is always only a means, thus spake Zarathustra. 'The emancipation of women' – this is the instinctive hatred of physiologically botched – that is to say, barren – women for those of their sisters who are well constituted: the fight against 'man' is always only a means, a pretext, a piece of strategy. By trying to rise to 'Woman *per se*', to 'Higher Woman', to the 'Ideal Woman', all they wish to do is to lower the general level of women's rank: and there are no more certain means to this end than university education, trousers, and the rights of voting cattle. Truth to tell, the emancipated are the anarchists in the 'eternally feminine' world, the physiological mishaps, the most deep-rooted instinct of whom is revenge. A whole species of the most malicious 'idealism' – which, by the bye, also manifests itself in men, in Henrik Ibsen for instance, that typical old maid – whose object is to poison the clean conscience, the natural spirit, of sexual love . . . And in order to leave no doubt in your minds in regard to my opinion, which, on this matter, is as honest as it is severe, I will reveal to you one more clause out of my moral code against vice – with the word 'vice' I combat every kind of opposition to nature, or, if you prefer fine words, idealism. The clause reads: 'Preaching of chastity is a public incitement to unnatural practices. All depreci- ation of the sexual life, all the sullying of it by means of the concept 'impure', is the essential crime against Life – is the essential crime against the Holy Spirit of Life.'

6

In order to give you some idea of myself as a psychologist, let me take this curious piece of psychological analysis out of the book *Beyond Good and Evil*, in which it appears. I forbid, by the bye, any guessing as to whom I am describing in this passage. 'The genius of the heart, as that great anchorite possesses it, the divine tempter and born Pied Piper of consciences, whose voice knows how to sink into the inmost depths of every soul, who neither utters a word nor casts a glance, in which some seductive motive or trick does not lie: a part of whose masterliness is that he understands the art of seeming – not what he is, but that which will place a fresh constraint upon his followers to press ever more closely upon him, to follow him ever more enthusiastically and whole-heartedly . . . The genius of the heart, which makes all loud and self-conceited things hold their tongues and lend their ears, which polishes all rough souls and makes them taste a new longing – to lie placid as a mirror, that the deep heavens may be reflected in them . . . The genius of the heart, which teaches the clumsy and too hasty hand to hesitate and grasp more tenderly; which scents the hidden and forgotten treasure, the pearl of goodness and sweet spirituality, beneath thick black ice, and is a divining rod for every grain of gold, long buried and imprisoned in heaps of mud and sand . . . The genius of the heart, from contact with which every man goes away richer, not 'blessed' and overcome, not as though favoured and crushed by the good things of others; but richer in himself, fresher to himself than before, opened up, breathed upon and sounded by a thawing wind; more uncertain, perhaps, more delicate, more fragile, more bruised; but full of hopes which as yet lack names, full of a new will and striving, full of a new unwillingness and counter-striving.' . . .

The Birth of Tragedy

I

In order to be fair to the *Birth of Tragedy* (1872) it is necessary to forget a few things. It created a sensation and even fascinated by means of its mistakes – by means of its application to Wagnerism, as if the latter were the sign of an ascending tendency. On that account alone, this treatise was an event in Wagner's life: thenceforward great hopes surrounded the name of Wagner. Even to this day, people remind me, sometimes in the middle of *Parsifal*, that it rests on my conscience if the opinion that this movement is of great value to culture at length became prevalent. I have often seen the book quoted as 'The Second Birth of Tragedy from the Spirit of Music': people had ears only for new formulae for Wagner's art, his object and his mission – and in this way the real hidden value of the book was overlooked. 'Hellenism and Pessimism' – this would have been a less equivocal title, seeing that the book contains the first attempt at showing how the Greeks succeeded in disposing of pessimism – in what manner they overcame it . . . Tragedy itself is the proof of the fact that the Greeks were not pessimists: Schopenhauer blundered here as he blundered in everything else. – Regarded impartially, *The Birth of Tragedy* is a book quite strange to its age: no-one would dream that it was begun in the thunder of the battle of Worth. I thought out these problems on cold September nights beneath the walls of Metz, in the midst of my duties as nurse to the wounded; it would be easier to think that it was written fifty years earlier. Its attitude towards politics is one of indifference – 'un-German',* as people would say today – it smells offensively of Hegel; only in one or two formulae is it infected with the bitter odour of corpses which is peculiar to Schopenhauer. An idea – the antagonism of the two concepts Dionysian and Apollonian – is translated into metaphysics; history itself is depicted as the development of this idea; in tragedy this antithesis has become unity; from this standpoint things which theretofore had never been face to face are suddenly confronted, and understood and illuminated by each other . . . Opera and revolution, for instance . . . The two decisive innovations in the book are, first, the comprehension of the Dionysian phenomenon among the Greeks – it provides the first psychological analysis of this phenomenon, and sees in it the single root of all Greek art; and, secondly, the comprehension of Socraticism – Socrates being presented for the first time as the instrument of Greek dissolution, as a typical decadent. 'Reason' *versus* Instinct. 'Reason' at any cost, as a dangerous, life-undermining force. The whole book is profoundly and politely silent concerning Christianity: the latter is neither Apollonian nor Dionysian; it denies all aesthetic values, which are the only values that *The Birth of Tragedy* recognises. Christianity is most profoundly nihilistic, whereas in the Dionysian symbol, the most extreme limits of a yea-saying attitude to life are attained. In one part of the book the Christian priesthood is referred to as a 'perfidious order of goblins', as 'subterraneans'.

* Those Germans who, like Nietzsche or Goethe, recognised that politics constituted a danger to culture, and who appreciated the literature of maturer cultures, such as that of France, were called *un-deutsch* (un-German) by imperialistic Germans. – TR.

2

This start of mine was remarkable beyond measure. As a confirm-
ation of my inmost personal experience I had discovered the only
example of this fact that history possesses – with this I was the first to
understand the amazing Dionysian phenomenon. At the same time,
by recognising Socrates as a decadent, I proved most conclusively
that the certainty of my psychological grasp of things ran very little
risk at the hands of any sort of moral idiosyncrasy: to regard morality
itself as a symptom of degeneration is an innovation, a unique event
of the first order in the history of knowledge. How high I had
soared above the pitifully foolish gabble about Optimism and Pessimism with my two new doctrines! I was the first to see the actual
contrast: the degenerate instinct which turns upon life with a
subterranean lust of vengeance (Christianity, Schopenhauer's philosophy, and in some respects too even Plato's philosophy – in short,
the whole of idealism in its typical forms), as opposed to a formula
of the highest yea-saying to life, born of an abundance and a
superabundance of life – a yea-saying free from all reserve, applying
even to suffering, and guilt, and all that is questionable and strange
in existence . . . This last, most joyous, most exuberant and exultant
yea to life, is not only the highest, but also the profoundest conception, and one which is most strictly confirmed and supported by
truth and science. Nothing that exists must be suppressed, nothing
can be dispensed with. Those aspects of life which Christians and
other nihilists reject belong to an incalculably higher order in the
hierarchy of values than that which the instinct of degeneration
calls good, and *may* call good. In order to understand this, a certain
courage is necessary, and, as a prerequisite of this, a certain superfluity of strength: for a man can approach only as near to truth as he
has the courage to advance – that is to say, everything depends
strictly upon the measure of his strength. Knowledge, and the
affirmation of reality, are just as necessary to the strong man as
cowardice, the flight from reality – in fact, the 'ideal' – are necessary
to the weak inspired by weakness . . . These people are not at liberty
to 'know' – decadents stand in need of lies – it is one of their self-
preservative measures. He who not only understands the word
'Dionysian', but understands *himself* in that term, does not require
any refutation of Plato, or of Christianity, or of Schopenhauer – for
his nose *scents decomposition.*

3

The extent to which I had by means of these doctrines discovered the idea of 'tragedy', the ultimate explanation of what the psychology of tragedy is, I discussed finally in *Twilight of the Idols* (Aph. 5, part 10) . . . 'The saying of yea to life, including even its most strange and most terrible problems, the will to life rejoicing over its own inexhaustibleness in the *sacrifice* of its highest types – this is what I called Dionysian, this is what I divined as the bridge leading to the psychology of the *tragic* poet. Not in order to escape from terror and pity, not to purify one's self of a dangerous passion by discharging it with vehemence – this is how Aristotle* understood it – but to be far beyond terror and pity and to be the eternal lust of Becoming itself – that lust which also involves the *lust of destruction.*' . . . In this sense I have the right to regard myself as the first *tragic philosopher* – that is to say, the most extreme antithesis and antipodes of a pessimistic philosopher. Before my time no such thing existed as this translation of the Dionysian phenomenon into philosophic emotion: tragic wisdom was lacking; in vain have I sought for signs of it even among the great Greeks in philosophy – those belonging to the two centuries before Socrates. I still remained a little doubtful about Heraclitus, in whose presence alone I felt warmer and more at ease than anywhere else. The yea-saying to the impermanence and annihilation of things, which is the decisive feature of a Dionysian philosophy; the yea-saying to contradiction and war, the postulation of Becoming, together with the radical rejection even of the concept *Being* – in all these things, at all events, I must recognise him who has come nearest to me in thought hitherto. The doctrine of the 'Eternal Recurrence' – that is to say, of the absolute and eternal repetition of all things in periodical cycles – this doctrine of Zarathustra's might, it is true, have been taught before. In any case, the Stoics, who derived nearly all their fundamental ideas from Heraclitus, show traces of it.

4

A tremendous hope finds expression in this work. After all, I have absolutely no reason to renounce the hope for a Dionysian future of music. Let us look a century ahead, and let us suppose that my attempt to destroy two millennia of hostility to nature and of the

* *Poetics*, c. VI. – Tr.

violation of humanity be crowned with success. That new party of life-advocates, which will undertake the greatest of all tasks, the elevation and perfection of mankind, as well as the relentless destruction of all degenerate and parasitical elements, will make that *superabundance of life* on earth once more possible, out of which the Dionysian state will perforce arise again. I promise the advent of a tragic age: the highest art in the saying of yea to life, 'tragedy', will be born again when mankind has the knowledge of the hardest but most necessary of wars behind it, without however suffering from that knowledge . . . A psychologist might add that what I heard in Wagnerian music in my youth and early manhood had nothing whatsoever to do with Wagner; that when I described Dionysian music, I described merely what *I* personally had heard – that I was compelled instinctively to translate and transfigure everything into the new spirit which filled my breast. A proof of this, and as strong a proof as you could have, is my essay, *Wagner in Bayreuth*: in all its decisive psychological passages I am the only person concerned – without any hesitation you may read my name or the word 'Zarathustra' wherever the text contains the name of Wagner. The whole panorama of the *dithyrambic* artist is the representation of the already existing author of *Zarathustra*, and it is drawn with an abysmal depth which does not even once come into contact with the real Wagner. Wagner himself had a notion of the truth; he did not recognise himself in the essay. – In this way, 'the idea of Bayreuth' was changed into something which to those who are acquainted with my *Zarathustra* will be no riddle – that is to say, into the Great Noon when the highest of the elect will consecrate themselves for the greatest of all duties – who knows? the vision of a feast which I may live to see . . . The pathos of the first few pages is universal history; the look which is discussed on page 105 of the book, is the actual look of *Zarathustra*; Wagner, Bayreuth, the whole of this petty German wretchedness, is a cloud upon which an infinite Fata Morgana of the future is reflected. Even from the psychological standpoint, all the decisive traits in my character are introduced into Wagner's nature – the juxtaposition of the most brilliant and most fatal forces, a Will to Power such as no man has ever possessed – inexorable bravery in matters spiritual, an un-limited power of learning unaccompanied by depressed powers for action. Everything in this essay is a prophecy: the proximity of the resurrection of the Greek spirit, the need of men who will be counter-Alexanders, who will once more tie the Gordian knot of Greek culture, after it has been cut. Listen to the world-historic accent with which the concept 'sense for the tragic' is introduced on page 180: there are little else but world-historic accents in this essay. This is the strangest kind of 'objectivity' that ever existed: my absolute certainty in regard to what I *am*, projected itself into any chance reality – truth about myself was voiced from out appalling depths. On pages 174 and 175 the style of *Zarathustra* is described and foretold with incisive certainty, and no more magnificent expression will ever he found than that on pages 144–147 for the event for which *Zarathustra* stands – that prodigious act of the purification and consecration of mankind.

Thoughts out of Season

I

The four essays composing the *Thoughts out of Season* are thoroughly warlike in tone. They prove that I was no mere dreamer, that I delight in drawing the sword – and perhaps, also, that my wrist is dangerously supple. The first onslaught (1873) was directed against German culture, upon which I looked down even at that time with unmitigated contempt. Without either sense, substance, or goal, it was simply 'public opinion'. There could be no more dangerous misunderstanding than to suppose that Germany's success at arms proved anything in favour of German culture – and still less the triumph of this culture over that of France. The second essay (1874) brings to light that which is dangerous, that which corrodes and poisons life in our manner of pursuing scientific study: Life is diseased, thanks to this dehumanised piece of clockwork and mechanism, thanks to the 'impersonality' of the workman, and the false economy of the 'division of labour'. The object, which is culture, is lost sight of: modern scientific activity as a means thereto simply produces barbarism. In this treatise, the 'historical sense', of which this century is so proud, is for the first time recognised as sickness, as a typical symptom of decay. In the third and fourth essays, a signpost is set up pointing to a higher concept of culture, to a re-establishment of the notion 'culture'; and two pictures of the hardest self-love and self-discipline are presented, two essentially un-modern types, full of the most sovereign contempt for all that which lay around them and was called 'empire', 'culture', 'Christianity', 'Bismarck', and 'success' – these two types were Schopenhauer and Wagner, *or*, in a word, Nietzsche . . .

2

Of these four attacks, the first met with extraordinary success. The stir which it created was in every way gorgeous. I had put my finger on the vulnerable spot of a triumphant nation – I had told it that its victory was not a red-letter day for culture, but, perhaps, something very different. The reply rang out from all sides, and certainly not only from old friends of David Strauss, whom I had made ridiculous as the type of a German Philistine of culture and a man of smug self-content – in short, as the author of that suburban gospel of his, called *The Old and the New Faith* (the term 'Philistine of culture' passed into the current language of Germany after the appearance of my book). These old friends, whose vanity as Würtembergians and Swabians I had deeply wounded in regarding their unique animal, their bird of Paradise, as a trifle comic, replied to me as ingenuously and as grossly as I could have wished. The Prussian replies were smarter; they contained more 'Prussian blue'. The most disreputable attitude was assumed by a Leipzig paper, the egregious *Grentzboten*; and it cost me some pains to prevent my indignant friends in Basle from taking action against it. Only a few old gentlemen decided in my favour, and for very diverse and sometimes unaccountable reasons. Among them was one, Ewald of Göttingen, who made it clear that my attack on Strauss had been deadly. There was also the Hegelian, Bruno Bauer, who from that time became one of my most attentive readers. In his later years he liked to refer to me, when, for instance, he wanted to give Herr von Treitschke, the Prussian historiographer, a hint as to where he could obtain information about the notion 'culture', of which he (Herr von T.) had completely lost sight. The weightiest and longest notice of my book and its author appeared in Würzburg, and was written by Professor Hoffmann, an old pupil of the philosopher von Baader. The essays made him foresee a great future for me, namely, that of bringing about a sort of crisis and decisive turning-point in the problem of atheism, of which he recognised in me the most instinctive and most radical advocate. It was atheism that had drawn me to Schopenhauer. The review which received by far the most attention, and which excited the most bitterness, was an extraordinarily powerful and plucky appreciation of my work by Carl Hillebrand, a man who was usually so mild, and the last *humane* German who knew how to wield a pen. The article appeared in the *Augsburg Gazette*, and it can be read today, couched in rather more cautious language, among his collected essays. In it my work was referred to as an event, as a decisive turning-point, as the first sign of an awakening, as an excellent symptom, and as an actual revival of German earnestness and of German passion in things spiritual. Hillebrand could speak only in the terms of the highest respect, of the form of my book, of its consummate taste, of its perfect tact in discriminating between persons and causes: he characterised it as the best polemical work in the German language – the best performance in the art of polemics, which for Germans is so dangerous and so strongly to be deprecated. Besides confirming my standpoint, he laid even greater stress upon what I had dared to say about the deterioration of language in Germany (nowadays writers assume the airs of Purists* and can no longer even construct a sentence); sharing my contempt for the literary stars of this nation, he concluded by expressing his admiration for my courage – that 'greatest courage of all which places the very favourites of the people in the dock', . . . The after-effects of this essay of mine proved invaluable to me in my life. No-one has ever tried to meddle with me since. People are silent. In Germany I am treated with gloomy caution: for years I have rejoiced in the privilege of such absolute freedom of speech, as no-one nowadays, least of all in the 'Empire', has enough liberty to claim. My paradise is 'in the shadow of my sword'. At bottom all I had done was to put one of Stendhal's maxims into practice:

* The Purists constituted a definite body in Germany, called the *Deutscher Sprach-Verein*. Their object was to banish every foreign word from the language, and they carried this process of ostracism even into the domain of the menu, where their efforts at rendering the meaning of French dishes were comical. Their principal organ, and their other publications, were by no means free either from solecisms or faults of style, and it is doubtless to this curious anomaly that Nietzsche here refers. – TR.

he advises one to make one's entrance into society by means of a
duel. And how well I had chosen my opponent! – the foremost
free-thinker of Germany. As a matter of fact, quite a novel kind of
free thought found its expression in this way: up to the present
nothing has been more strange and more foreign to my blood than
the whole of that European and American species known as *libres
penseurs*. Incorrigible blockheads and clowns of 'modern ideas' that
they are, I feel much more profoundly at variance with them than
with any one of their adversaries. They also wish to 'improve'
mankind, after their own fashion – that is to say, in their own
image; against that which I stand for and desire, they would wage
an implacable war, if only they understood it; the whole gang of
them still believe in an 'ideal'. . . . I am the first *Immoralist*.

3

I should not like to say that the last two essays in the *Thoughts out of
Season*, associated with the names of Schopenhauer and Wagner
respectively, serve any special purpose in throwing light upon
these two cases, or in formulating their psychological problems.
This of course does not apply to a few details. Thus, for instance,
in the second of the two essays, with a profound certainty of
instinct I already characterised the elementary factor in Wagner's
nature as a theatrical talent which in all his means and inspirations
only draws its final conclusions. At bottom, my desire in this essay
was to do something very different from writing psychology: an
unprecedented educational problem, a new understanding of self-
discipline and self-defence carried to the point of hardness, a road
to greatness and to world-historic duties, yearned to find expression. Roughly speaking, I seized two famous and, theretofore,
completely undefined types by the forelock, after the manner in
which one seizes opportunities, simply in order to speak my mind
on certain questions, in order to have a few more formulas, signs,
and means of expression at my disposal. Indeed I actually suggest
this, with most unearthly sagacity, on page 183 of *Schopenhauer as
Educator*. Plato made use of Socrates in the same way – that is to
say, as a cipher for Plato. Now that, from some distance, I can look
back upon the conditions of which these essays are the testimony,
I would be loth to deny that they refer simply to me. The essay
Wagner in Bayreuth is a vision of my own future; on the other hand,

my most secret history, my development, is written down in
Schopenhauer as Educator. But, above all, the *vow* I made! What I am
today, the place I now hold – at a height from which I speak no
longer with words but with thunderbolts – oh, how far I was from
all this in those days! But I saw the land – I did not deceive myself
for one moment as to the way, the sea, the danger – *and* success!
The great calm in promising, this happy prospect of a future which
must not remain only a promise! – In this book every word has been
lived, profoundly and intimately; the most painful things are not
lacking in it; it contains words which are positively running with
blood. But a wind of great freedom blows over the whole; even its
wounds do not constitute an objection. As to what I understand by
being a philosopher – that is to say, a terrible explosive in the
presence of which everything is in danger; as to how I sever my idea
of the philosopher by miles from that other idea of him which
includes even a Kant, not to speak of the academic 'ruminators' and
other professors of philosophy – concerning all these things this
essay provides invaluable information, even granting that at bottom,
it is not 'Schopenhauer as Educator' but 'Nietzsche as Educator',
who speaks his sentiments in it. Considering that, in those days, my
trade was that of a scholar, and perhaps, also, that I understood
my trade, the piece of austere scholar psychology which suddenly
makes its appearance in this essay is not without importance: it
expresses the feeling of distance, and my profound certainty regarding what was my real life-task, and what were merely means,
intervals, and accessory work to me. My wisdom consists in my
having been many things, and in many places, in order to become
one thing – in order to be able to attain to one thing. It was part of
my fate to be a scholar for a while.

Human, All-too-Human

I

Human, All-too-Human, with its two sequels, is the memorial of a
crisis. It is called a book for free spirits: almost every sentence in it
is the expression of a triumph – by means of it I purged myself of
everything in me which was foreign to my nature. Idealism is
foreign to me: the title of the book means: 'Where ye see ideal

things I see – human, alas! all-too-human things!' . . . I know men better. The word 'free spirit' in this book must not be understood as anything else than a spirit that has become free, that has once more taken possession of itself. My tone, the pitch of my voice, has completely changed; the book will be thought clever, cool, and at times both hard and scornful. A certain spirituality, of noble taste, seems to be ever struggling to dominate a passionate torrent at its feet. In this respect there is some sense in the fact that it was the hundredth anniversary of Voltaire's death that served, so to speak, as an excuse for the publication of the book as early as 1878. For Voltaire, as the opposite of everyone who wrote after him, was above all a grandee of the intellect: precisely what I am also. The name of Voltaire on one of my writings – that was verily a step forward – in my direction . . . Looking into this book a little more closely, you perceive a pitiless spirit who knows all the secret hiding-places in which ideals are wont to skulk – where they find their dungeons, and, as it were, their last refuge. With a torch in my hand, the light of which is not by any means a flickering one, I illuminate this nether world with beams that cut like blades. It is war, but war without powder and smoke, without warlike attitudes, without pathos and contorted limbs – all these things would still be 'idealism'. One error after the other is quietly laid upon ice; the ideal is not refuted – it freezes. Here, for instance, 'genius' freezes; round the corner the 'saint' freezes; under a thick icicle the 'hero' freezes; and in the end 'faith' itself freezes. So-called 'conviction' and also 'pity' are considerably cooled – and almost everywhere the 'thing in itself' is freezing to death.

2

This book was begun during the first musical festival at Bayreuth; a feeling of profound strangeness towards everything that surrounded me there, is one of its first conditions. He who has any notion of the visions which even at that time had flitted across my path, will be able to guess what I felt when one day I came to my senses in Bayreuth. It was just as if I had been dreaming. Where on earth was I? I recognised nothing that I saw; I scarcely recognised Wagner. It was in vain that I called up reminiscences. Tribschen – remote island of bliss: not the shadow of a resemblance! The incomparable days devoted to the laying of the first stone, the small group of the initiated who celebrated them, and who were far from lacking fingers for the handling of delicate things: not the shadow of a resemblance! *What had happened?* – Wagner had been translated into German! The Wagnerite had become master of Wagner! – *German* art! The German master! German beer! . . . We who know only too well the kind of refined artists and cosmopolitanism in taste, to which alone Wagner's art can appeal, were beside ourselves at the sight of Wagner bedecked with German virtues. I think I know the Wagnerite, I have experienced three generations of them, from Brendel of blessed memory, who confounded Wagner with Hegel, to the 'idealists' of the *Bayreuth Gazette*, who confound Wagner with themselves – I have been the recipient of every kind of confession about Wagner, from 'beautiful souls'. My kingdom for just one intelligent word! – In very truth, a blood–curdling company! Nohl, Pohl, and *Kohl*,* and others of their kidney to infinity! There was not a single abortion that was lacking among them – no, not even the anti-semite. – Poor Wagner! Into whose hands had he fallen? If only he had gone into a herd of swine! But among Germans! Some day, for the edification of posterity, one ought really to have a genuine Bayreuthian stuffed, or, better still, preserved in spirit – for it is precisely spirit that is lacking in this quarter – with this inscription at the foot of the jar: 'A sample of the spirit whereon the 'German Empire' was founded.' . . . But enough! In the middle of the festivities I suddenly packed my trunk and left the place for a few weeks, despite the fact that a charming Parisian lady sought to comfort me; I excused myself to Wagner simply by means of a fatalistic telegram. In a little spot called Klingenbrunn, deeply buried in the recesses of the Böhmerwald, I carried my melancholy and my contempt of Germans about with me like an illness – and, from time to time, under the general title of 'The Ploughshare', I wrote a sentence or two down in my notebook, nothing but severe psychological stuff, which it is possible may have found its way into *Human, all-too-Human*.

---

* Nohl and Pohl were both writers on music; Kohl, however, which literally means cabbage, is a slang expression, denoting superior nonsense. – Tr.

3

That which had taken place in me, then, was not only a breach with
Wagner – I was suffering from a general aberration of my instincts,
of which a mere isolated blunder, whether it were Wagner or my
professorship at Basle, was nothing more than a symptom. I was
seized with a fit of impatience with myself; I saw that it was high
time that I should turn my thoughts upon my own lot. In a trice I
realised, with appalling clearness, how much time had already been
squandered – how futile and how senseless my whole existence as a
philologist appeared by the side of my life-task. I was ashamed of
this false modesty . . . Ten years were behind me, during which, to
tell the truth, the nourishment of my spirit had been at a standstill,
during which I had added not a single useful fragment to my
knowledge, and had forgotten countless things in the pursuit of a
hotch-potch of dry-as-dust scholarship. To crawl with meticulous
care and short-sighted eyes through old Greek metricians – that is
what I had come to! . . . Moved to pity I saw myself quite thin, quite
emaciated: realities were only too plainly absent from my stock of
knowledge, and what the 'idealities' were worth the devil alone
knew! A positively burning thirst overcame me: and from that time
forward I have done literally nothing else than study physiology,
medicine, and natural science – I even returned to the actual study
of history only when my life-task compelled me to. It was at that
time, too, that I first divined the relation between an instinctively
repulsive occupation, a so-called vocation, which is the last thing to
which one is 'called', and that need of lulling a feeling of emptiness
and hunger, by means of an art which is a narcotic – by means of
Wagner's art, for instance. After looking carefully about me, I have
discovered that a large number of young men are all in the same
state of distress: one kind of unnatural practice perforce leads to
another. In Germany, or rather, to avoid all ambiguity, in the
Empire,* only too many are condemned to determine their choice
too soon, and then to pine away beneath a burden that they can no
longer throw off . . . Such creatures crave for Wagner as for an
opiate – they are thus able to forget themselves, to be rid of themselves for a moment . . . What am I saying! – for five or six hours.

* Nietzsche distinguishes between Bismarckian Germany and that other Germany
– Austria, Switzerland, and the Baltic Provinces – where the German language
was also spoken. – TR.

4

At this time my instincts turned resolutely against any further yielding or following on my part, and any further misunderstanding of myself. Every kind of life, the most unfavourable circumstances, illness, poverty – anything seemed to me preferable to that undignified 'selfishness' into which I had fallen; in the first place, thanks to my ignorance and youth, and in which I had afterwards remained owing to laziness – the so-called 'sense of duty'. At this juncture there came to my help, in a way that I cannot sufficiently admire, and precisely at the right time, that evil heritage which I derive from my father's side of the family, and which, at bottom, is no more than a predisposition to die young. Illness slowly liberated me from the toils, it spared me any sort of sudden breach, any sort of violent and offensive step. At that time I lost not a particle of the good will of others, but rather added to my store. Illness likewise gave me the right completely to reverse my mode of life; it not only allowed, it actually commanded, me to forget; it bestowed upon me the necessity of lying still, of having leisure, of waiting, and of exercising patience . . . But all this means thinking! . . . The state of my eyes alone put an end to all book-wormishness, or, in plain English – philology: I was thus delivered from books; for years I ceased from reading, and this was the greatest boon I ever conferred upon myself! That nethermost self, which was, as it were, entombed, and which had grown dumb because it had been forced to listen perpetually to other selves (for that is what reading means!), slowly awakened; at first it was shy and doubtful, but at last it *spoke again*. Never have I rejoiced more over my condition than during the sickest and most painful moments of my life. You have only to examine *The Dawn of Day*, or, perhaps, *The Wanderer and his Shadow*,* in order to understand what this 'return to myself' actually meant: in itself it was the highest kind of recovery! . . . My cure was simply the result of it.

5

Human, All-too-Human, this monument of a course of vigorous self-discipline, by means of which I put an abrupt end to all the 'Superior Bunkum', 'Idealism', 'Beautiful Feelings', and other effeminacies that had percolated into my being, was written

* *Human, all-too-Human*, Part II. – Tr.

principally in Sorrento; it was finished and given definite shape
during a winter at Basle, under conditions far less favourable than
those in Sorrento. Truth to tell, it was Peter Gast, at that time a
student at the University of Basle, and a devoted friend of mine,
who was responsible for the book. With my head wrapped in
bandages, and extremely painful, I dictated while he wrote and
corrected as he went along – to be accurate, he was the real
composer, whereas I was only the author. When the completed
book ultimately reached me – to the great surprise of the serious
invalid I then was – I sent, among others, two copies to Bayreuth.
Thanks to a miraculous flash of intelligence on the part of chance,
there reached me precisely at the same time a splendid copy of the
Parsifal text, with the following inscription from Wagner's pen:
'To his dear friend Friedrich Nietzsche, from Richard Wagner,
Ecclesiastical Councillor.' At this crossing of the two books I
seemed to hear an ominous note. Did it not sound as if two swords
had crossed? At all events we both felt this was so, for each of us
remained silent. At about this time the first Bayreuth pamphlets
appeared: and I then understood the move on my part for which it
was high time. Incredible! Wagner had become pious.

6

My attitude to myself at that time (1876), and the unearthly
certitude with which I grasped my life-task and all its world-
historic consequences, is well revealed throughout the book, but
more particularly in one very significant passage, despite the fact
that, with my instinctive cunning, I once more circumvented the
use of the little word 'I' – not however, this time, in order to shed
world-historic glory on the names of Schopenhauer and Wagner,
but on that of another of my friends, the excellent Dr Paul Rée –
fortunately much too acute a creature to be deceived – others
were less subtle. Among my readers I have a number of hopeless
people, the typical German professor for instance, who can always
be recognised from the fact that, judging from the passage in
question, he feels compelled to regard the whole book as a sort
of superior Réealism. As a matter of fact it contradicts five or six
of my friend's utterances: only read the introduction to *The
Genealogy of Morals* on this question. – The passage above referred
to reads: 'What, after all, is the principal axiom to which the

boldest and coldest thinker, the author of the book *On the Origin of Moral Sensations*' (read Nietzsche, the first Immoralist), 'has attained by means of his incisive and decisive analysis of human actions? "The moral man," he says, "is no nearer to the intelligible (metaphysical) world than is the physical man, for there is no intelligible world." This theory, hardened and sharpened under the hammer-blow of historical knowledge' (read *The Transvaluation of all Values*), 'may some time or other, perhaps in some future period – 1890! – serve as the axe which is applied to the root of the "metaphysical need" of man – whether more as a blessing than a curse to the general welfare it is not easy to say; but in any case as a theory with the most important consequences, at once fruitful and terrible, and looking into the world with that Janus-face which all great knowledge possesses.'*

The Dawn of Day: Thoughts about Morality as a Prejudice

I

With this book I open my campaign against morality. Not that it is at all redolent of powder – you will find quite other and much nicer smells in it, provided that you have any keenness in your nostrils. There is nothing either of light or of heavy artillery in its composition, and if its general end be a negative one, its means are not so – means out of which the end follows like a logical conclusion, *not* like a cannon-shot. And if the reader takes leave of this book with a feeling of timid caution in regard to everything which has hitherto been honoured and even worshipped under the name of morality, it does not alter the fact that there is not one negative word, not one attack, and not one single piece of malice in the whole work – on the contrary, it lies in the sunshine, smooth and happy, like a marine animal, basking in the sun between two rocks. For, after all, I was this marine animal: almost every sentence in the book was thought out, or rather *caught*, among that medley of rocks in the neighbourhood of Genoa, where I lived quite alone, and exchanged secrets with the ocean. Even to this day, when by chance I happen to turn over the leaves of this book, almost every sentence seems to me like a hook by

* *Human, All-too-Human*, Vol. i. Aph. 37.

means of which I draw something incomparable out of the depths; its whole skin quivers with delicate shudders of recollection. This book is conspicuous for no little art in gently catching things which whisk rapidly and silently away, moments which I call godlike lizards – not with the cruelty of that young Greek god who simply transfixed the poor little beast; but nevertheless with something pointed – with a pen. 'There are so many dawns which have not yet shed their light' – this Indian maxim is written over the doorway of this book. Where does its author seek that new morning, that delicate red, as yet undiscovered, with which another day – ah! a whole series of days, a whole world of new days! – will begin? In the *Transvaluation of all Values*, in an emancipation from all moral values, in a saying of yea, and in an attitude of trust, to all that which hitherto has been forbidden, despised, and damned. This yea-saying book projects its light, its love, its tenderness, over all evil things, it restores to them their soul, their clear conscience, and their superior right and privilege to exist on earth. Morality is not assailed, it simply ceases to be considered. This book closes with the word 'or?' – it is the only book which closes with an 'or?'

2

My life-task is to prepare for humanity one supreme moment in which it can come to its senses, a Great Noon in which it will turn its gaze backwards and forwards, in which it will step from under the yoke of accident and of priests, and for the first time set the question of the Why and Wherefore of humanity as a whole – this life-task naturally follows out of the conviction that mankind does *not* get on the right road of its own accord, that it is by no means divinely ruled, but rather that it is precisely under the cover of its most holy valuations that the instinct of negation, of corruption, and of degeneration has held such a seductive sway. The question concerning the origin of moral valuations is therefore a matter of the highest importance to me because it determines the future of mankind. The demand made upon us to believe that everything is really in the best hands, that a certain book, the Bible, gives us the definite and comforting assurance that there is a Providence that wisely rules the fate of man – when translated back into reality amounts simply to this, namely, the will to stifle the truth which maintains the reverse of all this, which is that hitherto man has been in the *worst possible* hands, and that he has been governed by the physiologically botched, the men of cunning and burning revengefulness, and the so-called 'saints' – those slanderers of the world and traducers of humanity. The definite proof of the fact that the priest (including the priest in disguise, the philosopher) has become master, not only within a certain limited religious community, but everywhere, and that the morality of decadence, the will to nonentity, has become morality *per se*, is to be found in this: that altruism is now an absolute value, and egoism is regarded with hostility everywhere. He who disagrees with me on this point, I regard as infected. But all the world disagrees with me. To a physiologist a like antagonism between values admits of no doubt. If the most insignificant organ within the body neglects, however slightly, to assert with absolute certainty its self-preservative powers, its recuperative claims, and its egoism, the whole system degenerates. The physiologist insists upon the removal of degenerated parts, he denies all fellow-feeling for such parts, and has not the smallest feeling of pity for them. But the desire of the priest is precisely the degeneration of the whole of mankind; hence his preservation of that which is degenerate – this is what his dominion costs humanity. What meaning have those lying concepts, those handmaids of morality, 'soul', 'spirit', 'free will', 'God', if their aim is not the physiological ruin of mankind? When earnestness is diverted from the instincts that aim at self-preservation and an increase of bodily energy, i.e. at an *increase of life*; when anaemia is raised to an ideal and the contempt of the body is construed as 'the salvation of the soul', what is all this if it is not a recipe for decadence? Loss of ballast, resistance offered to natural instincts, selflessness, in fact – this is what has hitherto been known as morality. With *The Dawn of Day* I first engaged in a struggle against the morality of self-renunciation.

Joyful Wisdom: La Gaya Scienza

Dawn of Day is a yea-saying book, profound, but clear and kindly. The same applies once more and in the highest degree to *La Gaya Scienza*: in almost every sentence of this book, profundity and playfulness go gently hand in hand. A verse which expresses my gratitude for the most wonderful month of January which I have ever lived — the whole book is a gift — sufficiently reveals the abysmal depths from which 'wisdom' has here become joyful.

> Thou who with cleaving fiery lances
> The stream of my soul from its ice dost free,
> Till with a rush and a roar it advances
> To enter with glorious hoping the sea:
> Brighter to see and purer ever,
> Free in the bonds of thy sweet constraint —
> So it praises thy wondrous endeavour,
> January, thou beauteous saint! *

Who can be in any doubt as to what 'glorious hoping' means here, when he has realised the diamond beauty of the first of Zarathustra's words as they appear in a glow of light at the close of the fourth book? Or when he reads the granite sentences at the end of the third book, wherein a fate for all times is first given a formula? The songs of Prince Free-as-a-Bird, which, for the most part, were written in Sicily, remind me quite forcibly of that Provençal notion of '*Gaya Scienza*', of that union of *singer, knight, and free spirit*, which distinguishes that wonderfully early culture of the Provençals from all ambiguous cultures. The last poem of all, 'To the Mistral' — an exuberant dance song in which, if you please, the new spirit dances freely upon the corpse of morality — is a perfect Provençalism.

Thus Spake Zarathustra: A Book for All and None

I

I now wish to relate the history of *Zarathustra*. The fundamental idea of the work, the *Eternal Recurrence*, the highest formula of a yea-saying to life that can ever be attained, was first conceived in the month of August 1881. I made a note of the idea on a sheet of paper, with the postscript: 'Six thousand feet beyond man and time'. That day I happened to be wandering through the woods alongside of the Lake of Silvaplana, and I halted not far from Surlei, beside a huge rock that towered aloft like a pyramid. It was then that the thought struck me. Looking back now, I find

* Translated for *Joyful Wisdom* by Paul V. Cohn. — Tr.

that exactly two months before this inspiration I had an omen of its coming in the form of a sudden and decisive change in my tastes – more particularly in music. The whole of *Zarathustra* might perhaps be classified under the rubric music. At all events, the essential condition of its production was a second birth within me of the art of hearing. In Recoaro, a small mountain resort near Vicenza, where I spent the spring of 1881, I and my friend and maestro, Peter Gast – who was also one who had been born again – discovered that the phoenix music hovered over us, in lighter and brighter plumage than it had ever worn before. If, therefore, I now calculate from that day forward the sudden production of the book, under the most unlikely circumstances, in February 1883 – the last part, out of which I quoted a few lines in my preface, was written precisely in the hallowed hour when Richard Wagner gave up the ghost in Venice – I come to the conclusion that the period of gestation covered eighteen months. This period of exactly eighteen months might suggest, at least to Buddhists, that I am in reality a female elephant. The interval was devoted to the *Gaya Scienza*, which contains hundreds of indications of the proximity of something unparalleled; for, after all, it shows the beginning of *Zarathustra*, since it presents *Zarathustra's* fundamental thought in the last aphorism but one of the fourth book. To this interval also belongs that *Hymn to Life* (for a mixed choir and orchestra), the score of which was published in Leipzig two years ago by E. W. Fritsch, and which gave perhaps no slight indication of my spiritual state during this year, in which the essentially yea-saying pathos, which I call the tragic pathos, completely filled me heart and limb. One day people will sing it to my memory. The text, let it be well understood, as there is some misunderstanding abroad on this point, is not by me; it was the astounding inspiration of a young Russian lady, Miss Lou von Salome, with whom I was then on friendly terms. He who is in any way able to make some sense of the last words of the poem will divine why I preferred and admired it: there is greatness in them. Pain is not regarded as an objection to existence: 'And if thou hast no bliss now left to crown me – Lead on! Thou hast thy sorrow still.'

Maybe that my music is also great in this passage. (The last note of the oboe, by the bye, is C sharp, not C. The latter is a misprint.) During the following winter, I was living on that charmingly peaceful Gulf of Rapallo, not far from Genoa, which cuts inland between Chiavari and Cape Porto Fino. My health was not very good; the winter was cold and exceptionally rainy; and the small *albergo* in which I lived was so close to the water that at night my sleep was disturbed if the sea was rough. These circumstances were surely the very reverse of favourable; and yet, in spite of it all, and as if in proof of my belief that everything decisive comes to life in defiance of every obstacle, it was precisely during this winter and in the midst of these unfavourable circumstances that my *Zarathustra* originated. In the morning I used to start out in a southerly direction up the glorious road to Zoagli, which rises up through a forest of pines and gives one a view far out to sea. In the afternoon, or as often as my health allowed, I walked round the whole bay from Santa Margherita to beyond Porto Fino. This spot affected me all the more deeply because it was so dearly loved by the Emperor Frederick III. In the autumn of 1886 I chanced to be there again when he was revisiting this small forgotten world of happiness for the last time. It was on these two roads that all *Zarathustra* came to me, above all, Zarathustra himself as a type – I ought rather to say that it was on these walks that *he waylaid me*.

2

In order to understand this type, you must first be quite clear concerning its fundamental physiological condition: this condition is what I call *great healthiness*. In regard to this idea I cannot make my meaning more plain or more personal than I have done already in one of the last aphorisms (No. 382) of the fifth book of the *Gaya Scienza*: 'We new, nameless, and unfathomable creatures,' so reads the passage, 'we firstlings of a future still unproved – we who have a new end in view also require new means to that end, that is to say, a new healthiness, a stronger, keener, tougher, bolder, and merrier healthiness than any that has existed heretofore. He who longs to feel in his own soul the whole range of values and aims that have prevailed on earth until his day, and to sail round all the coasts of this ideal 'Mediterranean Sea'; who, from the adventures of his own inmost experience, would fain know how it feels to be a conqueror and discoverer of the ideal; – as also how it is with the artist, the saint, the legislator, the sage, the scholar, the man of piety and the godlike anchorite of yore; – such a man requires one thing above all for his purpose, and that is, *great healthiness* – such healthiness as he not only possesses, but also constantly acquires and must acquire, because he is continually sacrificing it again, and is compelled to sacrifice it! And now, therefore, after having been long on the way, we Argonauts of the ideal, whose pluck is greater than prudence would allow, and who are often shipwrecked and bruised, but, as I have said, healthier than people would like to admit, dangerously healthy, and for ever recovering our health – it would seem as if we had before us, as a reward for all our toils, a country still undiscovered, the horizon of which no-one has yet seen, a beyond to every country and every refuge of the ideal that man has ever known, a world so overflowing with beauty, strangeness, doubt, terror, and divinity, that both our curiosity and our lust of possession are frantic with eagerness. Alas! how in the face of such vistas, and with such burning desire in our conscience and consciousness, could we still be content with *the man of the present day*? This is bad indeed; but, that we should regard his worthiest aims and hopes with ill-concealed amusement, or perhaps give them no thought at all, is inevitable. Another ideal now leads us on, a wonderful, seductive ideal, full of danger, the pursuit of which we should be loth to urge upon anyone, because we are not so ready to acknowledge any one's *right to it*: the ideal of a spirit who plays ingenuously (that is to say, involuntarily, and as the outcome of superabundant energy and power) with everything that, hitherto, has been called holy, good, inviolable, and divine; to whom even the loftiest thing that the people have with reason made their measure of value would be no better than a danger, a decay, and an abasement, or at least a relaxation and temporary forgetfulness of self: the ideal of a humanly superhuman well-being and goodwill, which often enough will seem inhuman – as when, for instance, it stands beside all past earnestness on earth, and all past solemnities in hearing, speech, tone, look, morality, and duty, as their most lifelike and unconscious parody – but with which, nevertheless, *great earnestness* perhaps alone begins, the first note of interrogation is affixed, the fate of the soul changes, the hour hand moves, and tragedy begins.'

3

Has anyone at the end of the nineteenth century any distinct notion of what poets of a stronger age understood by the word inspiration? If not, I will describe it. If one had the smallest vestige of superstition left in one, it would hardly be possible completely to set aside the idea that one is the mere incarnation, mouthpiece, or medium of an almighty power. The idea of revelation, in the sense that something which profoundly convulses and upsets one becomes suddenly visible and audible with indescribable certainty and accuracy – describes the simple fact. One hears – one does not seek; one takes – one does not ask who gives: a thought suddenly flashes up like lightning, it comes with necessity, without faltering – I have never had any choice in the matter. There is an ecstasy so great that the immense strain of it is sometimes relaxed by a flood of tears, during which one's steps now involuntarily rush and anon involuntarily lag. There is the feeling that one is utterly out of hand, with the very distinct consciousness of an endless number of fine thrills and titillations descending to one's very toes; – there is a depth of happiness in which the most painful and gloomy parts do not act as antitheses to the rest, but are produced and required as necessary shades of colour in such an overflow of light. There is an instinct for rhythmic relations which embraces a whole world of forms (length, the need of a wide-embracing rhythm, is almost the measure of the force of an inspiration, a sort of counterpart to its pressure and tension). Everything happens quite involuntarily, as if in a tempestuous outburst of freedom, of absoluteness, of power and divinity. The involuntary nature of the figures and similes is the most remarkable thing; one loses all perception of what is imagery and metaphor; everything seems to present itself as the readiest, the truest, and simplest means of expression. It actually seems, to use one of Zarathustra's own phrases, as if all things came to one, and offered themselves as similes. ('Here do all things come caressingly to thy discourse and flatter thee, for they would fain ride upon thy back. On every simile thou ridest here unto every truth. Here fly open unto thee all the speech and word shrines of the world, here would all existence become speech, here would all Becoming learn of thee how to speak.') This is my experience of inspiration. I do not doubt but that I should have to go back thousands of years before I could find another who could say to me: 'It is mine also!'

4

For a few weeks afterwards I lay an invalid, in Genoa. Then followed a melancholy spring in Rome, where I only just managed to live – and this was no easy matter. This city, which is absolutely unsuited to the poet-author of *Zarathustra*, and for the choice of which I was not responsible, made me inordinately miserable. I tried to leave it. I wanted to go to Aquila – the opposite of Rome in every respect, and actually founded in a spirit of hostility towards that city, just as I also shall found a city some day, as a memento of an atheist and genuine enemy of the Church, a person very closely related to me, the great Hohenstaufen, the Emperor Frederick II. But Fate lay behind it all: I had to return again to Rome. In the end I was obliged to be satisfied with the Piazza Barberini, after I had exerted myself in vain to find an anti-Christian quarter. I fear that on one occasion, to avoid bad smells as much as possible, I actually inquired at the Palazzo del Quirinale whether they could not provide a quiet room for a philosopher. In a chamber high above the Piazza just mentioned, from which one obtained a general view of Rome, and could hear the fountains plashing far below, the loneliest of all songs was composed – 'The Night-Song'. About this time I was obsessed by an unspeakably sad melody, the refrain of which I recognised in the words, 'dead through immortality' . . . In the summer, finding myself once more in the sacred place where the first thought of *Zarathustra* flashed like a light across my mind, I conceived the second part. Ten days sufficed. Neither for the second, the first, nor the third part, have I required a day longer. In the ensuing winter, beneath the halcyon sky of Nice, which then for the first time poured its light into my life, I found the third *Zarathustra* – and came to the end of my task: the whole having occupied me scarcely a year. Many hidden corners and heights in the country round about Nice are hallowed for me by moments that I can never forget. That decisive chapter, entitled 'Old and New Tables', was composed during the arduous ascent from the station to Eza – that wonderful Moorish village in the rocks. During those moments when my creative energy flowed most plentifully, my muscular activity was always greatest. The body is inspired: let us waive the question of 'soul'. I might often have been seen dancing in those days, and I could then walk for seven or eight hours on end over the hills without a suggestion of fatigue. I slept well and laughed a good deal – I was perfectly robust and patient.

5

With the exception of these periods of industry lasting ten days, the years I spent during the production of *Zarathustra*, and thereafter, were for me years of unparalleled distress. A man pays dearly for being immortal: to this end he must die many times over during his life. There is such a thing as what I call the rancour of greatness: everything great, whether a work or a deed, once it is completed, turns immediately against its author. The very fact that he is its author makes him weak at this time. He can no longer endure his deed. He can no longer look it full in the face. To have something at one's back which one could never have willed, something to which the knot of human destiny is attached – and to be forced thenceforward to bear it on one's shoulders! Why, it almost crushes one! The rancour of greatness! A somewhat different experience is the uncanny silence that reigns about one. Solitude has seven skins which nothing can penetrate. One goes among men; one greets friends: but these things are only new deserts, the looks of those one meets no longer bear a greeting. At the best one encounters a sort of revolt. This feeling of revolt I suffered, in varying degrees of intensity, at the hands of almost everyone who came near me; it would seem that nothing inflicts a deeper wound than suddenly to make one's distance felt. Those noble natures are scarce who know not how to live unless they can revere. A third thing is the absurd susceptibility of the skin to small pin-pricks, a kind of helplessness in the presence of all small things. This seems to me a necessary outcome of the appalling expenditure of all defensive forces, which is the first condition of every *creative* act, of every act which proceeds from the most intimate, most secret, and most concealed recesses of a man's being. The small defensive forces are thus, as it were, suspended, and no fresh energy reaches them. I even think it probable that one does not digest so well, that one is less willing to move, and that one is much too open to sensations of coldness and suspicion; for, in a large number of cases, suspicion is merely a blunder in aetiology. On one occasion when I felt like this I became conscious of the proximity of a herd of cows, some time before I could possibly have seen it with my eyes, simply owing to a return in me of milder and more humane sentiments: *they* communicated warmth to me . . .

6

This work stands alone. Do not let us mention the poets in the same breath: nothing perhaps has ever been produced out of such a superabundance of strength. My concept 'Dionysian' here became the *highest* deed; compared with it everything that other men have done seems poor and limited. The fact that a Goethe or a Shakespeare would not for an instant have known how to take breath in this atmosphere of passion and of the heights; the fact that by the side of Zarathustra, Dante is no more than a believer, and not one who first *creates* the truth – that is to say, not a world-ruling spirit, a *Fate*; the fact that the poets of the Veda were priests and not even fit to unfasten Zarathustra's sandal – all this is the least of things, and gives no idea of the distance, of the azure solitude, in which this work dwells. Zarathustra has an eternal right to say: 'I draw around me circles and holy boundaries. Ever fewer are they that mount with me to ever loftier heights. I build me a mountain range of ever holier mountains.' If all the spirit and goodness of every great soul were collected together, the whole could not create a single one of Zarathustra's discourses. The ladder upon which he rises and descends is of boundless length; he has seen further, he has willed further, and *gone* further than any other man. There is contradiction in every word that he utters, this most yea-saying of all spirits. Through him all contradictions are bound up into a new unity. The loftiest and the basest powers of human nature, the sweetest, the lightest, and the most terrible, rush forth from out one spring with everlasting certainty. Until his coming no-one knew what was height, or depth, and still less what was truth. There is not a single passage in this revelation of truth which had already been anticipated and divined by even the greatest among men. Before Zarathustra there was no wisdom, no probing of the soul, no art of speech: in his book, the most familiar and most vulgar thing utters unheard-of words. The sentence quivers with passion. Eloquence has become music. Forks of lightning are hurled towards futures of which no-one has ever dreamed before. The most powerful use of parables that has yet existed is poor beside it, and mere child's-play compared with this return of language to the nature of imagery. See how Zarathustra goes down from the mountain and speaks the kindest words to everyone! See with what delicate fingers he touches his very adversaries, the priests, and how he suffers with them from themselves! Here, at every moment, man is overcome, and the concept 'Superman' becomes the greatest reality – out of sight, almost far away beneath him, lies all that which heretofore has been called great in man. The halcyonic brightness, the light feet, the presence of wicked-ness and exuberance throughout, and all that is the essence of the type Zarathustra, was never dreamt of before as a prerequisite of greatness. In precisely these limits of space and in this accessibility to opposites Zarathustra feels himself the *highest of all living things*: and when you hear how he defines this highest, you will give up trying to find his equal.

> The soul which hath the longest ladder and can step down deepest,
> The vastest soul that can run and stray and rove furthest in its own domain,
> The most necessary soul, that out of desire flingeth itself to chance,
> The stable soul that plungeth into Becoming, the possessing soul that must needs taste of willing and longing,
> The soul that flyeth from itself, and overtaketh itself in the widest circle,
> The wisest soul that folly exhorteth most sweetly,
> The most self-loving soul, in whom all things have their rise, their ebb and flow.

But this is the very idea of Dionysus. Another consideration leads to this idea. The psychological problem presented by the type of Zarathustra is, how can he, who in an unprecedented manner says no, and *acts* no, in regard to all that which has been affirmed hitherto, remain nevertheless a yea-saying spirit? how can he who bears the heaviest destiny on his shoulders and whose very life-task is a fatality, yet be the brightest and the most transcendental of spirits – for Zarathustra is a dancer? How can he who has the hardest and most terrible grasp of reality, and who has thought the most 'abysmal thoughts', nevertheless avoid conceiving these things as objections to existence, or even as objections to the eternal recurrence of existence? – how is it that on the contrary he finds reasons for *being himself* the eternal affirmation of all things, 'the tremendous and unlimited saying of yea and amen'? . . . 'Into every abyss do I bear the benediction of my yea to life.' . . . But this, once more, is precisely the idea of Dionysus.

7

What language will such a spirit speak, when he speaks unto his soul? The language of the *dithyramb*. I am the inventor of the dithyramb. Hearken unto the manner in which Zarathustra speaks to his soul *Before Sunrise* (iii. 48). Before my time such emerald joys and divine tenderness had found no tongue. Even the profoundest melancholy of such a Dionysus takes shape as a dithyramb. As an example of this I take 'The Night-Song' – the immortal plaint of one who, thanks to his superabundance of light and power, thanks to the sun within him, is condemned never to love.

It is night: now do all gushing springs raise their voices. And my soul too is a gushing spring.

It is night: now only do all lovers burst into song. And my soul too is the song of a lover.

Something unquenched and unquenchable is within me, that would raise its voice. A craving for love is within me, which itself speaketh the languaage of love.

Light am I: would that I were night! But this is my loneliness, that I am begirt with light.

Alas, why am I not dark and like unto the night! How joyfully would I then suck at the breasts of light!

And even you would I bless, ye twinkling starlets and glow-worms on high! and be blessed in the gifts of your light.

But in mine own light do I live, ever back into myself do I drink the flames I send forth.

I know not the happiness of the hand stretched forth to grasp; and oft have I dreamt that stealing must be more blessed than taking.

Wretched am I that my hand may never rest from giving: an envious fate is mine that I see expectant eyes and nights made bright with longing.

Oh, the wretchedness of all them that give! Oh, the clouds that cover the face of my sun! That craving for desire! that burning hunger at the end of the feast!

They take what I give them; but do I touch their soul? A gulf is there 'twixt giving and taking; and the smallest gulf is the last to be bridged.

An appetite is born from out my beauty: would that I might do harm to them that I fill with light; would that I might rob them of the gifts I have given: thus do I thirst for wickedness.

To withdraw my hand when their hand is ready stretched forth like the waterfall that wavers, wavers even in its fall: thus do I thirst for wickedness.

For such vengeance doth my fulness yearn: to such tricks doth my loneliness give birth.

My joy in giving died with the deed. By its very fulness did my virtue grow weary of itself.

He who giveth risketh to lose his shame; he that is ever distributing groweth callous in hand and heart therefrom.

Mine eyes no longer melt into tears at the sight of the suppliant's shame; my hand hath become too hard to feel the quivering of laden hands.

Whither have ye fled, the tears of mine eyes and the bloom of my heart? Oh, the solitude of all givers! Oh, the silence of all beacons!

Many are the suns that circle in barren space; to all that is dark do they speak with their light – to me alone are they silent.

Alas, this is the hatred of light for that which shineth: pitiless it runneth its course.

Unfair in its inmost heart to that which shineth; cold toward suns – thus doth every sun go its way.

Like a tempest do the suns fly over their course: for such is their way. Their own unswerving will do they follow: that is their coldness.

Alas, it is ye alone, ye creatures of gloom, ye spirits of the night, that take your warmth from that which shineth. Ye alone suck your milk and comfort from the udders of light.

Alas, about me there is ice, my hand burneth itself against ice!

Alas, within me is a thirst that thirsteth for your thirst!

It is night: woe is me, that I must needs be light! And thirst after darkness! And loneliness!

It is night: now doth my longing burst forth like a spring – for speech
do I long.

It is night: now do all gushing springs raise their voices. And my soul
too is a gushing spring.

It is night: now only do all lovers burst into song. And my soul too is
the song of a lover.

8

Such things have never been written, never been felt, never
been *suffered*: only a God, only Dionysus suffers in this way.
The reply to such a dithyramb on the sun's solitude in light
would be Ariadne . . . Who knows, but I, who Ariadne is! To
all such riddles no-one heretofore had ever found an answer;
I doubt even whether anyone had ever seen a riddle here. One
day Zarathustra severely determines his life-task – and it is also
mine. Let no-one misunderstand its meaning. It is a yea-saying
to the point of justifying, to the point of redeeming even all that
is past.

I walk among men as among fragments of the future: of that future
which I see.

And all my creativeness and effort is but this, that I may be able to
think and recast all these fragments and riddles and dismal accidents
into one piece.

And how could I bear to be a man, if man were not also a poet, a
riddle reader, and a redeemer of chance!

To redeem all the past, and to transform every 'it was' into 'thus
would I have it' – that alone would be my salvation!

In another passage he defines as strictly as possible what to him
alone 'man' can be – not a subject for love nor yet for pity –
Zarathustra became master even of his loathing of man: man is to
him a thing unshaped, raw material, an ugly stone that needs the
sculptor's chisel.

No longer to will, no longer to value, no longer to create! Oh, that
this great weariness may never be mine!

Even in the lust of knowledge, I feel only the joy of my will to beget
and to grow; and if there be innocence in my knowledge, it is
because my procreative will is in it.

Away from God and gods did this will lure me: what would there be
  to create if there were gods?

'But to man doth it ever drive me anew, my burning, creative will.
  Thus driveth it the hammer to the stone.

Alas, ye men, within the stone there sleepeth an image for me, the
  image of all my dreams! Alas, that it should have to sleep in the
  hardest and ugliest stone!

Now rageth my hammer ruthlessly against its prison. From the stone the
  fragments fly: what's that to me?

I will finish it: for a shadow came unto me – the stillest and lightest
  thing on earth once came unto me!

The beauty of the Superman came unto me as a shadow. Alas, my
  brethren! What are the – gods to me now?

Let me call attention to one last point of view. The line in italics
is my pretext for this remark. A Dionysian life-task needs the
hardness of the hammer, and one of its first essentials is without
doubt the *joy even of destruction*. The command, 'Harden yourselves!' and the deep conviction that *all creators are hard*, is the really
distinctive sign of a Dionysian nature.

Beyond Good and Evil: the Prelude to a Philosophy of the Future

I

My work for the years that followed was prescribed as distinctly
as possible. Now that the yea-saying part of my life-task was
accomplished, there came the turn of the negative portion, both
in word and deed: the transvaluation of all values that had existed
hitherto, the great war – the conjuring-up of the day when the
fatal outcome of the struggle would be decided. Meanwhile, I
had slowly to look about me for my peers, for those who, *out
of strength*, would proffer me a helping hand in my work of
destruction. From that time onward, all my writings are so much
bait: maybe I understand as much about fishing as most people? If
nothing was *caught*, it was not I who was at fault. *There were no fish
to come and bite.*

2

In all its essential points, this book (1886) is a criticism of *modernity*, embracing the modern sciences, arts, even politics, together with certain indications as to a type which would be the reverse of modern man, or as little like him as possible, a noble and yea-saying type. In this last respect the book is a *school for gentlemen* – the term *gentleman* being understood here in a much more spiritual and radical sense than it has implied hither-to. All those things of which the age is proud – as, for instance, far-famed 'objectivity', 'sympathy with all that suffers', 'the historical sense', with its sub-jection to foreign tastes, with its lying-in-the-dust before *petits faits*, and the rage for science – are shown to be the contradiction of the type recommended, and are regarded as almost ill-bred. If you remember that this book follows upon *Zarathustra*, you may possibly guess to what system of diet it owes its life. The eye which, owing to tremendous constraint, has become accustomed to see at a great distance – *Zarathustra* is even more far-sighted than the Tsar – is here forced to focus sharply that which is close at hand, the present time, the things that lie about him. In all the aphorisms and more particularly in the form of this book, the reader will find the same *voluntary* turning away from those instincts which made a *Zarathustra* a possible feat. Refinement in form, in aspiration, and in the art of keeping silent, are its more or less obvious qualities; psychology is handled with deliberate hard-ness and cruelty – the whole book does not contain one single good-natured word . . . All this sort of thing refreshes a man. Who can guess the kind of recreation that is necessary after such an expenditure of goodness as is to be found in *Zarathustra*? From a theological standpoint – now pay ye heed; for it is but on rare occasions that I speak as a theologian – it was God Himself who, at the end of His great work, coiled Himself up in the form of a serpent at the foot of the tree of knowledge. It was thus that He recovered from being a God . . . He had made everything too beautiful . . . The devil is simply God's moment of idleness, on that seventh day.

The Genealogy of Morals: A Polemic

The three essays which constitute this genealogy are, as regards expression, aspiration, and the art of the unexpected, perhaps the most curious things that have ever been written. Dionysus, as you know, is also the god of darkness. In each case the beginning is calculated to mystify; it is cool, scientific, even ironical, intentionally thrust to the fore, intentionally reticent. Gradually less calmness prevails; here and there a flash of lightning defines the horizon; exceedingly unpleasant truths break upon your ears from out remote distances with a dull, rumbling sound – until very soon a fierce tempo is attained in which everything presses forward at a terrible degree of tension. At the end, in each case, amid fearful thunderclaps, a new truth shines out between thick clouds. The truth of the first essay is the psychology of Christianity: the birth of Christianity out of the spirit of resentment, not, as is supposed, out of the 'Spirit' – in all its essentials, a counter-movement, the great insurrection against the dominion of noble values. The second essay contains the psychology of conscience: this is not, as you may believe, 'the voice of God in man'; it is the instinct of cruelty, which turns inwards once it is unable to discharge itself outwardly. Cruelty is here exposed, for the first time, as one of the oldest and most indispensable elements in the foundation of culture. The third essay replies to the question as to the origin of the formidable power of the ascetic ideal, of the priest ideal, despite the fact that this ideal is essentially detrimental, that it is a will to nonentity and to decadence. Reply: it flourished not because God was active behind the priests, as is generally believed, but because it was a *faute de mieux* – from the fact that hitherto it has been the only ideal and has had no competitors. 'For man prefers to aspire to nonentity than not to aspire at all.' But above all, until the time of *Zarathustra* there was no such thing as a counter-ideal. You have understood my meaning. Three decisive overtures on the part of a psychologist to a *Transvaluation of all Values*. – This book contains the first psychology of the priest.

The Twilight of the Idols:
How to Philosophise with the Hammer

I

This work – which covers scarcely one hundred and fifty pages, with its cheerful and fateful tone, like a laughing demon, and the production of which occupied so few days that I hesitate to give their number – is altogether an exception among books: there is no work more rich in substance, more independent, more up-setting – more wicked. If anyone should desire to obtain a rapid sketch of how everything, before my time, was standing on its head, he should begin reading me in this book. That which is called 'Idols' on the title page is simply the old truth that has been believed in hitherto. In plain English, *The Twilight of the Idols* means that the old truth is on its last legs.

2

There is no reality, no 'ideality', which has not been touched in this book (touched! what a cautious euphemism!). Not only the eternal idols, but also the youngest – that is to say, the most senile: modern ideas, for instance. A strong wind blows between the trees and in all directions fall the fruit – the truths. There is the waste of an all-too-rich autumn in this book: you trip over truths. You even crush some to death, there are too many of them. Those things that you can grasp, however, are quite unquestionable; they are irrevocable decrees. I alone have the criterion of 'truths' in my possession. I alone *can* decide. It would seem as if a second consciousness had grown up in me, as if the 'life-will' in me had thrown a light upon the downward path along which it has been running throughout the ages. The *downward path* – hitherto this had been called the road to 'Truth'. All obscure impulse – 'darkness and dismay' – is at an end, the *'good man'* was precisely he who was least aware of the proper way.* And, speaking in all earnestness, no-one before me knew the proper way, the way upwards: only after my time could men

* A witty reference to Goethe's well-known passage in the Prologue to *Faust*:

    'A good man, though in darkness and dismay,
    May still be conscious of the proper way.'

The words are spoken by the Lord. – Tr.

once more find hope, life-tasks, and roads mapped out that lead
to culture – *I am the joyful harbinger of this culture* . . . On this
account alone I am also a fatality.

3

Immediately after the completion of the above-named work, and
without letting even one day go by, I tackled the formidable task of
the *Transvaluation* with a supreme feeling of pride which nothing
could equal; and, certain at each moment of my immortality, I cut
sign after sign upon tablets of brass with the sureness of Fate. The
Preface came into being on 3 September 1888. When, after having
written it down, I went out into the open that morning, I was
greeted by the most beautiful day I had ever seen in the Upper
Engadine – clear, glowing with colour, and presenting all the
contrasts and all the intermediary gradations between ice and the
south. I left Sils-Maria only on 20th September. I had been forced
to delay my departure owing to floods, and I was very soon, and
for some days, the only visitor in this wonderful spot, on which
my gratitude bestows the gift of an immortal name. After a journey
that was full of incidents, and not without danger to life – as
for instance at Como, which was flooded when I reached it in
the dead of night – I got to Turin on the afternoon of the 21st.
Turin is the only suitable place for me, and it shall be my
home henceforward. I took the same lodgings as I had occupied
in the spring, 6[III] Via Carlo Alberto, opposite the mighty Palazzo
Carignano, in which Vittorio Emanuele was born; and I had a
view of the Piazza Carlo Alberto and above it across to the hills.
Without hesitating, or allowing myself to be disturbed for a single
moment, I returned to my work, only the last quarter of which
had still to be written. On 30 September, tremendous triumph; the
seventh day; the leisure of a god on the banks of the Po.[*] On the
same day, I wrote the Preface to *The Twilight of the Idols*, the
correction of the proofs of which provided me with recreation
during the month of September. Never in my life have I experienced such an autumn; nor had I ever imagined that such things
were possible on earth – a Claude Lorrain extended to infinity,
each day equal to the last in its wild perfection.

---

[*] There is a wonderful promenade along the banks of the Po, for which Turin is
famous, and of which Nietzsche was particularly fond. – Tr.

The Case of Wagner: A Musician's Problem

I

In order to do justice to this essay a man ought to suffer from the fate of music as from an open wound. – From what do I suffer when I suffer from the fate of music? From the fact that music has lost its world-transfiguring, yea-saying character – that it is decadent music and no longer the flute of Dionysus. Supposing, however, that the fate of music be as dear to man as his own life, because joy and suffering are alike bound up with it; then he will find this pamphlet comparatively mild and full of consideration. To be cheerful in such circumstances, and laugh good-naturedly with others at one's self – *ridendo dicere severum*,* when the *verum dicere* would justify every sort of hardness – is humanity itself. Who doubts that I, old artillery-man that I am, would be able if I liked to point my *heavy* guns at Wagner ? – Everything decisive in this question I kept to myself – I have loved Wagner. – After all, an attack upon a more than usually subtle 'unknown person' whom another would not have divined so easily, lies in the meaning and path of my life-task. Oh, I have still quite a number of other 'unknown persons' to unmask besides a Cagliostro of Music! Above all, I have to direct an attack against the German people, who, in matters of the spirit, grow every day more indolent, poorer in instincts, and more *honest*; who, with an appetite for which they are to be envied, continue to diet themselves on contradictions, and gulp down 'Faith' in company with science, Christian love together with anti-semitism, and the will to power (to the 'Empire'), dished up with the gospel of the humble, without showing the slightest signs of indigestion. Fancy this absence of party-feeling in the presence of opposites! Fancy this gastric neutrality and 'disinterestedness'! Behold this sense of justice in the German palate, which can grant equal rights to all – which finds everything tasteful! Without a shadow of a doubt the Germans are idealists. When I was last in Germany, I found German taste striving to grant Wagner and the *Trumpeter of Säkkingen*† equal rights; while I myself witnessed the attempts of the people of Leipzig to do honour to one of the most genuine and most

* The motto of *The Case of Wagner*. – Tr.
† An opera by Nessler. – Tr.

German of musicians – using German here in the old sense of the word – a man who was no mere German of the Empire, the master Heinrich Schütz, by founding a Liszt Society, the object of which was to cultivate and spread artful (*listige*) * Church music. Without a shadow of doubt the Germans are idealists.

2

But here nothing shall stop me from being rude, and from telling the Germans one or two unpleasant home truths: who else would do it if I did not? I refer to their laxity in matters historical. Not only have the Germans entirely lost the *breadth of vision* which enables one to grasp the course of culture and the values of culture; not only are they one and all political (or Church) puppets; but they have also actually *put a ban upon* this very breadth of vision. A man must first and foremost be 'German', he must belong to '*the* race'; then only can he pass judgment upon all values and lack of values in history – then only can he establish them . . . To be German is in itself an argument, 'Germany, Germany above all' † is a principle; the Germans stand for the 'moral order of the universe' in history; compared with the Roman Empire, they are the up-holders of freedom; compared with the eighteenth century, they are the restorers of morality, of the 'categorical imperative'. There is such a thing as the writing of history according to the lights of Imperial Germany; there is, I fear, anti-semitic history – there is also history written with an eye to the Court, and Herr von Treitschke is not ashamed of himself. Quite recently an idiotic opinion *in historicis*, an observation of Vischer the Swabian aesthete, since happily deceased, made the round of the German newspapers as a 'truth' to which every German *must assent*. The observation was this: 'The Renaissance *and* the Reformation only together constitute a whole – the aesthetic rebirth, and the moral rebirth.' When I listen to such things, I lose all patience, and I feel inclined, I even feel it my duty, to tell the Germans, for once in a way, all that they have on their conscience. *Every great crime against culture for the last four centuries lies on their conscience* . . . And always for the same reason, always owing to their bottomless cowardice in the face of reality, which is also cowardice in the face of truth; always

---

* Unfortunately it is impossible to render this play on the words in English. – Tr.
† The German national anthem (*Deutschland, Deutschland über alles*). – Tr.

owing to the love of falsehood which has become almost instinctive in them – in short, 'idealism'. It was the Germans who caused
Europe to lose the fruits, the whole meaning of her last period of
greatness – the period of the Renaissance. At a moment when a
higher order of values, values that were noble, that said yea to life,
and that guaranteed a future, had succeeded in triumphing over
the opposite values, the values of degeneration, in the very seat of
Christianity itself – and *even in the hearts of those sitting there* –
Luther, that cursed monk, not only restored the Church, but,
what was a thousand times worse, restored Christianity, and at a
time too when it lay defeated. Christianity, the *Denial of the Will to
Live*, exalted to a religion! Luther was an impossible monk who,
thanks to his own 'impossibility', attacked the Church, and in so
doing restored it! Catholics would be perfectly justified in celebrating feasts in honour of Luther, and in producing festival plays*
in his honour. Luther and the 'rebirth of morality'! May all
psychology go to the devil! Without a shadow of a doubt the
Germans are idealists. On two occasions when, at the cost of
enormous courage and self-control, an upright, unequivocal, and
perfectly scientific attitude of mind had been attained, the Germans
were able to discover back stairs leading down to the old 'ideal'
again, compromises between truth and the 'ideal', and, in short,
formulae for the right to reject science and to perpetrate falsehoods.
Leibniz and Kant – these two great breaks upon the intellectual
honesty of Europe! Finally, at a moment when there appeared on
the bridge that spanned two centuries of decadence, a superior
force of genius and will which was strong enough to consolidate
Europe and to convert it into a political and economic unit, with
the object of ruling the world, the Germans, with their Wars of
Independence, robbed Europe of the significance – the marvellous
significance – of Napoleon's life. And in so doing they laid on their
conscience everything that followed, everything that exists today –
this sickliness and want of reason which is most opposed to
culture, and which is called Nationalism – this *névrose nationale*
from which Europe is suffering acutely; this eternal subdivision of
Europe into petty states, with politics on a municipal scale: they
have robbed Europe itself of its significance, of its reason – and

* Ever since the year 1617 such plays have been produced by the Protestants of
Germany. – Tr.

have stuffed it into a cul-de-sac. Is there anyone except me who knows the way out of this cul-de-sac? Does anyone except me know of an aspiration which would be great enough to bind the people of Europe once more together?

3

And after all, why should I not express my suspicions? In my case, too, the Germans will attempt to make a great fate give birth merely to a mouse. Up to the present they have compromised themselves with me; I doubt whether the future will improve them. Alas! how happy I should be to prove a false prophet in this matter! My natural readers and listeners are already Russians, Scandinavians, and Frenchmen – will they always be the same? In the history of know-ledge, Germans are represented only by doubtful names, they have been able to produce only '*unconscious*' swindlers (this word applies to Fichte, Schelling, Schopenhauer, Hegel, and Schleiermacher, just as well as to Kant or Leibniz; they were all mere *Schleier-machers*).* The Germans must not have the honour of seeing the first upright intellect in their history of intellects, that intellect in which truth ultimately got the better of the fraud of four thousand years, reckoned as one with the German intellect. 'German intellect' is my foul air: I breathe with difficulty in the neighbourhood of this psychological uncleanliness that has now become instinctive – an uncleanliness which in every word and expression betrays a German. They have never undergone a seventeenth century of hard self-examination, as the French have – a La Rochefoucauld, a Descartes, are a thousand times more upright than the very first among Germans – the latter have not yet had any psychologists. But psychology is almost the standard of measurement for the cleanliness or uncleanliness of a race ... For if a man is not even clean, how can he be deep? The Germans are like women, you can scarcely ever fathom their depths – they haven't any, and that's the end of it. Thus they cannot even be called shallow. That which is called 'deep' in Germany, is precisely this instinctive uncleanliness towards one's self, of which I have just spoken: people refuse to be clear in regard to their own natures. Might I be allowed, perhaps, to suggest the word 'German' as an international epithet denoting this psycho-logical depravity? – At the moment of writing, for instance, the

* *Schleiermacher* literally means a weaver or maker of veils. – Tr.

German Emperor is declaring it to be his Christian duty to liberate the slaves in Africa; among us Europeans, then, this would be called simply 'German' . . . Have the Germans ever produced even a book that had depth? They are lacking in the mere idea of what constitutes a book. I have known scholars who thought that Kant was deep. At the Court of Prussia I fear that Herr von Treitschke is regarded as deep. And when I happen to praise Stendhal as a deep psychologist, I have often been compelled, in the company of German university professors, to spell his name aloud.

4

And why should I not proceed to the end? I am fond of clearing the air. It is even part of my ambition to be considered as essentially a despiser of Germans. I expressed my suspicions of the German character even at the age of six-and-twenty (see *Thoughts out of Season*, Vol. ii. pp. 164, 165) – to my mind the Germans are impossible. When I try to think of the kind of man who is opposed to me in all my instincts, my mental image takes the form of a German. The first thing I ask myself when I begin analysing a man, is, whether he has a feeling for distance in him; whether he sees rank, gradation, and order everywhere between man and man; whether he makes distinctions; for this is what constitutes a gentleman. Otherwise he belongs hopelessly to that open-hearted, open-minded – alas! and always very good-natured species, *la canaille*! But the Germans are *canaille* – alas! they are so good-natured! A man lowers himself by frequenting the society of Germans: the German places everyone on an equal footing. With the exception of my intercourse with one or two artists, and above all with Richard Wagner, I cannot say that I have spent one pleasant hour with Germans. Suppose, for one moment, that the profoundest spirit of all ages were to appear among Germans, then one of the saviours of the Capitol would be sure to arise and declare that his own ugly soul was just as great. I can no longer abide this race with which a man is always in bad company, which has no idea of nuances – woe to me! I am a nuance – and which has not *esprit* in its feet, and cannot even walk withal! In short, the Germans have no feet at all, they simply have legs. The Germans have not the faintest idea of how vulgar they are – but this in itself is the acme of vulgarity – they are not even ashamed of being merely Germans. They will have their say in everything, they regard themselves as fit to decide all questions; I even fear that they have decided about me. My whole life is essentially a proof of this remark. In vain have I sought among them for a sign of tact and delicacy towards myself. Among Jews I did indeed find it, but not among Germans. I am so constituted as to be gentle and kindly to everyone – I have the right not to draw distinctions – but this does not prevent my eyes from being open. I except no-one, and least of all my friends – I only trust that this has not prejudiced my reputation for humanity among them? There are five or six things which I have always made points of honour. Albeit, the truth remains that for many years I have considered almost every letter that has reached me as a piece of cynicism. There is more cynicism in an attitude of goodwill towards me than in any sort of hatred. I tell every friend to his face that he has never thought it worth his while to *study* any one of my writings: from the slightest hints I gather that they do not even know what lies hidden in my books. And with regard even to my *Zarathustra*, which of my friends would have seen more in it than a piece of unwarrantable, though fortunately harmless, arrogance? Ten years have elapsed, and no-one has yet felt it a duty to his conscience to defend my name against the absurd silence beneath which it has been entombed. It was a foreigner, a Dane, who first showed sufficient keenness of instinct and of courage to do this, and who protested indignantly against my so-called friends. At what German university today would such lectures on my philosophy be possible, as those which Dr Brandes delivered last spring in Copenhagen, thus proving once more his right to the title psychologist? For my part, these things have never caused me any pain; that which is *necessary* does not offend me. *Amor fati* is the core of my nature. This, however, does not alter the fact that I love irony and even world-historic irony. And thus, about two years before hurling the destructive thunder-bolt of the *Transvaluation*, which will send the whole of civilisation into convulsions, I sent my *Case of Wagner* out into the world. The Germans were given the chance of blundering and immortalising their stupidity once more on my account, and they still have just enough time to do it in. And have they fallen in with my plans? Admirably! my dear Germans. Allow me to congratulate you.

I

I know my destiny. There will come a day when my name will recall the memory of something formidable – a crisis the like of which has never been known on earth, the memory of the most profound clash of consciences, and the passing of a sentence upon all that which theretofore had been believed, exacted, and hallowed. I am not a man, I am dynamite. And with it all there is nought of the founder of a religion in me. Religions are matters for the mob; after coming in contact with a religious man, I always feel that I must wash my hands . . . I require no 'believers', it is my opinion that I am too full of malice to believe even in myself; I never address myself to masses. I am horribly frightened that one day I shall be pronounced 'holy'. You will understand why I publish this book beforehand – it is to prevent people from wronging me. I refuse to be a saint; I would rather be a clown. Maybe I am a clown. And I am notwithstanding, or rather not *not*withstanding, the mouthpiece of truth; for nothing more blown-out with falsehood has ever existed than a saint. But my truth is terrible: for hitherto *lies* have been called truth. *The Transvaluation of all Values*, this is my formula for mankind's greatest step towards coming to its senses – a step which in me became flesh and genius. My destiny ordained that I should be the first decent human being, and that I should feel myself opposed to the falsehood of millenniums. I was the first to discover truth, and for the simple reason that I was the first who became conscious of falsehood as falsehood – that is to say, I smelt it as such. My genius resides in my nostrils. I contradict as no-one has contradicted hitherto, and am nevertheless the reverse of a negative spirit. I am the harbinger of joy, the like of which has never existed before; I have discovered tasks of such lofty greatness that, until my time, no-one had any idea of such things. Mankind can begin to have fresh hopes, only now that I have lived. Thus, I am necessarily a man of Fate. For when Truth enters the lists against the falsehood of ages, shocks are bound to ensue, and a spell of earthquakes, followed by the transposition of hills and valleys, such as the world has never yet imagined even in its dreams. The concept 'politics' then becomes elevated entirely to the sphere of spiritual warfare. All the mighty realms of the ancient order of society are blown into space – for they are all based on falsehood: there will be wars, the like of which have never been seen on earth before. Only from my time and after me will politics on a large scale exist on earth.

2

If you should require a formula for a destiny of this kind that has taken human form, you will find it in my *Zarathustra*.

> And he who would be a creator in good and evil – verily, he must
>   first be a destroyer, and break values into pieces.
> Thus the greatest evil belongeth unto the greatest good: but this is
>   the creative good.

I am by far the most terrible man that has ever existed; but this does not alter the fact that I shall become the most beneficent. I know the joy of *annihilation* to a degree which is commensurate with my power to annihilate. In both cases I obey my Dionysian nature, which knows not how to separate the negative deed from the saying of yea. I am the first immoralist, and in this sense I am essentially the annihilator.

3

People have never asked me as they should have done, what the name of Zarathustra precisely meant in my mouth, in the mouth of the first immoralist; for that which distinguishes this Persian from all others in the past is the very fact that he was the exact reverse of an immoralist. Zarathustra was the first to see in the struggle between good and evil the essential wheel in the working of things. The translation of morality into the realm of meta-physics, as force, cause, end-in-itself, is his work. But the very question suggests its own answer. Zarathustra created this most portentous of all errors – morality; therefore he must be the first to expose it. Not only because he has had longer and greater experience of the subject than any other thinker – all history is indeed the experimental refutation of the theory of the so-called moral order of things – but because of the more important fact that Zarathustra was the most truthful of thinkers. In his teaching alone is truthfulness upheld as the highest virtue – that is to say, as the reverse of the cowardice of the 'idealist' who takes to his heels at the sight of reality. Zarathustra has more pluck in his body than all other thinkers put together. To tell the truth and to aim straight: that is the first Persian virtue. Have I made myself clear? . . . The overcoming of morality by itself, through truthfulness, the moralist's overcoming of himself in his opposite – in me – that is what the name Zarathustra means in my mouth.

4

In reality two negations are involved in my title Immoralist. I first of all deny the type of man that has hitherto been regarded as the highest – the *good*, the *kind*, and the *charitable*; and I also deny that kind of morality which has become recognised and paramount as morality-in-itself – I speak of the morality of decadence, or, to use a still cruder term, Christian morality. I would agree to the second of the two negations being regarded as the more decisive, for, reckoned as a whole, the overestimation of goodness and kindness seems to me already a consequence of decadence, a symptom of weakness, and incompatible with any ascending and yea-saying life. Negation and annihilation are inseparable from a yea-saying attitude towards life. Let me halt for a moment at the question of the psychology of the good man. In order to appraise the value of a certain type of man, the cost of his maintenance must be calculated – and the conditions of his existence must be known. The condition of the existence of the *good* is falsehood: or, otherwise expressed, the refusal at any price to see how reality is actually constituted. The refusal to see that this reality is not so constituted as always to be stimulating beneficent instincts, and still less, so as to suffer at all moments the intrusion of ignorant and good-natured hands. To consider distress of all kinds as an objection, as something which must be done away with, is the greatest nonsense on earth; generally speaking, it is nonsense of the most disastrous sort, fatal in its stupidity – almost as mad as the will to abolish bad weather, out of pity for the poor, so to speak. In the great economy of the whole universe, the terrors of reality (in the passions, in the desires, in the will to power) are incalculably more necessary than that form of petty happiness which is called 'goodness'; it is even needful to practise leniency in order so much as to allow the latter a place at all, seeing that it is based upon a falsification of the instincts. I shall have an excellent opportunity of showing the incalculably calamitous consequences to the whole of history, of the credo of optimism, this monstrous offspring of the *homines optimi*. Zarathustra,* the first who recognised that the optimist is just as degenerate as the pessimist, though perhaps more detrimental, says: '*Good men never speak the truth. False shores and false harbours were ye taught by the good. In the lies of the good were ye born and bred. Through the good everything hath become false and crooked from the roots.*' Fortunately the world is not built merely upon those instincts which would secure to the good-natured herd animal his paltry happiness. To desire everybody to become a 'good man', 'a gregarious animal', 'a blue-eyed, bene-volent, beautiful soul', or – as Herbert Spencer wished – a creature of altruism, would mean robbing existence of its greatest character, castrating man, and reducing humanity to a sort of wretched China-dom. *And this some have tried to do! It is precisely this that men called morality.* In this sense Zarathustra calls 'the good' now 'the last men', and anon 'the beginning of the end'; and above all, he con-siders them as *the most detrimental kind of men*, because they secure their existence at the cost of Truth and at the cost of the Future.

> The good – they cannot create; they are ever the beginning of the end.
> They crucify him who writeth new values on new tables; they sacrifice *unto themselves* the future; they crucify the whole future of humanity!
> The good – they are ever the beginning of the end.
> And whatever harm the slanderers of the world may do, *the harm of the good is the most calamitous of all harm.*

5

Zarathustra, as the first psychologist of the good man, is perforce the friend of the evil man. When a degenerate kind of man has succeeded to the highest rank among the human species, his position must have been gained at the cost of the reverse type – at the cost of the strong man who is certain of life. When the gregarious animal stands in the glorious rays of the purest virtue,

---

* Needless to say this is Nietzsche, and no longer the Persian. – Tr.

the exceptional man must be degraded to the rank of the evil. If falsehood insists at all costs on claiming the word 'truth' for its own particular standpoint, the really truthful man must be sought out among the despised. Zarathustra allows of no doubt here; he says that it was precisely the knowledge of the good, of the 'best', which inspired his absolute horror of men. And it was out of this feeling of repulsion that he grew the wings which allowed him to soar into remote futures. He does not conceal the fact that his type of man is one which is relatively superhuman – especially as opposed to the 'good' man, and that the good and the just would regard his Superman as the *devil*.

> Ye higher men, on whom my gaze now falls, this is the doubt that ye wake in my breast, and this is my secret laughter: methinks ye would call my Superman – the devil! So strange are ye in your souls to all that is great, that the Superman would be terrible in your eyes for his goodness.

It is from this passage, and from no other, that you must set out to understand the goal to which Zarathustra aspires – the kind of man that he conceives sees reality *as it is*; he is strong enough for this – he is not estranged or far removed from it, he is that reality himself, in his own nature can be found all the terrible and questionable character of reality: *only thus can man have greatness*.

6

But I have chosen the title of Immoralist as a surname and as a badge of honour in yet another sense; I am very proud to possess this name which distinguishes me from all the rest of mankind. No-one hitherto has felt Christian morality beneath him; to that end there were needed height, a remoteness of vision, and an abysmal psychological depth, not believed to be possible hitherto. Up to the present Christian morality has been the Circe of all thinkers – they stood at her service. What man, before my time, had descended into the underground caverns from out of which the poisonous fumes of this ideal – of this slandering of the world – burst forth? What man had even dared to suppose that they were underground caverns? Was a single one of the philosophers who preceded me a psychologist at all, and not the very reverse of a psychologist – that is to say, a 'superior swindler', an 'Idealist'? Before my time there was no psychology.

To be the first in this new realm may amount to a curse; at all events, it is a fatality: *for one is also the first to despise*. My danger is the loathing of mankind.

7

Have you understood me? That which defines me, that which makes me stand apart from the whole of the rest of humanity, is the fact that I *unmasked* Christian morality. For this reason I was in need of a word which conveyed the idea of a challenge to everybody. Not to have awakened to these discoveries before, struck me as being the sign of the greatest uncleanliness that mankind has on its conscience, as self-deception become instinctive, as the fundamental will to be blind to every phenomenon, all causality and all reality; in fact, as an almost criminal fraud *in psychologicis*. Blindness in regard to Christianity is the essence of criminality – for it is the crime *against* life. Ages and peoples, the first as well as the last, philosophers and old women, with the exception of five or six moments in history (and of myself, the seventh), are all alike in this. Hitherto the Christian has been *the* 'moral being', a peerless oddity, and, *as* 'a moral being', he was more absurd, more vain, more thoughtless, and a greater disadvantage to himself, than the greatest despiser of humanity could have deemed possible. Christian morality is the most malignant form of all falsehood, the actual Circe of humanity: that which has corrupted mankind. It is not error as error which infuriates me at the sight of this spectacle; it is not the millennia of absence of 'goodwill', of discipline, of decency, and of bravery in spiritual things, which betrays itself in the triumph of Christianity; it is rather the absence of nature, it is the perfectly ghastly fact that *anti-nature* itself received the highest honours as morality and as law, and remained suspended over man as the categorical imperative. Fancy blundering in this way, *not* as an individual, *not* as a people, but as a whole species! as *humanity*! To teach the contempt of all the principal instincts of life; to posit falsely the existence of a 'soul', of a 'spirit', in order to be able to defy the body; to spread the feeling that there is something impure in the very first prerequisite of life – in sex; to seek the principle of evil in the profound need of growth and expansion – that is to say, in severe self-love (the term itself is slanderous); and conversely to see a higher moral value – but what am I talking about? – I mean the *moral value per se*, in the typical signs of decline, in the antagonism of the instincts, in 'selflessness', in the loss of ballast, in 'the suppression of the personal element', and in 'love of one's neighbour' (neighbour-itis!). What! is humanity itself in a state of degeneration? Has it always been in this state? One thing is certain, that ye are taught only the values of decadence as the highest values. The morality of self-renunciation is essentially the morality of degeneration; the fact, 'I am going to the dogs', is translated into the imperative, 'Ye shall all go to the dogs' – and not only into the imperative. This morality of self-renunciation, which is the only kind of morality that has been taught hitherto, betrays the will to nonentity – it denies life to the very roots. There still remains the possibility that it is not mankind that is in a state of degeneration, but only that parasitical kind of man – the priest, who, by means of morality and lies, has climbed up to his position of determinator of values, who divined in Christian morality his road to power. And, to tell the truth, this is my opinion. The teachers and leaders of mankind – including the theologians – have been, every one of them, decadents: hence their transvaluation of all values into a hostility towards life; hence morality. *The definition of morality:* Morality is the idiosyncrasy of decadents, actuated by a desire *to avenge themselves with success upon life.* I attach great value to this definition.

8

Have you understood me? I have not uttered a single word which I had not already said five years ago through my mouthpiece Zarathustra. The unmasking of Christian morality is an event which is unequalled in history, it is a real catastrophe. The man who throws light upon it is a *force majeure*, a fatality; he breaks the history of man into two. Time is reckoned up before him and after him. The lightning flash of truth struck precisely that which theretofore had stood highest: he who understands what was destroyed by that flash should look to see whether he still holds anything in his hands. Everything which until then was called truth, has been revealed as the most detrimental, most spiteful, and most subterranean form of life; the holy pretext, which was the 'improvement' of man, has been recognised as a ruse for draining life of its energy and of its blood. Morality conceived as

Vampirism . . . The man who unmasks morality has also unmasked the worthlessness of the values in which men either believe or have believed; he no longer sees anything to be revered in the most venerable man – even in the types of men that have been pronounced holy; all he can see in them is the most fatal kind of abortions, fatal, *because they fascinate*. The concept 'God' was invented as the opposite of the concept life – everything detrimental, poisonous, and slanderous, and all deadly hostility to life, was bound together in one horrible unit in Him. The concepts 'beyond' and 'true world' were invented in order to depreciate the only world that exists – in order that no goal or aim, no sense or task, might be left to earthly reality. The concepts 'soul', 'spirit', and last of all the concept 'immortal soul', were invented in order to throw contempt on the body, in order to make it sick and 'holy', in order to cultivate an attitude of appalling levity towards all things in life which deserve to be treated seriously, i.e. the questions of nutrition and habitation, of intellectual diet, the treatment of the sick, cleanliness, and weather. Instead of health, we find the 'salvation of the soul' – that is to say, a *folie circulaire* fluctuating between convulsions and penitence and the hysteria of redemption. The concept 'sin', together with the torture instrument appertaining to it, which is the concept 'free will', was invented in order to confuse and muddle our instincts, and to render the mistrust of them man's second nature! In the concepts 'disinterestedness' and 'self-denial', the actual signs of decadence are to be found. The allurement of that which is detrimental, the inability to discover one's own advantage and self-destruction, are made into absolute qualities, into the 'duty', the 'holiness', and the 'divinity' of man. Finally – to keep the worst to the last – by the notion of the *good* man, all that is favoured which is weak, ill, botched, and sick-in-itself, which *ought to be wiped out*. The law of selection is thwarted, an ideal is made out of opposition to the proud, well-constituted man, to him who says yea to life, to him who is certain of the future, and who guarantees the future – this man is henceforth called the *evil* one. And all this was believed in as *morality*! – *Ecrasez l'infâme!*

9

Have you understood me? *Dionysus* versus *Christ*.